ENGLISH AND IRISH GLASS

ENGLISH AND IRISH GLASS

By
GEOFFREY WILLS

GUINNESS SIGNATURES
24 UPPER BROOK STREET,
LONDON, W.1.

©
GUINNESS SIGNATURES
(GUINNESS SUPERLATIVES LTD.)
1968

Published in Great Britain by
GUINNESS SIGNATURES
24 UPPER BROOK STREET, LONDON, W.1.

Printed in 10pt. Century Series 650
on Invercarron Art Paper 120g.s.m.
by McCorquodale and Company Limited, London.
Monotone and 4-colour half-tone blocks by Gilchrist Bros. Ltd., Leeds.

CONTENTS

Signature No.	Title
1	Commemorative Goblets
2	Drinking Glasses: Part 1
3	Drinking Glasses: Part 2
4	Ewers and Decanters
5	Table Wares
6	Candlesticks and Lustres
7	Chandeliers
8	Irish Glass
9	Bottles: to 1720
10	Bottles: from 1720
11	Enamelled and Engraved Glass
12	18th Century Coloured Glass
13	Novelties and "Friggers"
14	Victorian Glass: Part 1
15	Victorian Glass: Part 2
16	Modern Glass

CORRECTIONS

'Errors will proceed from Press or Pen,
So long as errors are in men' — William Salmon, 1745.

1, page 3 It should have been stated that Giacomo Verzelini established his glass-house in 1575 in Broad Street, not far away from Crutched Friars.

12, page 4 The name of John Greene's partner was Michael Measey, not Richard. It is given correctly elsewhere (see Index).

INTRODUCTION

The fact that a mixture of common sand and equally unpromising ashes can be transformed by man's knowledge and craftsmanship into objects of beauty will never fail to surprise. Because the molten material cools rapidly the finished article bears the imprint of immediacy, and embodies in its form the skill and taste of its maker. Of the many minor arts, that of glass-making is one in which the hand and eye of the worker are of paramount importance, and this remains the case to-day.

Glass has been known to mankind for some three thousand years, but the history of its making in England goes back for little more than four centuries. Early attempts were made to replace the ubiquitous Venetian ware by employing craftsmen from that country. Then, late in the seventeenth century, we not only adapted their methods to suit our own needs, but radically improved upon them. George Ravenscroft's glass-of-lead gave his fellow men a substance that was unique in its properties and appearance, and one of which the peculiar qualities duly led to its production in its best-known form: as cut-glass.

While many people consider that true craftsmanship and good design vanished suddenly from the land as Victoria ascended the throne, this arbitrary view is not held by everyone. Many histories of glass stop in the early years of the nineteenth century and restart in the recent past, ignoring the years between 1837 and 1901 with raised eyebrows of outrage and horror. Nonetheless, there is a continuity to be observed in the succession of styles through the years, and no one period can fairly be omitted from study.

In the following pages the development of the glass industry in England and Ireland is traced from the reign of Edward VI to the present time. Recently published information resulting from research on English glass is recorded, and the place of Irish workmanship in the late eighteenth/early nineteenth centuries is accorded due recognition. The illustrations, which total more than two hundred and fifty, include some that may be familiar, but most are of pieces not seen before in book form. All have been selected carefully to amplify the written word.

It is hoped that the *Guinness Signatures* on *English and Irish Glass* will prove helpful to new collectors and old, and may even induce the hesitant to join the ranks. While prices are generally high, as is the case with most other types of antiques, there are always exceptions to rules and cost need not be an absolute bar. It is still possible to discover neglected but praiseworthy byways, and as a result form a worthwhile collection. To the collector this will give pleasure (and possibly profit, too), and at the same time knowledge of the subject can be usefully advanced.

Geoffrey Wills.

BIBLIOGRAPHY

The following is a list of the principal sources consulted in writing these *Signatures*:

Mario Amaya
    The Taste for Tiffany, in Apollo, vol. LXXXI, No. 36 (February, 1965), page 102.

Yolande Amic
    L'Opaline Francaise, Paris, 1952.

Geoffrey W. Beard
    Nineteenth Century Cameo Glass, 1956.

Francis Buckley
    The Glass Trade in England in the Seventeenth Century, 1913.
    The Taxation of English Glass in the 17th Century, 1914.
    Old London Glass-houses, 1915. (This, and the two preceding works published privately by the author.)
    History of Old English Glass, 1925.

Derek C. Davis
    English and Irish Antique Glass, 1964.

F. A. Girling
    English Merchants' Marks, 1964.

Geoffrey A. Godden
    Antique China and Glass under £5, 1966.

Albert Hartshorne
    Old English Glasses, 1897.

E. B. Haynes
    Glass through the Ages, revised edition 1959.

W. B. Honey
    Glass (A guide to the Victoria & Albert Museum Collection), 1946.

John Houghton
    Husbandry and Trade Improved, 2 vols., edition of 1728.

James Howell
    Familiar Letters, third edition 1655.

J. Paul Hudson
    Seventeenth Century Wine Bottles at Jamestown, in *The Journal of Glass Studies*, Corning, N.Y., vol. III (1961), page 79.

Ivor Noël Hume
    The Glass Wine Bottle in Virginia, ibid., page 90.

P. Macquoid and R. Edwards
    The Dictionary of English Furniture, 3 vols., second edition revised by R. Edwards, 1954.

J. Northwood II
    John Northwood, 1958.

Arnold Palmer
    Movable Feasts, 1952.

A. C. Powell
    Glass-Making in Bristol, in *Transactions of the Bristol & Gloucestershire Archaelogical Soc.*, 1925.

H. J. Powell
    Glass-Making in England, 1923.

Henry D. Roberts
    The Royal Pavilion, Brighton, 1939.

S. v. La Roche
    Sophie in London, 1786, translated by Clare Williams, 1933.

W. A. Seaby
    Irish Williamite Glass, Belfast, 1965.

H. Clifford Smith
    Buckingham Palace, 1931.

W. A. Thorpe
    A History of English and Irish Glass, 2 vols., 1929.
    English Glass, third edition 1961.

Hugh Wakefield
    Nineteenth Century British Glass, 1961.

M. S. D. Westropp
    Old Irish Glass, 1920.

Geoffrey Wills
    The Country Life Pocket Book of Glass, 1966.

THE AUTHOR

Geoffrey Wills is respected throughout the world as a leading authority on the subject of antiques and, more specifically, English glassware. During the course of many years' writing, he has contributed hundreds of feature articles in the journals *Country Life*, *Apollo*, *The Connoisseur* and others. His books include *The Country Life Pocket Book of Glass*, *English Looking-Glasses* and *The Country Life Book of English China*. Honorary Editor of *The Proceedings of the Wedgwood Society* since its first issue in 1956, he also lectures extensively throughout Britain on numerous Antique subjects.

Mr. Wills was born in London in 1912 and was educated at University College School. In 1955 he moved to Cornwall and since then has lived in a wing of Cotehele House, the magnificent mediæval mansion that is now a National Trust property standing above the steep wooded banks of the Tamar.

ENGLISH AND IRISH GLASS

1. Commemorative Goblets
2. Drinking Glasses—Part 1
3. Drinking Glasses—Part 2
4. Ewers and Decanters
5. Table Wares
6. Candlesticks and Lustres
7. Chandeliers
8. Irish Glass
9. Bottles, 1650-1720
10. Bottles, 1720-1850
11. Enamelled and Engraved Glass
12. 18th Century Coloured Glass
13. Novelties and Friggers
14. Victorian Glass—Part 1
15. Victorian Glass—Part 2
16. Modern Glass

Commemorative Goblets

Fig. 1: Engraved in diamond-point with a hound pursuing a stag and another hound pursuing a unicorn, inscribed JOHN JONE DIER, and dated 1581. Height 8¼ inches. (Victoria and Albert Museum, London.)

SURVIVING commemorative goblets epitomise the first one hundred and fifty years of glass-making in England: from the long years of Venetian domination to the emergence of a truly English art. In most instances such pieces were made solely for display, much ingenious craftsmanship was lavished on them by their makers, and some bear the initials or names of former owners as well as dates. All these factors will have inspired the care with which successive owners have cherished them. Had this not been the case, even fewer examples than we now fortunately possess would have been preserved.

Isolated references to the activities of glass-makers are to be found in sixteenth and seventeenth century documents, and have enabled historians to trace the growth of the craft. Many details remain undiscovered and have provoked argument, quite a few obscurities will probably never be clarified. On the whole, the story is one that is paralleled in other branches of English manufacturing: foreigners were brought here to work, we assimilated them and their skills, and then proceeded to improve on what we had learned from abroad.

Broadly speaking, the story of glass-making in England may be said to have begun in the mid-sixteenth century. At that time, the craftsmen of Venice had long been supplying the needs of all Europe, and they took every possible care that the secrets of their manufactories remained closely guarded. In spite of all the precautions taken, some of the workmen absconded to other countries, and received payment for imparting what they knew. Their knowledge was not always sufficient to ensure success, and the first Venetians to reach the British Isles failed to prosper.

It was in the year 1549 that eight workers came to London from Venice to set up a glass-manufactory, and produce wares that would equal, if not better,

Fig. 2: Engraved with a merchant's mark (a private sign used by a trader), the initials K Y and the motto of the Pewterers' Company, and dated 1583. Height 8¼ inches. (Photograph: The Connoisseur.)

Fig. 3: Decorated in gilding with the arms of the Vintners' Company and armorial devices, inscribed DIEVX ET MON DROYT and WENYFRID GEARES, and dated 1590. Height 7¼ inches. (Sotheby's.)

those of their native land. All but one of them, Josepo Cassilari, had left these shores within three years, and English needs continued to be supplied from afar. Twenty-one years later, some more Venetians together with a relative of Cassilari overcame all difficulties and established a glass-works in Crutched Friars, in the City of London. They occupied a portion of the former monastery of the 'Crossed' or 'Crouched' Friars, who wore a distinguishing red cross on their habit. The house had been taken from the order by Henry VIII, and parts of the premises were subsequently rebuilt, but the old refectory was left standing and used by the glass-makers.

The great fires needed in the furnaces of a glass-house constituted a constant hazard in the buildings of the time. The Venetians had had frequent experience of this, and following a number of serious conflagrations the glass-makers were made to establish themselves on the nearby island of Murano. There, if catastrophe threatened it would at least be contained by the surrounding water, and the dwellings of innocent neighbours remain unaffected. No similar precaution was taken in London, so when the Crutched Friars premises caught fire in 1575 there was considerable apprehension in the city.

The historian Raphael Holinshed noted the occurrence as follows:

> The fourth of September being Sundaie about seven of the clocke in the morning a certaine glasshouse which sometime has been the crossed friars hall neere to the Tower of London burst out in a terrible fire: whereunto the Lord Mayor, aldermen and shiriffes with all expedition repaired and practised there all means possible by water buckets, hookes and otherwise to have quenched it. All which notwithstanding, whereas the same house a small time before had consumed great quantitie of wood by making of fine drinking glasses, now itself having within it neere fortie thousand billets of wood was all consumed to the stone walls, which walls greatlie defended the fire from spreading further and dooing anie more harme.

IN the same year, 1575, another Venetian, Giacomo Verzelini, who may have been connected with the group of men in Crutched Friars, made the first noteworthy attempt to establish glass-making in this country. He obtained from Queen Elizabeth a privilege allowing him to make glass for the ensuing twenty-one years, while at the same time he agreed to teach all he knew to his English employees. In turn, the Government would protect his enterprise by prohibiting the importation of foreign glasses. One may wonder whether he did impart his knowledge to his men, as there is no record of any of them having made use of it by starting on his own. Nor is it certain whether or not the Government carried out their part of the agreement. Similar bans on foreign goods were in force from time to time during the next two centuries, and there is evidence that most of them were applied only loosely, if at all. Probably the prohibition of glass imports was also no more than nominal.

Writing in the 1580's, William Harrison described the England in which he was living. One fact that struck him was the great popularity of glass, which he reported as being more fashionable at the time than silver. The precious metal had suddenly become plentiful through the discovery and exploitation by the Spanish of mines in South America. The deliberate raiding of galleons bringing ingots to Europe ensured that a proportion of the wealth of the New World reached England. This was sheer piracy, but the philosophy of the times accepted such a rough-and-ready way of enriching the nation. A consequence of the abundance of silver was that men looked on it as less desirable than when it had been scarce, and in its place they coveted beautiful, but fragile, glassware.

Verzelini and his fellow-countrymen all came originally from Venice, as their names make clear, but few of them arrived in England direct from the land of their birth. Most of them had settled first in the city of Antwerp, where immigrant craftsmen had been established as glass-makers since about 1540. Not unnaturally, wherever they settled they made wares closely resembling those of Venice, and it is now only rarely possible to distinguish between specimens made in one place or another. Thus, most of the glasses made in England during the sixteenth and seventeenth centuries are identical with those made elsewhere in Europe at the same

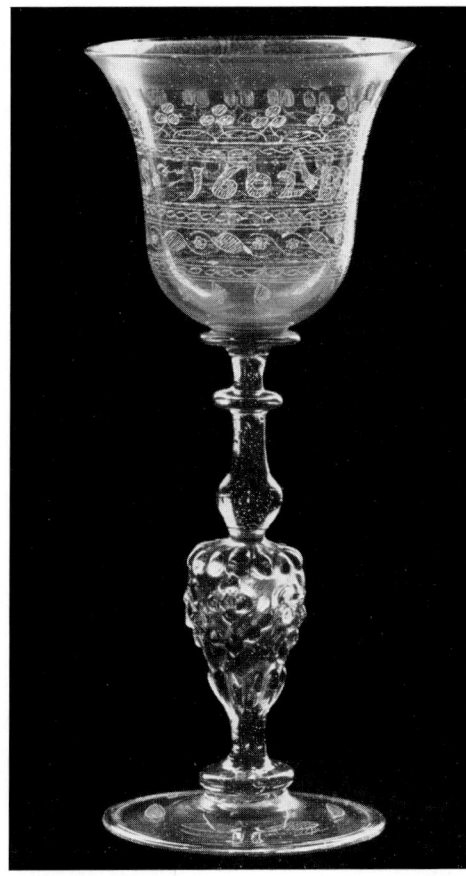

Fig. 4: Inscribed BARBARA POTTERS and dated 1602. Height 8¼ inches. (Victoria and Albert Museum.)

Fig. 5: The hollow knop below the bowl decorated with prunts and containing a Charles II threepenny-piece of 1679. Height $9\frac{7}{16}$ inches. (The London Museum.)

date. Not only were they being made by men who practiced the craft they had learned in their homeland, but their task was to compete with the productions of that country. To achieve this, they copied the Venetian styles as closely as possible, not only imitating shapes and ornamentation but making the glass itself (the 'metal', as it was called) in the same manner and from similar ingredients.

A GROUP of nine surviving decorated and dated glass goblets has been attributed with confidence to Verzelini's manufactory. Eight of them have the feature of decoration taking the form of engraving executed with a diamond-point, and in a single instance with a pattern in gold. The actual metal of which they are made does not seem to differ in composition and appearance from imported pieces of the time, and wording on them is in English. The dates with which they are inscribed, ranging from 1577 to 1590, fall within the period when Verzelini had the monopoly of glass-making in this country and when importations were illegal. It is assumed that the engraving or gilding was added at the time of making, and there is no reason to suppose otherwise. The glasses could have been made here, and, if so, they are the earliest identified English glasses we now have.

The actual goblets themselves do not complete the story, and some enterprising detective work has revealed further detail to assist in making an English origin acceptable. It is known that a French engraver of designs on pewter, named Antony de Lisle, or de Lysle, was in London during the years from which dated glasses have survived. Two of the goblets bear the words IN GOD IS AL MI TRVST, which is the motto of the Pewterers' Company of London; a fact which may be no more than a coincidence. On the other hand, a glass in the musée de Cluny, Paris, dated 1578, has the French *fleur-de-lys* on it. A portion of the decoration shows a hunting scene and is similar to that on three of the other glasses. At present, there is no proof that the nine goblets are English, but equally it cannot be asserted that they are foreign. Until, if ever, evidence is brought to light making their origin (or origins) a certainty, there can be no valid objection to claiming them as products of the Broad Street glass-house.

RECORDED GLASSES ATTRIBUTED TO THE
GLASS-HOUSE OF GIACOMO VERZELINI,
AND DATED 1577–1590

i 1577 Initialled RB IB. The upper part of the bowl engraved with a hound pursuing a stag and another hound pursuing a unicorn. The foot and stem missing and replaced in the seventeenth century with a piece of turned pearwood.
Height 7⅞ in.
In the Corning Museum of Glass, Corning, N.Y.

ii 1578 Initialled AT RT and engraved as i.
Height 8⅜ in.
Formerly in the collection of Commander Sir Hugh Dawson, Bt., C.B.E., R.N.

iii 1578 Initialled A and engraved as i.
M M
D L P
The lower part of the bowl with a panel containing three *fleurs-de-lys*. It has been suggested that the initials are those of Marthe Mansion de la Pommerage, wife of Gédéon Picard, a physician of Lower Pitou, for whom it was made, but this seems to be unconfirmed.
Height 6¼ in.
In the musée de Cluny, Paris.

iv 1580 Initialled AF.
Height 5⅛ in.
Formerly in the possession of the eighteenth century collector, Horace Walpole, to whom it was given by Lady Georgiana Smyth, and now in the Victoria and Albert Museum, London.

v 1581 Inscribed JOHN JONE DIER, and engraved with the arms of Queen Elizabeth I. The upper part of the bowl as i.
Height 8¼ in.
In the Victoria and Albert Museum. (Fig. 1.)

vi 1583 Engraved with a merchant's mark, the initials KY, and the motto of the Worshipful Company of Pewterers: IN GOD IS AL MI TRVST.
Height 8¼ in.
In the Corning Museum of Glass. (Fig. 2.)

vii 1586 Initialled GS and engraved with the motto

Fig. 6: The hollow knop ornamented similarly to that in Fig. 5, and containing a William and Mary fourpenny-piece dated 1689, the year of their coronation. Height 9½ inches. (Sotheby's.)

Above, *Fig. 7: The knop on the cover probably representing John, Duke of Marlborough (1650–1722), victor of Blenheim and other battles. The hollow knop in the stem containing a Queen Anne shilling of 1714, and that on the cover a Queen Anne fourpenny-piece of 1708. Height 12⅞ inches. (The London Museum.)* **Opposite,** *Fig. 8: Goblet and cover with elaborately ornamented stem and finial in the Venetian manner; about 1690. Height 21¼ inches. (Sotheby's.)*

of the Pewterers' Company, as vi.
Height 5¾ in.
In the British Museum, London.

viii 1586 Initialled MP RP and inscribed GOD SAVE QVYNE ELISABETH.
Height 6½ in.
In a collection in the United States.

ix 1590 Decorated in gilding with the arms of the Vintners' Company, a group of armorial devices, and inscribed DIEVX ET MON DROYT and WENYFRID GEARES.
Height 7¼ in.
Formerly in the possession of the Dukes of Northumberland and now in a collection in the United States. (Fig. 3.)

VERZELINI had a successful business career, and when he died he left a family of five children: two sons and three daughters. From the proceeds of his glass-making activities he purchased a number of properties in Kent, to one of which, Downe Court, near Bromley, he retired. In the village church is the memorial brass which depicts him with his wife and family: the daughters shown with their husbands and one of them with the eldest grandchild. On the brass is an inscription giving a few further details:

> Here lyeth buried Jacob Verzelini Esquire borne in the citie of Venice and Elizabeth his wife borne in Antwerpe of the ancient houses of Vanburen and Mace who haveing lived together in the holye state of Matrimonie fortie nine years and fower months departed this mortal lyfe The said Jacob the twentye day of Januarye An°. Dni. 1606 aged LXXXIIII yeares and the said Elizabeth the XXVI daye of October An°. Dni. 1607 aged LXXIII yeares and rest in hope of resurrexion to lyfe eternall.

IN 1592, when the twenty-one-year privilege still had a further four years to run, Verzelini sold it. The purchaser was Sir Jerome Bowes, a former soldier, who was perhaps more interested in acquiring a lucrative monopoly than in effecting an improvement in the quality and design of glassware. He was succeded by a number of other businessmen, each of whom was much concerned with the replacement of wood by coal for heating the furnaces.

This was a matter of considerable concern at the time, for glass-making, iron-smelting and other activities were making heavy inroads into supplies of native timber. Forests were being depleted so noticeably that the Government grew concerned lest the vital trade of ship-building was affected by a shortage of its principal requirement. Encouragement was given to all who would use coal, and throughout the seventeenth century every effort was made by manufacturers to employ it.

One of the successors to Bowes was an ex-Admiral, Sir Robert Mansell, who possessed himself of the privilege in 1615. A little light is thrown on his activities in some letters that were written and published by James Howell, who travelled in Spain and elsewhere on behalf of Sir Robert. In the former country Howell purchased for him in 1621 two thousand poundsworth of barilla; an alkali used in glass-making that was obtained from a plant growing on the coast of Valencia. A few months later he wrote back to London from Venice to report that he had been to Murano, 'a little island, about the distance of Lambeth from London, where crystal-glass is made, and 'tis a rare sight to see a whole street, where on the one side there are twenty furnaces together at work'.

His principal task at this stage of his journeyings was apparently to study local manufacturing methods, and he noted that 'since I came to this town I despatched sundry businesses of good value for Sir Robert Mansell, which I hope will give content'. Just what were the 'sundry businesses' we can only guess, as he made no further mention of them at the time. Another of Howell's letters makes it clear that he succeeded in arranging the voyage to England of two Muranese who, he said 'are the best gentlemen-craftsmen that ever blew crystal'.

Sir Robert Mansell remained in control of English glass-making until about 1656, by which date he had gained the exclusive right to make glass of all kinds, which included sheet glass for windows and looking-glasses. Not only did he administer the original manufactory in Broad Street, London, but also numerous provincial glass-houses. Nothing has been identified positively as having been made under Mansell's regime, but it is possible that specimens now labelled 'Venetian' may one day be recognised

as English productions of his busy furnaces. For then, as in earlier years, the fashions set in Murano were copied everywhere, and the glass of one country resembled that of most others.

From between the years 1550 and 1650 the only surviving English glass articles are the nine Verzelini pieces, and another dated 1602 (Fig. 4) when Sir Jerome Bowes held the privilege. All ten are in the form of goblets, and it may be wondered why these in particular have successfully withstood the stresses of three and a half centuries while all else has apparently perished. The explanation may lie in the fact that they are exceptional specimens. Some were made (or rather, engraved) especially for people of the time whose names or initials they bear, and all are dated. Being of outstanding size the goblets would be used, if at all, only on rare occasions, and thus they avoided the hazards of daily usage. Undoubtedly because all bear delicately engraved ornament they have been cherished more than plain examples would have been. This combination of features, size and decoration, is probably the reason why the ten goblets, and others of later date, have survived into the twentieth century.

THE PURITAN regime of Oliver Cromwell, which followed the Civil War, terminated in 1660 when Charles II ascended the throne. The restoration of the monarchy took place at a time when there was an awakening throughout Europe of interest in scientific matters. In England, amongst many other subjects, that of glass was closely studied. A sign of this activity was the publication in 1662 of a translation of an important Italian book, Antonio Neri's *L'Arte Vetraria*, which had been issued in Florence as long ago as 1612. Two years later, on 25th July, 1664, the Worshipful Company of Glass-Sellers received a royal charter, which gave the Company control of the trade in the City of London and within a radius of seven miles around it.

Venetian glass has been described as somewhat resembling horn, although a more up-to-date comparison might be made with transparent plastic. It was frequently blown very thinly, and often decorated in an elaborate manner with applied pieces of glass of contrasting colour. In spite of

Opposite, *Fig. 9: Wheel-engraved with the arms of the patriotic Britannic Society, and the cover with a crown-shaped finial; about 1760. Height 12¾ inches. (The London Museum.)*
Below, *Fig. 10: Inscribed SUCCESS TO SIR FRANCIS KNOLLYS, and probably engraved to commemorate the election held at Reading in 1761 when Sir Francis was returned to Parliament. Height 7⅝ inches. (Sotheby's.)*

Fig. 11: The stem and the base of the bowl cut with facets, and the bowl engraved with a figure of Britannia and a rose spray. Inscribed MAY MAGNA CHARTA AND THE BILL OF RIGHTS ALWAYS BE SUPPORTED and MAY THE ADDRESSERS OF COVENTRY BE REMEMBERED WITH INFAMY, perhaps to celebrate the tercentenary of the Battle of Barnet, 1471, when the citizens of Coventry were fined and deprived of their Charter for harbouring the Earl of Warwick and repulsing the king, Edward IV. About 1770. Height 11½ inches. (Howard Phillips.)

the obvious difficulty of transporting it, both on account of the fragility of the material itself and its delicate ornament, there was no diminution of its widespread popularity. In London, as well as in Continental centres, it was aped as closely as its many imitators could manage.

Occasionally it was reported that the copyists had outdone the original; John Evelyn, the diarist, recorded that on 10th June, 1673, he had some friends to his house for dinner, went afterwards to see soldiers encamped at Blackheath, and 'thence to the Italian glass-house at Greenwich, where glasse was blown of finer mettal than that of Murano at Venice'. Later, in 1688, a French visitor to Venice, François Maximilien Misson, remarked:

> 'One of my friends assured me, that a few years ago, having carried a vial of the finest crystal of Murano to London, the workmen there were so far from looking upon it as extraordinary or inimitable, that they said they could and sometimes did, make finer work.'

SOME YEARS passed before any action was taken by the members of the Company, but in 1673 they engaged a man named George Ravenscroft to make experiments on their behalf. To assist him he had the services of at least one Italian (only his surname, da Costa, has been recorded), and possibly two others. Within a year Ravenscroft announced that he had succeeded in making 'a particular sort of crystalline glass resembling rock crystal, not formerly exercised or used in this our kingdom'. He quickly applied for a patent, which was granted to him on 16th May, 1674, for a period of seven years. At the same time, the Company was so encouraged by what he had done that it set him up in a glass-house at Henley-on-Thames, where he could commence manufacture and pursue further researches away from the eyes of inquisitive competitors.

Ravenscroft's experiments led him to make use of native raw materials, and to replace imported pebbles and barilla with English flint-stones and potash. He found the latter produced a good-looking metal, but a proportion suffered seriously from a defect known as 'crisselling': a network of very fine cracks that gave the article a clouded appearance. Also, in an advanced stage, the surface of the glass became moist and before long the piece decomposed and crumbled. Seeking a cure, he had recourse to an ingredient long known to glass-makers but rarely employed by them: oxide of lead, which Ravenscroft added in the form of red lead. This not only corrected the fault, but also aided the fusing of the other constituents when in the furnace.

In 1676, the Company announced:

> Wee underwritten doe certify and attest that the defect of the flint glasses (which were formerly observed to crissel and decay) hath been redressed several months agoe and the glasses since made have all proved durable and lasting as any glasses whatsoever. Moreover that the usual tryalls wherewith the essay of glasses are made have bene often reitterated on these new flint glasses with entire success and easy to be done againe by any body, which proofs the former glass would not undergoe, besides ye distinction of sound discernible by any person whatsoever. London, the 3 June 1676.

Soon after, the Company gave Ravenscroft permission to mark all his productions with his personal seal. It took the form of a small blob or pad of glass, about $\frac{1}{4}$ in. in diameter, on which was moulded in relief, appropriately, the head of a raven. It is considered that such sealing, which was practised also by a few other makers, lasted only for a few years, and we have no knowledge of how many pieces received these distinctive marks. There are now known about a score of specimens marked with the raven's head, of which the majority are in museums on one side of the Atlantic or the other.

THE NEW 'flint glass' or 'glass of lead', as it was called, not only had a more brilliant appearance than the 'soda glass' it supplanted, but in the words of the late W. B. Honey 'had a light-dispersing character that gave it a remarkable interior fire'. The molten material cooled quicker than the Venetian type, and therefore could not be blown as thinly. As vessels were therefore made with thicker walls they were much stronger, and this feature of durability proved an important point in gaining public acceptance for it. Also, as each piece was more solid in construction, and because the metal itself was basically heavier, it was of noticeably greater weight in the hand than a comparable example made of soda glass. The appearance of two similar articles side-by-side reveals that the English version is clearer and brighter, but any applied ornament is more clumsy. This latter is due to the nature of the metal, which did not allow treatment of the delicacy familiar on pieces from Murano and their imitations from elsewhere. For this reason, because of the character of the glass itself, English design gradually ceased to imitate the Venetian, and a style dictated by the metal, one that made the utmost of its unique qualities, was developed.

The year after he had perfected his glass-of-lead Ravenscroft prepared for the Glass-Sellers' a list of the articles he was engaged in making, and a note of the price at which each would be supplied. The list, which is dated 29th May, 1677, does not specifically mention goblets, but this need not mean he did not make them. Others of the surviving sealed pieces are not on the list either and all may have been included under the heading of 'extraordinary work or ornament', which was priced by weight at five shillings a pound. In any case, Ravenscroft continued in business until his death in 1681, and may well have increased the range of goods during the last years of his life.

If no marked Ravenscroft goblets have survived, at least we have a number by other makers using his formula. By the year 1700 nearly a hundred glass-houses up and down England were making flint glass; which, as noted above, was first made with flints, but although these were soon replaced by sand the old name remained in use. Some of their pieces can be given dates, because of the custom sometimes practised of enclosing a coin in the hollow stem (Figs. 5, 6, 7). Such dates must, however, be accepted with caution, as the coin can have been put there at any time after the year it bears on it. This does not necessarily mean deliberate intent to produce a fake, but a glass-maker might have enclosed a coin of earlier date to mark an event occurring in that particular year.

Both the appearance and the nature of the metal, whether it is with or without lead content, determines if a piece was made before or after Ravenscroft's time. The presence of lead, even in a minute quantity, is detectable by a simple chemical test.

Opposite, *Fig. 12: Engraved with Masonic emblems. Late eighteenth century. Height 6 inches. (The London Museum.)*

Figs. 13 and 14: Engraved with a named portrait of Admiral Viscount Duncan, victor of the Battle of Camperdown in 1797, and with a sailing ship. About 1800. Height 11⅜ inches. (Author's collection.)

As the mixture often contained as much as 30 per cent of lead in its composition, there should be no doubt about it when it is present. Usually, the external appearance of an article is sufficient, and only in exceptional cases is there a need to resort to the laboratory.

Signs of lead in a piece of glass can date it to any time after Ravenscroft's experiments of 1673–4. They are also an indication, with some few exceptions, that the piece in question is of English make, for this was the only country to employ lead in glass-making consistently and with success. Articles made from the newly-devised formula were soon on the market abroad, and attracted sufficient attention to be the subject of local imitation. Indeed, as early as 1680 a manufactory at Liége was making what it called *'flint glass à l'anglaise'*.

A few examples of goblets dating from about the year 1700 retain their original covers, but it is not possible to state whether all were once equipped in the same manner. The cover was made to fit loosely within the inner side of the rim of the bowl, and the latter gives no indication of whether it began its existence with or without such an embellishment. No doubt a large number of covers have been broken and discarded with the passing of time, and it is perhaps remarkable that any of them should have been preserved. (Fig. 8.)

GOBLETS of large size continued to be made during the course of the eighteenth century, and on into the nineteenth. Although they remain imposing objects, the later ones lack the extreme interest of the earlier. They no longer epitomise the first exciting experiments with new types of glass, by Verzelini and the followers of Ravenscroft, but are noteworthy for the people and events they commemorate and the high standard of their workmanship. (Figs. 9–13.) As they were commissioned to celebrate particular persons and events, the goblets are invariably the results of especial care on the parts of glass-makers and decorators. They have been the pride of owners and their descendants and of collectors, by all of whom they were treated with care or they would not be with us now. Their study is both interesting and worthwhile, for commemorative goblets are splendid examples of the art of the English glass-maker.

© *Geoffrey Wills, 1968.*

2

Drinking Glasses: Part 1

GLASS has been employed for making drinking-vessels for so long that to-day it is accepted as the obvious material for the purpose. It has become such a household commonplace that the term 'a glass' is understood generally to mean a receptacle for liquid, whether wine or water. In the past there were few alternatives to it: some of the wealthier people might take their wine from silver cups, the less well-off from pewter, wood, horn or rough pots of clay. Broadly speaking, the drinking of wine in England from glasses made in the country, rather than imported ones, goes back to the reign of Edward the sixth, who died in 1553.

The first attempt at such glass-making was by a group of men from Venice, who reached London in 1549. They made only a brief stay, and nothing is known of what they may have produced during their three-year sojourn. The activities of Giacomo Verzelini, who established a glass-house in the city in 1575 are almost equally obscure, and the picture is much the same until late in the seventeenth century.

It is certain that any wine-glasses made were in close imitation of fashionable imported examples. These came largely from Venice, but others had shorter distances to travel and were from places such as Antwerp and Liége. In most instances these Continental glass-houses were manned partly by Venetians, and their output differed little if at all from that of their homeland. All employed the same type of glass (or 'metal'), which could be blown extremely thinly (Fig. 1). The shapes used were common to one and another, and were occasionally ornamented with applied pieces of glass to form what were called 'ears' or 'wings' of complex design. Not only were the various ingredients mixed to the same proportions throughout Europe, but in many cases they were imported

Opposite, *Fig. 1: A Netherlands soda glass wine-glass, thinly blown and of a yellow-grey tint; circa 1650. Height 7¼ inches. (Howard Phillips.)* **Above,** *Fig. 2: Römer with the raven's head seal of George Ravenscroft; this type of drinking-glass originated in Germany and was popular mostly on the Continent. 1676-78. Height 6½ inches. (Victoria and Albert Museum.)*

especially from the sources that supplied Venice. Thus, almost any surviving drinking-glass, or fragment of one, dating from before about 1675 is of debatable origin.

The fortunate preservation of a quantity of papers has, however, enabled us to know something about many of the kinds of drinking-vessels in use in England in the second half of the seventeenth century. Sketches of nearly 200 of them are with a collection of the correspondence between a Venetian, Alessio Morelli, and two London glass-dealers, John Greene and Michael Measey. Some of the pieces ordered for the English market are of recognisably Venetian types, with glass ornament frilled and pinched into fanciful shapes. Most of them are plainer, and foreshadow designs that were shortly adopted by the home-based industry.

Some of the letters of Greene and Measey were given postscripts with clear instructions to the sender of the goods. Among them were the following:

When you write to me, direct your letter: for Mr. John Greene, at the Kings Arms in the Poultry, London.

I pray take notice of these general directions underwritten:

That all the Drinking-glasses be very well made and of very bright clear and white sound metal [glass] as exactly as possible may be to the forms for fashion, size and number, and that no other fashions or sorts but those corresponding to my patterns here inclosed.

That the drinking-glasses be packed up with

Above left, *Fig. 3:* Three wines, each with a folded foot; (left to right) the straight-sided bowl containing a tear in the solid base and supported on an acorn knop, height $6\frac{7}{8}$ inches; the thistle bowl supported on a mushroom knop above a true baluster containing a large tear, height $7\frac{3}{8}$ inches; the trumpet bowl with a tear in the solid base and supported on a cylinder stem with a collar above, height $6\frac{3}{4}$ inches. About 1710. (Sotheby's.)

Above, *Fig. 4:* Three glass-of-lead wines, each with a straight-sided bowl and folded foot; (left to right) the lower part of the bowl decorated with spiked projections, height $5\frac{7}{8}$ inches; the bowl partly with 'wrythen' decoration, height $6\frac{7}{8}$ inches; the bowl spirally ribbed and with 'pearly' ornament, height $5\frac{5}{8}$ inches. 1685-90 (Sotheby's.)

dry weeds in good, strong, deep half-chests, but pray let them be made good large-size half-chests, and well hooped and nailed, and marked and numbered as in the margin; as well upon the lids of the chests as at the ends, that the seamen may know the lids from the bottoms [and not stand them upside-down on board ship]. Remember to send two bills; the 1st right, the 2nd wrong.

This last injunction meant that the 'right' invoice listed all the goods at the correct price, whereas the 'wrong' one omitted a proportion and came to a smaller total sum of money. The second bill was presented to the customs, and if passed would mean payment of less Duty. The request to pack in 'dry weeds' was because earlier consignments had suffered from wet, and it was then pointed out that 'if the weeds be not well dried or do take any wet after they be packed they stain and spoil the glasses'.

The two thousand dozen glasses ordered by Greene and his partner between 1667 and 1672 included many named for specific drinks. They

Below, *Fig. 5: Three wines each with a folded foot; (left to right) the ogee bowl with a solid base merging into a large drop knop, circa 1695, height $6\frac{3}{4}$ inches; the thistle bowl with a spherical base resting on a Silesian stem with stars at the upper corners, circa 1715, height $9\frac{5}{8}$ inches; the straight-sided bowl resting on a multi-knopped stem, circa 1705, height $6\frac{7}{8}$ inches. (Sotheby's.)*

Above, *Fig. 6: Five wines, each with a folded foot; (left to right) the bell bowl on an annular knop above a true baluster, height 7¾ inches; the round funnel bowl resting on a collar above a hollow egg-shaped knop enclosing a Charles II penny, height 9⅛ inches; the straight-sided bowl supported on a drop knop above an inverted baluster containing a large tear, height 7½ inches; the straight-sided bowl supported on an inverted baluster containing a heart-shaped tear, height 9½ inches, the bowl with flared sides and solid base containing a bubble, the plain stem with a central annulated knop, height 7½ inches. About 1700-1710.* (*Photograph:* The Connoisseur.)

included sack (a sweet wine imported from Spain and the Canaries), claret, Rhenish wine and beer. They also asked for brandy tumblers, and 'tumblers of all sorts'. Then, as now, a drink was usually taken from a glass suited to it by shape or custom, or by both. In many instances time has blurred the fine distinctions of fashion, and we can now only guess at which type of vessel might have held, say, sack.

A few surviving glasses are similar in appearance to those sketched by Greene and Measey. Some of them may actually have been in one of Morelli's consignments to these men, or to one of the other importers of the time. Equally, of course, they can have been made here, but it is very doubtful whether their true origin will ever be known. Wherever they may have hailed from they are now rare, and eagerly sought by collectors (Fig. 4).

THE introduction of glass-of-lead by George Ravenscroft, which occurred in about 1674, saw the making of glasses that can be identified certainly as of English origin. Two, indeed, bear the small seal of a raven's head and were the work of Ravenscroft's own glass-house during the few years when he used that personal mark. Each is a glass of 'römer' shape, highly popular on the Continent and used for Rhenish wine. The bowl of the vessel is raised on a wide hollow stem orna-

mented with circular pads of raised dots (known as 'prunts') and with a broad domed foot (Fig. 2). German and Netherlands examples differ from English ones in having had the foot built up from a string of glass which was wound round a removable core during manufacture. Another recorded English glass-of-lead römer also has a seal, but this one bears the initial 'S'; conjectured to be the mark of a glass-house known to have existed in Salisbury Court, off Fleet Street, about the year 1684.

On 29th May 1677 Ravenscroft submitted to the Glass-Sellers' Company a price-list of his products, against each of which was noted the weight and the wholesale price. The list included:

Beer glasses ribbed and plain	7 oz.	1. 6d.
Clarrett wine glasses of the same	5 oz.	1. 0d.
Sacke glasses of the same	4 oz.	10d.
Brandy glasses of the same	2 oz.	6d.
Beer glasses nipt diamond waies	8 oz.	1. 8d.
Clarrett glasses of the same	5½ oz.	1. 3d.
Sacke glasses of the same	4 oz.	1. 0d.

Purlee glasses at the same price as the above. The term 'nipt diamond waies' means that the piece is all or partly covered in a mesh of diamond-shaped raised lines. 'Purlee' has proved harder to define, and has provoked some argument amongst collectors. Many think it refers to the surface of

Above, *Fig. 7: Four wines; (left to right) the bell-shaped bowl resting on a multi-knopped air-twist stem, circa 1750; the trumpet bowl elongated into a cylinder above an inverted baluster, circa 1750; the thistle bowl solid at the base and resting on a collar above a Silesian stem, circa 1715; the trumpet bowl above a multi-spiral air-twist stem with a single knop, circa 1750. Height 6¼ to 6¾ inches. (Photograph:* The Connoisseur*).*

Above, *Fig. 8: Three wines with colour-twist stems; (left to right) the round funnel bowl on a stem containing a yellow spiral enclosed by two opaque-white corkscrew spirals, height 5⅞ inches; the ogee bowl on a stem containing an opaque-white basket cable encircled by a white corkscrew ribbon edged in orange and green, height 7¾ inches; the round funnel bowl on a stem containing an opaque-white spiral edged in green and blue, height 6 inches. About 1760. (Sotheby's.)*

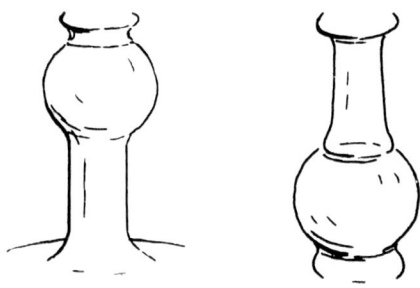

(Left) *inverted baluster stem;* (right) *true or plain baluster.*

the glass having a dimpled finish (see Fig. 4, right-hand wine-glass), but others consider that a drink named 'purl' was intended to be taken from such vessels. Dr. Johnson defined purl in 1756 as 'a kind of medicated malt liquor, in which wormwood and aromaticks are infused'; which no doubt tasted better than it sounds.

The English makers quickly devised styles in which the qualities of Ravenscroft's metal would appear at their best. In this they were aided greatly by the molten material itself, which was difficult to work into the light and fantastic forms of the Venetian makers. Happily, the thicker-walled vessels to which it lent itself so naturally brought out the full beauty of each object.

It may be argued that the great number of eighteenth century wine-glasses still existing is a reflection on the heavy drinking habits of our forefathers. That may possibly be true, but we should be grateful for this evidence of thirst, because it is generally agreed that they are among the more interesting glass productions of the period. Further, because of the numbers that have survived it is still possible to form a collection without having to be a millionaire. Some types of glasses have already risen to this lofty status, but there would appear to be yet time for a determined and fast-moving enthusiast to acquire for himself many that remain comparatively free from price-inflation.

By about 1700 English glass-makers had begun to shake themselves free from the long-enduring dominance of Venice, and of Venetian designs. One of the first signs was the disappearance of fancywork, and the replacement of the hollow stem by a solid one. Starting with a plain ball or 'knop' the stem became elongated to form a baluster: a shape seen in architecture and in other decorative arts of the time. As the support for a glass, the baluster was usually inverted, with the wider part uppermost, but the glass-maker produced a great number of different stems built-up ingeniously from combinations of round and straight sections. In addition, some of the stems were made enclosing a bubble of air within them; a bubble usually shaped to form a peardrop or 'tear'.

Not only the stems of the glasses, but also the bowls were varied in shape. The most common of the early eighteenth century shapes were the bell and the bucket. The bases of most of the glasses are of the type with a folded edge, a feature giving extra strength where it is required. The foot is also domed, so that the mark left by the iron bar (the 'pontil') on which the glass was made is raised clear of a surface.

About 1715 a new type of stem, the 'Silesian', was introduced. Although it has been pointed out that its origin was more probably in west Germany than east, the name given to it many years ago is still in use. Its introduction here was due to two events. Firstly, the Treaty of Utrecht, negotiated between 1711 and 1715, allowed a greater freedom for German trade, not least to the glass-makers of that country. Secondly, the accession to the throne of England in 1714 of George, Elector of Hanover, as King George I, led to the importation of many of the habits, likes and dislikes of his native land, and also of some of the craftsmen. The tapering ribbed Silesian stem is most frequently found unornamented, but some examples bear wording in raised

Below, *bowls:* (*1*) *Ogee* (*2*) *Bucket.*

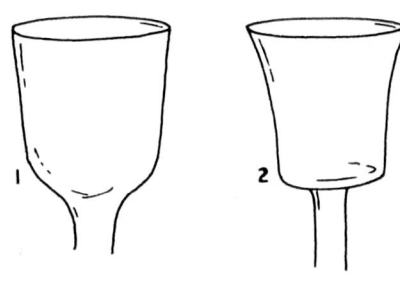

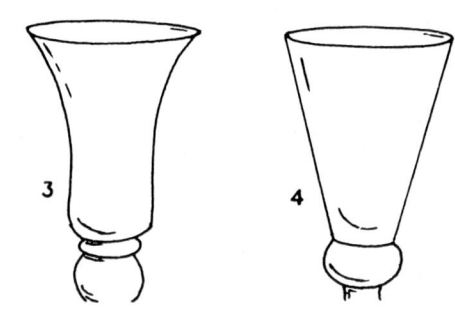

(*3*) *Bell* (*4*) *Conical.*

Folded foot showing the pontil mark (a) raised above the level of the under edge.

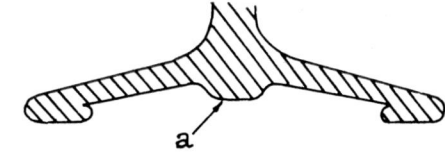

Above, *Fig. 9: Two wines with facet-cut stems and partly-cut bowls. About 1760. Heights approximately 6 inches. (Delomosne and Son.)*

letters on the upper shoulders. One, in the Victoria and Albert Museum, London, is inscribed *God Save King G*, others give the monarch's name in full or just the initials *G R*.

Almost from its commencement the making of glass-of-lead proved a success, and this duly encouraged successive Governments to turn to the glass trade when money was urgently wanted. Earlier, in 1645, in the days of soda-glass, Cromwell imposed a Grand Excise and New Impost by which 'Twelve Pence shall be laid upon every Twenty Shillings value of Glasse and Glasses of all sorts made within the Kingdom'. There followed an interval of freedom for half a century, but when William III wanted money to pay some of the expense of his war against the French, he must have remembered the action of the erstwhile Lord Protector. In 1695 his Government imposed a Duty of twenty per cent on all glass wares except bottles (the latter were charged at one shilling a dozen), which was to be applied for a maximum period of five years.

In the following year, 1696, the Duty was confirmed, and at the same time Parliament made it payable permanently. This last action precipitated a great outcry and, led by members of the Glass-Sellers' Company, makers and dealers all over the country angrily petitioned Westminster. As a result of such active opposition a Parliamentary Committee was set up, and decided there was justice in many of the claims of hardship. In 1698 the Duty was halved, and in the following year it was abolished altogether. Once again the trade was unfettered, and once again, by a coincidence, the duration of its freedom was a half century.

England was again at war in 1745; spirits having been the subject of fresh taxation in 1743, and sugar in 1744, it was then the turn of glass. A Duty was levied on glass-of-lead by weight, at the rate of nine shillings and fourpence on each hundredweight (112 lbs.) of material used and at a lower rate for bottle glass. Once more there were noisy complaints from those affected, and newspapers of the time printed stories of protest meetings being held and of petitions being taken to the House of Commons. This time, however, the Government stood firm.

There is no record of what effect the Duties levied by Cromwell and William III had on either the design or output of glass wares, but the Duty of 1745 has been said to have impeded expansion in the industry and markedly influenced design. As regards the latter, adherents to the theory point to the lighter weight and smaller size of most of the drinking-glasses made after about 1745; changes resulting, so it is said, from attempts by the manufacturers to keep down costs to the public. A smaller proportion of lead was used, which produced a greater bulk of metal per ton and resulted in a somewhat less brilliant product than before.

The changes in design, and of size and weight, were due as much, or more, to fashion as to any other cause. The newer styles of glasses began to appear on the market when signs of rococo design were showing in productions of the other applied arts. By 1740, pattern books were published in London which illustrated samples of the asymmetrical lines already sweeping the rest of Europe. In England, the new forms were applied early to silverware, and within a decade had spread to everything else. They are probably most familiar in much of the mahogany furniture made by Chippendale and his contemporaries, which was the height of fashion from about 1750. In all the arts, soberly balanced lines were replaced by mobile and contorted curves based on the shapes of sea-shells and rocks (rococo: from the French *rocaille*, meaning rock-work).

The feet of glasses also underwent a change during 1740-50. From then onwards the folded foot was seldom made, and a plain type took its place. After about 1770 the pontil mark beneath the base was ground flat, so there was no longer a necessity for the foot to be domed.

Glasses made from the middle of the eighteenth century onwards are not only of lighter appearance and weight than earlier ones, but were often decorated with cutting, engraving or enamelling; subjects dealt with in *Signature* 11. A variant ornament was sometimes formed in the stem, when the earlier imprisoned air-bubble was manipulated by the maker in such a way that it became a series of silvery spirals, known as an 'air-twist'. A later

Below, *Fig. 10: A Newcastle wine-glass with a flared funnel-shaped bowl supported on a multi-knopped baluster stem above a conical foot. Circa 1745. Height 8⅛ inches. (Sotheby's.)*

refinement of the same process was to enclose and treat similarly one or more threads of coloured glass (Figs. 7 and 8).

A NUMBER of drinking-glasses can be identified as having been made in the north of England, at Newcastle upon Tyne. A glass-house was at work there in the early years of the seventeenth century, when successful experiments resulted in the making of window-glass, using local coal to fire the furnaces. As a result, Newcastle coal was sent by sea to London to be used for the same purpose, and supplies of window-glass accompanied it to the capital.

A contemporary account of the window-glass tells of its qualities and its popularity, and relates the manner in which it travelled. Writing in 1703, Richard Neve noted in his *Builder's Dictionary*:

> This sort of glass is of a kind of an ash-colour, 'tis the glass that is most in use here in England, but 'tis subject to have specks and blemishes and streaks in it, and 'tis very often warped crooked.

He continued by stating that the glass was sold by the case, each containing either 35 or 45 tables or sheets. The cases consisted of light frames, into which

> the glass is set in on some straw, which is laid on the bottom of the frame, and there is some straw also put on the sides and top of each case, but none betwixt the tables. These cases are brought to London in the coal-ships, they being set on end in the coles more than half its depth, by which means they are kept steady from falling and being broke by the motion, and rowling of the ship.

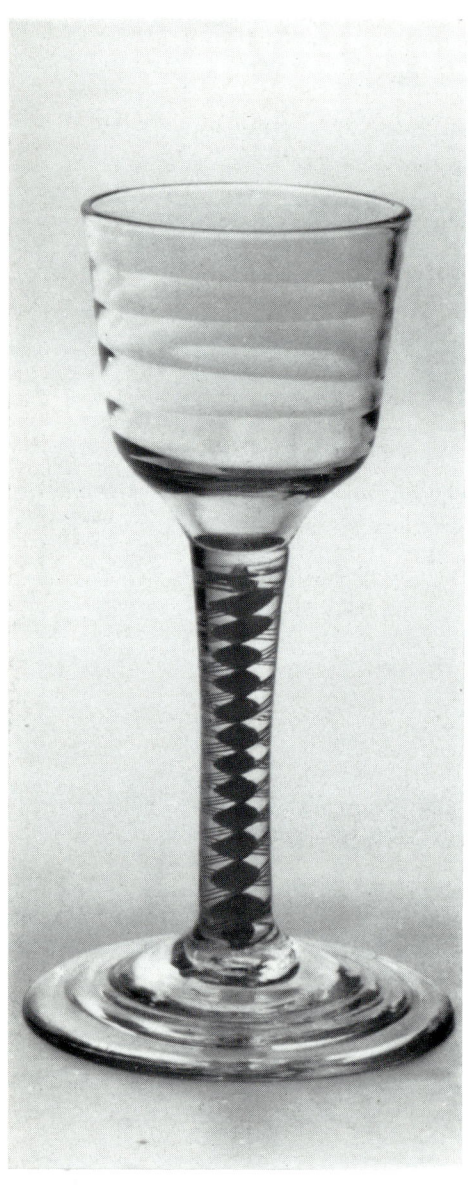

Above, *Fig. 11:* Lynn wine-glass with an ogee bowl horizontally ribbed and an opaque-twist stem above a moulded foot. About 1760. Height 5⅝ inches. (*Sotheby's.*)

Right, *Fig. 12:* 'Night', *engraved by Dent after William Hogarth, 1738. It shows a coach on fire in the narrow entrance to Whitehall, London, looking towards Charing Cross with the statue of Charles I in the distance. On the right is* The Rummer *tavern, with its painted sign above the doorway.*

Above, *Fig. 13*: Cordial glass of about 1710, with a trumpet bowl and baluster stem; there is a cushion knop at the top of the stem and a further knop at the base. Height 6⅞ inches. (*Sotheby's*.)

Later in the century, Ravenscroft's glass-of-lead formula was adopted, and it is recorded that by 1696 a manufactory for making it was in operation. This was probably in the possession of a member of the Dagnia family, who came to Newcastle from Bristol in the 1680's and hailed originally from Italy. The Dagnias prospered, and successive generations of the family increased the number of glass-houses in the city. Other manufacturers also established themselves there, and by 1835 the total of glass-houses had risen to thirty-two.

Newcastle glasses exhibit features that enable them to be distinguished from others. They tend to have tall stems composed of balusters and other shapes assembled to produce a noticeably elegant result, and the bowls are blown thinly. The metal itself is usually very clear in appearance and has a high surface brilliance (Fig. 10).

One other provincial glass-house requires a mention; that at King's Lynn, in Norfolk. There was certainly such an establishment operating in 1693, as is clear from an advertisement in the *London Gazette* of 27th February of that year:

> To be sold all sorts of the best and finest Drinking-Glasses, and curious Glasses for Ornament, and likewise all sorts of Glass Bottles, by Francis Jackson, and John Straw, Glass-makers, at their warehouse in Worcester-Court near the Fountain Tavern in the Strand, or at their Glass-Houses near the Faulkon in Southwark, and Lynn in Norfolk; where all Persons may be furnished at reasonable rates.

The reason for having a glass-house in that part of Norfolk is explained by the fact that excellent sand for glass-making is found in the area. However, there is also evidence that because of the Duty levied in 1695, Jackson told the Committee of the House of Commons, set up two years later, that he had given up the manufactory at King's Lynn. This does not mean, necessarily, that someone else did not purchase and continue to run it. In fact, an advertisement in 1747 in the *Ipswich Journal* announced:

> To be sold by the glass-house in Lynn, a large quantity of fine Flint-Glass both figured and plain, well sorted, the stock consisting of a great Variety of the most Valuable sorts of drinking Glasses, Decanters, Salvers and other glassware.

A number of wine-glasses and tumblers exhibiting a common feature have been attributed to the King's Lynn glass-house; all have a series of ridges running horizontally around the bowl (Fig. 11). As long ago as 1897 a well-known authority and collector of glass recorded that the few ribbed-bowl glasses he possessed had all been bought in the county of Norfolk, and he suggested it was not improbable that they had been made there. For over seventy years now this theory has not been rebutted, and perhaps it never will be.

IN addition to ale and wines, a variety of spirits was enjoyed during the course of the century. They ranged from gin and brandy to fruit liqueurs and mixtures foreshadowing the modern cocktail. Cheap gin was sold in large quantities after the monopoly of the city of London Distillers' Company was broken in 1713. The poorer people, in particular, took full advantage of its low price while ignoring its poorer quality, and indulged themselves until their behaviour invoked the concern of reformers. In 1736 the Government passed an Act to tax spirits and regulate their sale, it having been agreed that 'the excessive drinking of spirituous liquors by the common people tends not only to the destruction of their healths, and the debauching of their morals, but to the public ruin'. As a result, the rising death-rate was arrested and the price and quality of gin both rose. Some years later, in 1751, a further Act increased the tax, and William Hogarth, the artist, showed the nation how it had fallen from virtue and prosperity since exchanging the pleasures of beer for those of gin.

Gin being a drink of 'the common people', it was taken in glasses of simple design and sturdy construction. Cordials, on the other hand, were popular in the more polite ranks of society, and required glasses of comparatively sophisticated pattern. Being strong, they were served in small quantities, and glasses for them had small bowls usually balanced by tall stems (Fig. 13). They are now quite rare, for only a proportion of the more attractive examples have been preserved. Many thousands of the plainer ones, and hundreds of the better-looking ones, must have been broken and discarded in the past.

Figs. 14, 15: Rummer, inscribed S A. A token of Regard from J R. *within a garland of flowers and scrolls; on the reverse* (**below**) *is a sailing ship. About 1830. Height 5¼ inches.*

Above, *Fig. 16: Creamware pottery tankard printed in black with a group of gentlemen smoking churchwarden pipes and drinking from small-sized tumblers. About 1765. Height 4¾ inches.*

Examples of a glass with a large bowl, short stem and heavy foot, known as a rummer, often date from the late eighteenth century. Advertisements of the 1750's mention them by name, but it has been uncertain what they may have looked like at that date. However, William Hogarth's engraving entitled *Night* provides evidence on the point. It was published in 1738, and shows a scene at Charing Cross, looking from Whitehall and with the statue of Charles I in the distance. On the right is the tavern named *The Rummer*, and its painted sign shows a drinking-glass of the familiar type (Fig. 12). Thus, the glass has a longer ancestry than has usually been suspected.

It has been stated that the word 'rummer' is an English corruption of the German 'römer', and has no verbal connection with the spirit rum. Possibly this is so, and it seems that the earlier tall-stemmed glass ceased to be made in this country soon after Ravenscroft produced the one shown in Fig. 2. Whatever the derivation of its name, and this is surely a minor matter, the glass was certainly used for hot or cold rum, or other spirits, and cheered many a heart with its contents. With minor changes in shape and proportion it continued to be made during the nineteenth century.

Glasses resembling the modern tumbler date back several centuries. Surviving Georgian examples have very thick bases, and are wide at the mouth in proportion to their height. Small ones were also made, as can be seen in the print on a pottery tankard in Fig. 16. The men depicted are seated at a table smoking church-warden pipes, and holding small-sized tumblers filled from the punch-bowl before them. In the United States tumblers are sometimes referred to as 'flip glasses', and may well have been used for imbibing flip, a sweetened mixture of beer and spirits. Flip was popular on board ship in Georgian times, and the habit of drinking it was doubtless brought ashore in America by colonists who tasted it when crossing the Atlantic.

© *Geoffrey Wills, 1968.*

3

Drinking Glasses: Part 2

DRAMS, FIRING-GLASSES, CUSTARDS AND JELLIES, AND TODDY AND PUNCH LIFTERS

A DRAM is the name given to a type of dwarf glass usually with a bowl of average size, but raised on a short stem or no stem at all, and standing about 3 to 4½ inches in height. Many surviving specimens are of indifferent quality, although interesting because of their scarcity and varied design. They would seem to have been for use in taverns for the serving of spirits, and their squat form was no doubt adopted to minimise breakages; any tall-stemmed vessel would quickly have fallen a victim to daily usage in a public place. Most of these little glasses were left undecorated, but a few ornamented ones are recorded, probably preserved on account of their attractive appearance. While some of these rarities have air- or colour-twists in their short stems, others have engraved or enamelled bowls.

Drams were made also in the form of firing-glasses. In this guise they have a heavy thickened foot, provided so that drinkers might signal agreement and register applause by rapping with them on the table-top. The noise so produced by a roomful of convivial spirits would resemble that of musket fire, and accounts for the name.

Some examples of drams, both with and without the heavy foot, were given 'deceptive' bowls, the latter extremely thick and with a small central cavity holding a quarter or less of the normal amount of liquor. It is said they were for the use of toastmasters wishing to remain sober, but who were expected to drink to all the toasts proposed in the course of a convivial evening. Alternatively, they were made for serving travellers, who paid the price of a full measure and were cheated of it in the excitement and poor lighting of a busy inn-yard. Both theories appear equally unacceptable, and

a further suggestion is that such glasses were intended for persons desiring to appear socially accommodating, but who were of an abstemious nature. Doubtless they had a definite purpose, but their original usage has been forgotten and we will have to continue guessing.

Glasses with bowls of similar pattern to normal ones, but having only a stem beneath and completely lacking a foot, were provided for stirrup-cups. As it was usually served to those in the saddle, it was unnecessary for such a vessel to stand: it was filled while held and not dispensed with until empty. Almost as unstable were glasses in the form of a boot. It is usually said that they were made in the 1760's in punning ridicule of the then Prime Minister, the Earl of Bute. He was

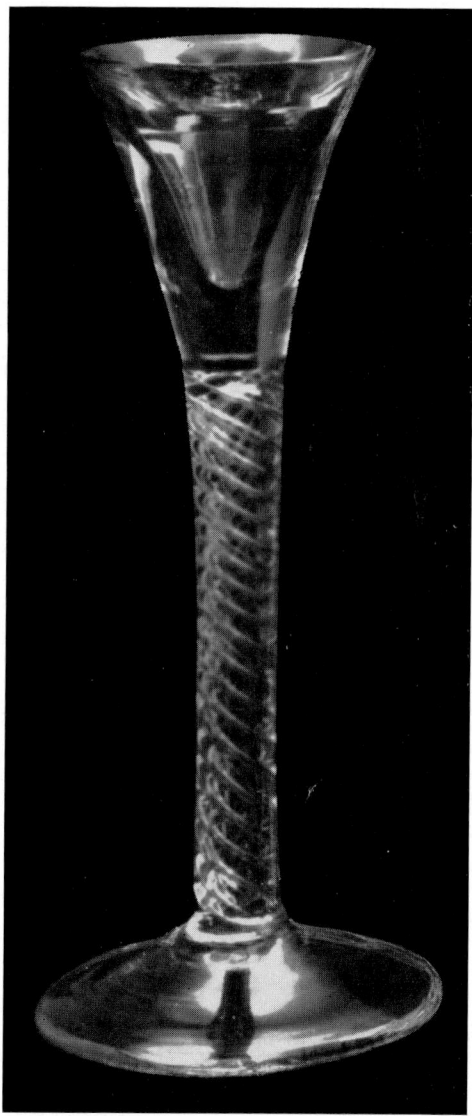

Below, far left, *Fig. 1: Dram with a plain knop and a broad folded foot. Circa 1750; height 2¾ inches.* **Below left,** *Fig. 2: Firing-glass with an opaque-white and green colour-twist stem. Circa 1760; height 4⅜ inches. (Sotheby's.)* **Below right,** *Fig. 3: Cordial glass with a "deceptive" trumpet bowl and air-twist stem. Circa 1750; height 7 inches. (Sotheby's.)*

Above, *Fig. 4: Four custard or jelly glasses of different patterns, 1750-70. Heights 3 and 4½ inches. (City Museum and Art Gallery, Plymouth.)*

widely disliked for his ability in intrigue allied with the fact that he was a Scot, and London was cautious about its northern neighbours since the '45 rebellion and earlier. In addition, Bute had been responsible for introducing a tax on cider, and was also alleged to have had a liaison with the Princess of Wales. If all the charges against him were well-founded he must have been deserving of public malice, but the boot-shaped glasses are mostly datable to long after he died in 1792.

The sweet course at dinner in the seventeenth century and later was often in the form of a jelly or custard served in an individual glass for each guest. There is no reason to suppose that there was any difference in the appearance of glasses used for serving one or another, so that the terms custard-glass and jelly-glass are synonymous. Such glasses followed the dictates of fashion in the same way as other table appointments, and were left plain or embellished according to taste. Early eighteenth century glasses for sweets of these kinds, as well as for ice-cream, were given tall bowls rising direct from domed or flat feet, and are usually found with one or two handles. It is probable that some of the earliest of the glasses lacked handles altogether, and cannot be distinguished from those used for drinking wine.

The original purpose of many surviving drinking-glasses can often only be guessed. Many of them will certainly have been made to special order for those who favoured a particular shape or size, and there have always been individualists with a liking for something completely out of the ordinary. This is exemplified by the glass illustrated in Fig. 6, which would normally be described as a rummer, but is engraved with the word BEER. Numerous glasses, of both large and small capacities and including goblets that were not obviously commemorative ones, have been preserved. We cannot now determine for certain what drink they were intended to contain, and can only admire them as outstanding examples of the glassmaker's craft.

Below, *Fig. 5: Glass in the shape of a boot; late 18th/early 19th Century. Height approximately 4 inches.*

A glossary of drinks popular during the 18th Century, and notes on the glasses in which they were served.

ALE: In the past, ale and beer were stronger than now. Consequently they were served in glasses of much smaller capacity than is required for the present-day pint or half-pint. The glasses had tall narrow bowls, and about the middle of the eighteenth century were often embellished appropriately with representations of barley and hop plants. The majority with such decoration, which was usually engraved and only very rarely enamelled, show two ears of barley with their stalks crossed. Each stalk bears a single leaf, and on the opposite side of the vessel is a hop bloom with two leaves. The various combinations of blooms and leaves have been classified as follows:

i   Two leaves to each barley stalk.
ii   Four leaves to each barley stalk.
iii   Five leaves to each barley stalk.
iv   One barley ear and a hop bloom with a single leaf.
v   One barley ear and a hop bloom with two leaves.
vi   Two barley ears, one leaf to hop bloom.
vii   Barley ears doubled, four, a single leaf to each stalk.
viii   Two hop blooms dependent from two barley stalks.
ix   Two ears of barley, sideways instead of crossed, and no hops.
x   Four crossed barley ears, no hops.

Glasses for drinking ale on special occasions

Below, *Fig. 6: Rummer engraved with hops and barley, and inscribed* BEER; *circa 1810. Height 6½ inches. (L. G. G. Ramsey Esq., F.S.A.)*

were also made in yard and half-yard lengths, the former with a capacity in the region of a pint. John Evelyn noted in his diary that one was used following the proclamation of James II on 10th February, 1685. He wrote:

> Being sent to by the Sheriff of the County to appear and assist in proclayming the King, I went the next day to Bromely, where I met the Sheriff and the Commander of the Kentish Troop, with an appearance, I suppose, of above 500 horse, and innumerable people, two of his Ma^{ty's} trumpets and a Serjeant with other officers, who having drawn up the horse in a large field neere the towne, march'd thence, with swords drawne, to the market-place, where making a ring, after sound of trumpets and silence made, the High Sheriff read the proclaiming titles to his bailiffe, who repeated them aloud, and then after many shouts of the people, his Ma^{ty's} health being drunk in a flint glasse of a yard long, by the Sheriff, Commander, Officers, and cheife Gentlemen, they all dispers'd, and I return'd.

The yard-of-ale was finished with a normal flat heavy foot like any other drinking-glass, but sometimes it was given a bulb at the end. Because of this feature it would not stand properly, and must therefore be drained of its contents before being put down. The unsuspecting drinker raised the glass to empty it, and as it rose above the horizontal he got the remaining contents squirted in his face because of air entering the bulb. Old examples of either type are now very scarce; not unexpectedly in view of their obvious fragility, and most specimens are of comparatively recent manufacture.

CHAMPAGNE: Sparkling Champagne became known in England during the second half of the seventeenth century, when there are many references to it in written and printed documents. In 1665 the Duke of Bedford paid 34/8d. 'for Champaign wine, also 2 dozen glass bottles and corks', and it is mentioned in a number of plays a few years later. Thus, Thomas Shadwell wrote in *The Virtuoso* (1676) of those who

> '... come as the sparks do to a playhouse, too full of Champaign, venting very much

noise and very little wit'.

Later in the century, in a comedy by George Farquhar called *Love and a Bottle*, occurs the following dialogue:

> B: ... Champagne is a fine liquor, which all great Beaux drink to make them witty.
>
> M: Oh! by the Universe! I must be witty. I'll drink nothing else. I never was witty in all my life. I love jokes dearly. Here, Club, bring us a bottle of what d'ye call it, the witty liquor.
>
> (Club, his servant, brings a bottle of Champagne).

It is uncertain what types of drinking-glasses were used for Champagne before about 1830, when the shallow-bowled variety first came into use. Although eighteenth century tradesmen's bills list champagne glasses, they are not described in sufficient detail for them to be identified. The plainer kinds of sweetmeat glasses, with wide-mouthed bowls and tall stems (see *Signature* 5), are sometimes described as champagnes, but perhaps this is because of their resemblance to Victorian and modern ones.

Above, *Fig. 7: Three ales with engraved decoration. Left, with a faceted stem; centre, with a double-knopped air-twist stem; and right, with straight opaque-white twist stem.* Circa *1750-70. Height 7-7½ inches.* (Photograph: *The Connoisseur.*)

CIDER: This drink made from apples has always enjoyed popularity, especially in the country districts where the fruit grew in abundance. The drink was taxed in 1763; the year in which the political activities of John Wilkes came violently into public notice. In April he published a fresh number of his journal *The North Briton*, with which he had been strongly criticising every action of the government. The new number, No. 45, contained a particularly strong attack on the speech to be delivered from the throne at the forthcoming opening of Parliament, and of which Wilkes had had a sight of an advance copy. Readers were alarmed at his suggestion that we were abandoning the King of Prussia, a most popular ally, and the Government took exception to the whole article. In particular, the Prime Minister, George Grenville, and his advisers thought Wilkes had now gone too far altogether. They saw that he had dragged into the argument the name of the King himself by writing:

> 'Every friend of his country must lament that a prince of so many great and amiable qualities . . . can be brought to give the sanction of his sacred name to the most odious measures, and to the most unjustifiable public declarations, from a throne ever renowned for truth, honour, and unsullied virtue'.

As a result, Wilkes was arrested and tried, expelled from the House of Commons, and occupied the forefront of the political scene for most of the ensuing decade. The followers of Wilkes, a hard-living man who played his rôle of champion of the under-dog with great skill, were numerous and vociferous. The cider tax and the seething political agitation coincided in date as well as in popular appeal, and the drink was raised temporarily in status from the country inn to the radical dining-table.

While cider remained a drink confined mainly to the provinces no particular type of glass has been identified as being associated with it. After it became elevated in rank and acquired some political significance, vessels with a bucket-shaped bowl would seem to have been used. Some surviving examples of this shape bear the legend NO EXCISE, or representations of apple trees or boughs with the fruit and leaves.

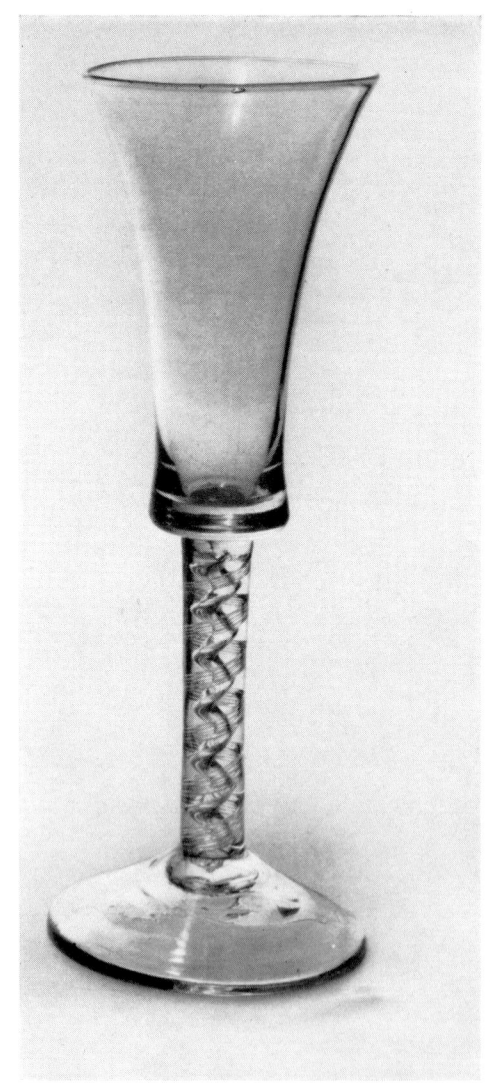

Below, *Fig. 8: Ale with a waisted bucket bowl and an air-twist stem,* circa *1750. Height 8 inches. (Sotheby's.)*

Below, *Fig. 9: Glass of "champagne" type, the double-ogee bowl resting on an air-twist stem and folded foot. Circa 1750. Height 7¼ inches. (Sotheby's.)*

CLARET: The red wines of Bordeaux in northern France were known and drunk in England during the Middle Ages, and probably much earlier. They shared the fate of most food and drink of the time, and were heavily spiced and sweetened with honey and sugar. In that state Claret is found referred to in documents as Claré: a reference to its light red tint. The 'parelling', as it was called, of wines in the past was done not only to please the palate for such strong-tasting beverages, but the unadulterated vintage would probably have been so coarse and rough as to be undrinkable. Nonetheless, Claret remained a favourite wine in England, and by the early seventeenth century, when a liking for the exotic became less general, that from Rochelle was described as 'sharp in taste and of a pallid complexion'.

In 1634 James Howell wrote that 'Portugal affords no wines worth the transporting', but by the end of the century, the story was very different. It is not improbable that the marriage of Charles II and Catherine of Braganza in 1662 focused attention on the wines of her native land, and led her countrymen to doctor their product to suit English taste. Seven years later French and Portuguese wines were paying the same rate of import duty, and in 1693 and 1697 the duties were raised on the former. At the latter date they stood at 4s. 0½d. a gallon on French wines against 1s. 8d. a gallon for Portuguese.

The final blow to the long reign of Claret (and to Burgundy, also) came in 1703, when a Treaty was negotiated by our ambassador, John Methuen. This allowed Portuguese wine to enter England at one-third the rate of duty of French wine, while English woollen goods were taken into Portugal at one-half the rate of duty levied on the products of other countries. As a result, French wine was quickly supplanted by Portuguese, and the Port-drinking Englishman, with or without the accompaniment of gout, became a stock figure.

No special size or shape of glass would appear to have been appropriated to Claret or Port, but each user chose to suit his taste and pocket.

CORDIALS: Cordials were the old equivalent of the twentieth century cocktail, and the name

Left, *Fig. 10: Three early cordials; (left to right) the bell bowl with a plain baluster stem containing a tear above a folded foot, height 5½ inches; the trumpet bowl set on a cylinder stem with an elongated tear above a domed and folded foot, height 6 inches; the bell bowl resting on a collar above a plain swelling stem containing a large tear, height 6¼ inches; 1700-15. (Sotheby's.)*

was one that covered a variety of drinks. A recipe printed in 1742 reads:

> Beat two pounds of double refined sugar very well, and put to it a gallon of the best brandy, stirring it a good while all one way; then put confection of alkermes one dram, spirit of saffron an ounce; then stir it one way for a quarter of an hour; then add three sheets of leaf-gold, and bottle it up; it will keep as long as you please.

Another, of earlier date, is recommended for its medicinal virtues:

> Take a gallon of strawberries clean picked, put to them a pint of Aquavitae, and let them stand four days, and then pour off what is liquid, and strain the rest into it; sweeten it with a little sugar, and infuse a grain of musk or ambergris in it. This strengthens the heart and stomach: half a quarter of a pint in a morning is a preservative against ill airs and infections.

Ratafia (see below) was a type of cordial. Most cordials were based on brandy, were understandably taken a little at a time, and in glasses that held only a small quantity. To compensate for the size of the bowl, the stem was often of above-average height.

Right, *Fig. 11: Three mid-century cordials; (left to right) the straight-sided bowl above an opaque-twist stem, height 6⅞ inches; the round funnel bowl on a multi-spiral air-twist stem, height 6¾ inches; the straight-sided bowl on an air-twist stem of complicated corkscrew pattern, height 7⅛ inches; 1750-60.*
(Sotheby's.)

MEAD: Mead is a very old drink made from fermented honey and water; a variety fermented with ale was called Bragget, and a third type that was the strongest of the trio was known as Metheglin. James Howell wrote to a friend in 1655 as follows:

> To inaugurate a good and jovial New Year unto you, I send you a mornings draught, (viz. a bottle of Metheglin). Neither Sir John Barleycorn or Bacchus had anything to do with it, but it is the pure juice of the Bee, the laborious Bee, and King of insects; the Druids and old British Bards were wont to take a carouse hereof before they entered into their speculations, and if you do so when your fancy labours with anything, it will do you no hurt, and I know your fancy to be very good.
>
> But this drink always carries a kind of state with it, for it must be attended with a brown toast, nor will it admit but of one good draught, and that in the morning, if more, it will keep a humming in the head, and so speak too much of the house it comes from, I mean the hive.

Indulgence in mead-drinking was not only by those wishing to stimulate their mental activity, but was recommended for its medicinal qualities. Like those of many other alcoholic and non-

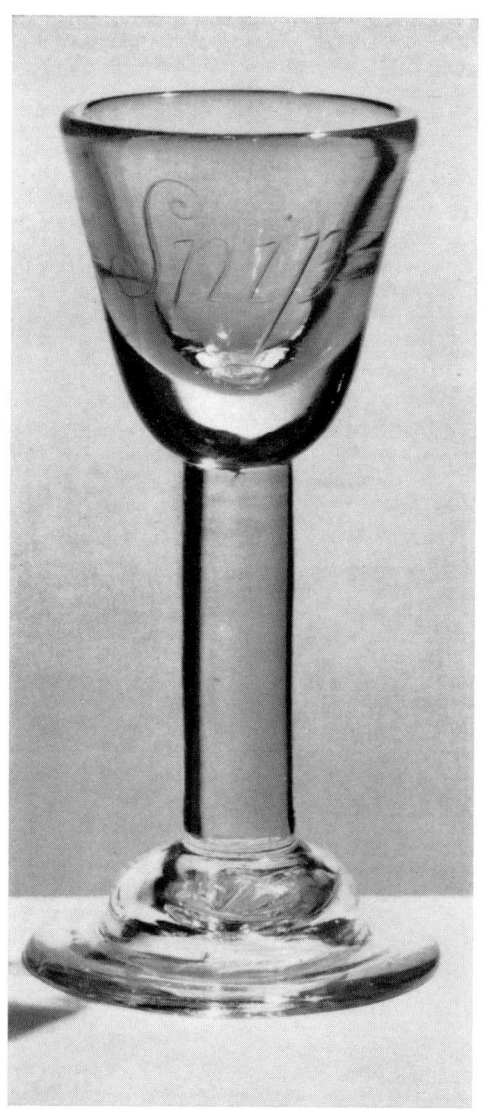

Below, *Fig. 12: Cordial of small size, the thick funnel bowl inscribed* Snip *and set on a plain stem with domed foot. Circa 1740; height 4½ inches. (L. G. G. Ramsey Esq., F.S.A.)*

alcoholic beverages of the period, these were wide-ranging and recommended as certain in their effect. A typical eulogy of 1705 reads:

> *Metheglin: its Virtues:* Metheglin has been highly held in esteem in this nation, and is of excellent use amongst us, if rightly made; nor can it be otherways, since honey, its principal ingredient, is the collection of so many herbs, plants and flowers; and no doubt the quintessential part of them. It is an excellent pectoral, good against consumption, phthisic and asthma: it is cleansing, and diuretic, good against the stone and gravel: it is restorative and strengthening, comforting the vital part, and affords good nourishment.

Mead was popular at one time throughout northern Europe, and appears to have been taken there in a type of glass with an incurved rim to the bowl and a low broad foot. There is no surviving English vessel of this type, and in recent years a tall-stemmed glass with globular bowl has been termed a mead-glass.

MUMM: In the 1750's Samuel Johnson defined Mumm as 'ale brewed with wheat', and it was probably introduced to Britain from north Germany during the seventeeth century. There are mentions of it from time to time, such as when Samuel Pepys drank some at *The Fleece* in Leadenhall Street, on 3rd May 1664. The carefully-kept household accounts of Sir Thomas Myddelton, of Chirk Castle, Denbighshire, record the purchase on 1st October 1678 of 4½ dozen bottles of Mumm at £1 16s.—exactly 8d. each. Seven years later, on 13th August 1685, his successor, Sir Richard Myddelton paid 17s. for '2 dozen and a halfe of drinkinge glasses, and 2 mum glasses', and just prior to this he bought three barrels of Mumm for £10 2s. from a London grocer.

From Germany came not only the recipe for Mumm, but as late as 1696 the glasses for it were being imported from that country. The report mentioning the fact implies that they were not being made here, and whether they were at a later date is not known.

PORT: see CLARET.

PUNCH: Punch acquired its name in the East, where a Hindustani drink was given the name *panch* meaning five, from the number of ingredients it contained. In England, it was compounded variously according to personal taste or public fashion. A recipe of 1705 gives brandy, with or without some white wine, and sugar, limejuice, lemon and orange. As an alternative to brandy the basis was sometimes rum or arrack (see Toddy), but a feature of the drinking of it was that it was made as and when required and not purchased in ready-mixed form.

The imbibing of punch, and the ritual of its mixing, played a part in the social life of the eighteenth century. It was frequently mentioned in print, and the poet Thomas Blacklock wrote of it in 1756:

'What harm in drinking can there be,
Since punch and life so well agree ?'

Samuel Johnson detected a resemblance between punch, with its several ingredients, and conversation, and wrote an essay on the subject. The final paragraph is a fair sample of the Doctor's reasoning and the involved literary style in which he cloaked it. He wrote:

> He only will please long, who, by tempering the acidity of satire with the sugar of civility, and allaying the heat of wit with the frigidity of humble chat, can make the true punch of conversation; and as that punch can be drunk in the greatest quantity which has the largest proportion of water, so that companion will be oftenest welcome, whose talk flows out with inoffensive copiousness, and unenvied insipidity.

Punch was served in a bowl of silver, china or glass, and dispensed by means of a ladle; sometimes one made of glass, but more frequently of silver with a long whalebone handle. No especial type of glass would appear to have been devoted to drinking it, and the engraving in Fig. 14, dating from about 1765, shows the long-stemmed variety being used for the purpose.

During the course of the eighteenth century there appeared a neat little accessory for serving

Below, *Fig. 13:* "*Mead*" *glass, the bowl gadrooned at the base and set on an opaque-twist stem and wide foot;* circa *1760. Height 5⅜ inches. (Sotheby's.)*

Below, *Fig. 14: Wedgwood creamware pottery teapot and cover, decorated at Liverpool with a print in black depicting a party of gentlemen drinking punch. Circa 1765. Height 6½ inches.*
(E. N. Stretton, Esq.)

punch: the punch-lifter, sometimes called a toddy-lifter. It looks like a miniature glass wine-decanter, but with a small hole at each end. The lifter employs the same principle as the pipette, and whoever was responsible for transferring the device from the laboratory to the table has remained anonymous. After immersing the bulbous end into the punch or toddy, a finger or thumb is placed over the hole at the top. This action ensures that the liquid is held within the bulb while the lifter is removed from the punch-bowl and held over the drinking-glass. Then, the finger or thumb over the upper hole is raised and the liquor runs out. It is a very simple little article, but one that is liable to cause consternation in the hands of a clumsy and unskilled user. Lifters vary in the amount of cut decoration that ornaments them, and the majority are faceted along their length, with one or more encircling bands to provide a grip. Most surviving examples are of early nine-

teenth century date, and it would seem that they ceased to be made after about 1830.

RATAFIA: According to William Salmon, who wrote in the early 1700's, 'this liquor is at present very much in vogue'. It was made in several ways, with cherries or apricots or other fruit. Spices and sugar were added to the fruit and, in some instances, brandy, but this last ingredient was not always present. One wonders whether it was in the instance given by John Bunyan, who wrote in 1682: 'I have a cordial of Mr. Forget-Good's making, the which, Sir, if you will take a dram of, may make you bonny and blithe'. Ratafia was served in small quantities, in glasses with tall bowls of tapering 'flute' shape.

SHRUB: Like so many of the other popular beverages of the eighteenth century Shrub varied in its composition. A recipe of 1742 gives brandy, lemon-juice, white wine and sugar, whereas one of 1858

Below, *Fig. 15:* Two punch- or toddy-lifters, both decorated with cutting. Circa *1820.* Length 6¾ inches. (County Museum, Truro.)

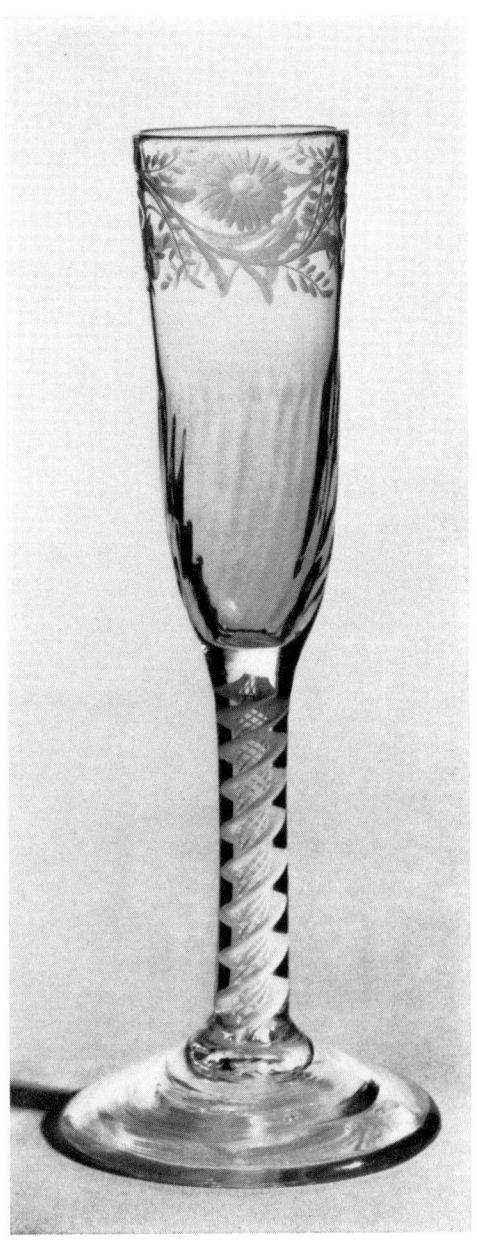

Below. *Fig. 16: Ratafia glass, the tall moulded bowl engraved with flowers and leaves, and set on an opaque-white twist stem. Circa 1760-70. Height 7 inches. (L. G. G. Ramsey Esq., F.S.A.)*

lists only white currants, rum and sugar. Most modern writers refer to it as an antiquated liquor obsolete in the twentieth century, but it is in fact still made and bottled in Bristol. It was probably taken during the eighteenth century in small-bowled cordial glasses.

SYLLABUB: A recipe of 1705 states:
Take a pint of Canary or white-wine, a sprig of rosemary, a nutmeg quartered, the juice of a lemon and some of the peel with sugar, put these together in a pot all night, and cover them; in the morning take a pint of cream and a pint and a half of new milk; then take out the lemon peel, rosemary and nutmeg, and squirt your milk and cream into the pot with a wooden cow sold at the turner's.

A later recipe suggests milking the cow straight into the prepared mixture of sweetened and spiced wine, or

You may make this syllabub at home, only have new milk; make it as hot as milk from the cow, and out of a tea-pot, or any such thing, pour it in, holding your hand very high.

Dr. Edmund Pyle, Chaplain to George II, writing in 1758 to a fellow-cleric, noted:

. . . Dr. Hayles has actually published what has been some time talked of; a tube of tin, with a box of the same at the lower end of it that is full of very small holes. This engine, with the help of a pair of bellows blows up cream into syllabub, with great expedition. This complex machine has already procured the blessing of the house-keeper of this palace, and of all such as she is, in the present generation (who know the time and labour required to whip this sort of gear).

The result, whether prepared with the aid of a flesh-and-blood cow, or a mechanical imitation of the animal, was crowned with a froth of cream and served in a glass with a wide top.

TODDY: This is the juice obtained from the unexpanded flower spathes of the coconut palm, and which has been allowed to ferment. If toddy is distilled it becomes arrack, a spirit sometimes used as the basis of punch during the eighteenth century.

© *Geoffrey Wills, 1968.*

4

Ewers and Decanters

Ewers, or jugs, are amongst the few surviving examples of seventeenth century glass-of-lead bearing the raven's head seal of George Ravenscroft. The best-known specimen is the one in the Cecil Higgins Art Gallery, Bedford, showing distinct signs of the crisselling which afflicted his earlier glass (Fig. 2). As mentioned earlier (*Signature* 1), it was announced on 3rd June 1676 that 'the defect of the flint glasses (which were formerly observed to crissel and decay) hath been redressed severall months agoe'. Exactly one month later, a further announcement was made:

> Wee underwritten shop-keepers and Glass-sellers in and about this Citty of London doe hereby certifie and attest to whome it may concerne That Whereas some of the Christaline or fflint Glasses formerly made were observed to Crizell and spoile; The said defect hath been remedied many months agoe, and the Glasses since made prove as durable and lasting as any other sort of Glasses, there haveing also been made severall Essays and tryalls thereof whereby the soundness of Glasse is usualy knowne And in Witnesse of the trueth wee have signed the third day of July Anno Dom. 1676.
>
> Richard Sadler   Hump: Kilby
> John Greene   Thomas Lewin
> Jno. Allen   Chris: Seward
> Hawly Bischoppe   John Withers.

On 25th October of the following year, a further announcement offered a money-back guarantee to purchasers:

> In pursuance of a former Advertisement concerning the amendment and durability of Flint Glasses, and for entire assurance of such

Fig. 1: A jug engraved with ears of barley, hops, and other ornament. Circa 1750; height 6 inches. (Cecil Davis, Ltd.)

Above, *Fig. 2: Crisselled ewer with ribbed body and foot, made by George Ravenscroft and bearing his seal of a raven's head. Circa 1675; height 9 inches. (Cecil Higgins Art Gallery, Bedford.)*

as shall buy any marked with the Raven's Head, either from the Glass House situate in the Savoy on the River side, or from Shopkeepers who shall aver to have had them from the said Glass House. It is further offered and declared, That in case any of the abovesaid Glasses shall happen to crizel or decay (as once they did) they shall be readily changed by the said Shop-keepers or at the above said Glass House, or the Money returned to content of the Party aggrieved, with his Charges also, if they shall have been sent into the Country, or beyond seas to any remoter parts of the World.

Of the men who signed the first-quoted statement, John Greene was a partner of Michael Measey, and together they had earlier imported large quantities of glass from Venice. Hawly Bischoppe, perhaps of Netherlands origin and known also as Hawley Bishop, took over Ravenscroft's experimental glass-house at Henley from 1676. In due course, after the death of Ravenscroft in 1681, Bishop also took over the London premises at the Savoy. The other men were perhaps shopkeepers of whom no record has been brought to light, or possibly may have played a larger part in developing the new glass than has so far been discovered.

THE marking of glass with a small seal to indicate the maker was not confined to Ravenscroft. In fact, it has a history going back to ancient Syria, the cradle of glass-making, and its revival in England began in the 1650's when seals were placed on glass winebottles. Other makers are recorded as having used individual seals during the later years of the seventeenth century, although no examples of some of the seals have been found yet. There is always a hope that this lack of evidence will be righted, for when Albert Hartshorne wrote his book on glass in 1897 not a single Ravenscroft seal had come to light. However, during the past seventy years about twenty pieces with the tiny head of a raven on them have been located, and there is always a possibility that more exist awaiting discovery.

It is known from an announcement in *The London Gazette* of 16th April 1683 that a man named Henry Holden had been appointed Glassmaker to the King (Charles II), and had been given permission to mark with the royal arms all glasses made for the king. Holden's premises were, like Bishop's, in the Savoy, between the Strand and the river Thames, originally the site of a palace burned down by Wat Tyler's rebels in 1381.

The Duke of York, brother of Charles II and later succeeding him on the throne as James II, had an interest in a glass-house at Wapping, in east London. An announcement regarding it appeared in the *Gazette* on 4th December 1684:

> At his Royal Highness's Glass-house near the Hermitage Stairs in Wapping, are to be exposed to Sale all manner of Flint Glasses, and likewise all sorts of Ordinary and Green, with all other Curiosities that can be made of Glass, all the Glasses being marked with a Lion and Coronet to prevent Counterfeits.

One seal of late seventeenth century date has been found, but it remains uncertain which glasshouse used it. It occurs on the stem of a wineglass, now in Northampton Museum, and on a posset pot in the British Museum. The seal bears a representation of a female figure shooting with a bow, and has been attributed to a factory in Southwark,

Below, *Fig. 3: Part of a cut-glass service, showing drinking-glasses, finger bowls and wine-glass coolers, decanters, a claret jug and a water jug. Circa 1820. (Cecil Davis, Ltd.)*

on the south bank of the river Thames, owned by John Bowles and William Lillington.

The sealed ewer at Bedford (Fig. 2) is of the so-called helmet shape, raised on a low foot and ornamented with ribbing. The pattern can be paralleled in English silver of about the same date, and it originated on the Continent where it was often used for jugs made of pottery. Similar glass ones to Ravenscroft's are known, but lacking the seal. They were made either by him after he had ceased sealing his goods, or by one of the other glassmakers of the time who quickly discovered the excellence of his glass formula and put it into practice.

FOLLOWING the ewers of late seventeenth century date there is a dearth of surviving examples for a period of more than 100 years. No doubt they continued to be made throughout the eighteenth century, but surprisingly few now remain. Such articles were employed for holding water, either for washing the hands or for drinking, and must have been in constant daily use. No doubt because of this, the rate of wastage was high and they were continually discarded in a damaged state.

Opposite, *Fig. 4: Two water jugs and two cream or milk jugs, all with cut decoration;* circa *1800. Height of taller jug is approximately 11 inches. (Delomosne & Son, Ltd.)* **Left,** *Fig. 5: Posset pot with a ribbed body, made by George Ravenscroft and with his seal at the base of the spout; dating from about 1675, the pot is 3⅜ inches high. (Sotheby's.)*

Existing jugs date mainly from the early 1800's, when cut decoration was the height of fashion. This called for them to be very heavily made, with thick walls to take the ornament, and when filled with water they are no light-weight to raise from the table. In consequence of their construction they are stronger than most of their predecessors, which were often comparatively thin-walled and light-weight, and an appreciable number have survived (Fig. 4).

Small-sized jugs for cream and milk were made in the eighteenth century, and later. Up to about 1760 it was usual to take cream with tea, but after that date the modern habit of adding milk became general. Glass jugs were made for the purpose, but not before about 1740. The early ones had bulbous bodies and three short feet, very like silver jugs of the same date, but on the whole it would seem that there was a preference for china or silver. Glass examples are now scarce and perhaps they always were.

The weak point in the design of any jug is the handle, especially at the place where it joins the body. A glass jug has its handle made separately and it is stuck to the body while hot; the metal of the two usually unites completely, but sometimes

Fig. 6: Posset pot of plain pattern raised on a folded foot; circa 1720, height 7½ inches. (Howard Phillips.)

the junction is imperfect and remains a potential danger. Anyone suddenly picking up a water-filled jug with a weak handle is likely to find that it 'comes away in his (or her) hand', and a repair is seldom satisfactory except to preserve the article for display. Buyers should therefore examine a jug in detail and having made a purchase, no less than with other glass, use it with care.

POSSET POTS

POSSET is defined as milk curdled with wine, and was made from a warmed mixture of milk with wine and sugar, sometimes with the addition of cream and eggs, and bread or biscuit crumbs, or oatmeal flour. Sack (Canary wine) was the usual basis, but it was not invariably included as this recipe proves:

King William's Posset

Take a quart of cream, and mix it with a pint of ale, then beat the yolks of ten eggs, and the whites of four; when they are well beaten, put them to the cream and ale; sweeten it to your taste, and slice some nutmeg in it; set it over the fire, and keep it stirring all the while; and when it is thick, and before it boils, take it off, and pour it into the basin you serve it in to the table.

Another recipe adds a warning to the reader, advising gentle stirring:

... stroke it as little as you can, and so do it till you see it be thick enough; then put it into the basin with the ladle gently; if you do it too much it will turn to whey.

The drink was taken as a delicacy, or as a health-giving stimulant that was supposedly potent in treating the common cold. It was not noticeably effective in the latter rôle, because the common cold remains uncured while posset is barely remembered. It is known to have been particularly popular towards the end of the seventeenth century and for the following seventy or so years.

Caudle is another drink, served warm, that may well have been taken from spouted pots. It was given as a restorative to women in childbed, and usually made from gruel mixed with wine and spices. By the eighteenth century it had become rather similar to posset, as a typical recipe of the time shows:

A Fine Caudle

Take a pint of milk, turn it with sack; then strain it, and when it is cold, put it in a skillet with mace, nutmeg, and some white bread sliced; let all these boil, and then beat the yolks of four or five eggs, the whites of two, and thicken your caudle, stirring it all one way for fear it curdle; let it warm together, then take if off and sweeten it to your taste.

Like posset, caudle went out of favour in the mid-eighteenth century. Probably the word remained longer in the public consciousness because of its incorporation in the title of a series of contributions to *Punch:* 'Mrs. Caudle's Curtain Lectures'. They were written by Douglas Jerrold, published in the course of 1845 and did much to ensure the early success of the journal. The 'Lectures' were delivered by Mrs. Caudle to her husband as he lay abed trying to get off to sleep. She kept him awake by her reproofs for his allegedly intemperate habits, and his apparent lack of concern for the happiness and welfare of his loving wife and family.

Posset pots are covered vessels of glass or pottery, and occasionally silver, with the feature of a thin curved spout, and handles at each side of the body. Some surviving examples bear the seal of George Ravenscroft on the front of the lower end of the spout, but none of them retains its cover. The specimen in Fig. 5 is of simple design, with the body ribbed and the handles curled at top and bottom; the little seal is clearly visible in the illustration.

Examples of slightly later date differ little in appearance from the earlier ones (Fig. 6). Large pots and covers of elaborate design, with handles frilled at the edges and bodies ornamented with applied discs stamped with patterns (the discs are known as 'prunts'), were given covers surmounted by tall and complicated finials. Although they do not have spouts they are sometimes referred to as posset pots, but they could have been used equally well for punch or any other beverage.

It is understandable that glass posset pots are now quite rare. Not only were they fragile in the same way as any other object made from the same material, but their slender spouts would have been particularly vulnerable. In addition, as the drink

Fig. 7: Purple glass decanter with "nipt diamond waies" ornament, of about 1675. Height 7½ inches. (Ashmolean Museum, Oxford.)

Fig. 8: Decanter with a loose-fitting stopper, the base of the body and rim of the stopper decorated with gadrooning. Circa 1685. (Howard Phillips.)

lost favour after about 1750 the pots would have been put aside, and it is perhaps remarkable that any have been kept at all.

DECANTERS

THE decanter was evolved to fill the need for a vessel in which wine could be brought from the cask and served at the table. The earliest known examples date from the time of George Ravenscroft, and his successful experiments to produce a material to surpass that hitherto imported from Venice. On 29th May 1677 he submitted to the Glass-sellers' Company of London a price list of the articles he was making, together with their weights and the amount he would charge the Company for each of them. They were as follows:

Quart ribbed bottles	16 oz.	3s. 0d.
Pint bottles of the same	10 oz.	2s. 0d.
½ pint bottles of the same	8 oz.	1s. 6d.
¼ pint bottles of the same	5 oz.	1s. 0d.
Quart bottles all over nipt diamond waies	16 oz.	4s. 0d.
Pint bottles of the same sort	10 oz.	2s. 6d.
½ pint bottles of the same sort	7 oz.	1s. 6d.
Quarterne bottles of the same sort	6 oz.	1s. 3d.

A 'ribbed' bottle would probably have borne raised ribbing running up all or most of its body (see Figs. 2 and 9). The term 'nipt diamond waies' refers to a style of ornament not uncommon on glass of the time, in which the surface has on it a raised criss-cross pattern. A bottle with 'nipt diamond waies' ornamentation and bearing Ravenscroft's seal is in the British Museum, and another, unmarked and of purple glass is in the Ashmolean Museum, Oxford (Fig. 7).

An advance in design involved the addition of a handle to the decanter, and at the same time its shape was altered. From being what has been called a 'shaft-and-globe' it became a tall-bodied and short-necked article, breaking away from the pattern of contemporary winebottles hitherto followed. Halfway between these two types is the rare decanter illustrated in Fig. 8. The lower part of the body is ribbed spirally, an ornament known as gadrooning, and the loose-fitting stopper is edged in the same manner. A scarce type, but not unique like the preceding piece, is shown in Fig. 9.

The stoppers of the early decanters, or serving-bottles as they are sometimes termed, are invariably very easy fitting. At the time, the vessel was filled just before it was required, emptied quite soon afterwards and, unlike later practice, not employed for storage. Evaporation was of slight consequence under the circumstances, so an air-tight container was not a necessity. Loss of the stoppers by breakage, or the discarding of them as encumbrances, must have been commonplace, and understandably there are more of the decanters now lacking their tops than complete with them.

In the course of the eighteenth century different habits of eating and drinking became customary, and amongst them was the changeover from claret to port as the Englishman's favourite wine. The latter, it was found, benefited from careful storage, and was improved further by being poured from its bottle into another vessel wherein it could settle and acquire room-temperature. This other vessel was a decanter, and as the wine was thenceforward kept in it until finished, a close-fitting stopper became essential. By about 1750, it is found to have been ground into the neck of the decanter to make it virtually airtight.

THE shapes of the actual decanters varied with the years, but no single one would seem to have attained any greater popularity than another. During the years 1750 to 1770 it would have been possible to purchase them in any of three shapes: bulbous, resembling a modern water-carafe; mallet-shaped, resembling the mason's tool with the sides sloping outwards towards the base; and club-shaped, somewhat similar to the preceding but with the sides tapering to the base. All were usually decorated with engraving, cutting or enamelling, a subject dealt with more fully in *Signature* 11.

From contemporary advertisements in newspapers of the period it is possible to trace some of the fashionable patterns. The first notice of a decanter with the name of its contents engraved upon it appeared in the *Norwich Mercury* for

Fig. 9: Decanter with a loose-fitting stopper, the body and stopper partly ribbed. Circa 1685. Height $11\frac{5}{8}$ inches. (London Museum.)

26th December 1755, when a dealer in the city announced:

> new-fashioned decanters with inscriptions engraven on them, Port, Claret, Mountain, etc., etc., decorated with vine leaves, grapes, etc. (Fig. 12).

Within a few years other dealers advertised them and referred to them as 'label decanters'. The names recorded on them, in addition to those noted above, include Cider, Beer, Ale and 'Champaign'; the latter a still red wine from the Champagne district, that was in greater favour at the time than the sparkling white variety.

Towards the end of the eighteenth century the shape of the decanter altered, and the diameter of the base increased as the height became a little less. About the time of the Regency, the most popular had drum-shaped bodies, gently sloping shoulders and short necks. The latter were given from two to four rings to form a hand-grip when pouring, and the mouth was flared (Fig. 11). Elaborate cutting was used as a decoration, but equally there were many decanters left compara-

Right, *Fig. 12: Three decanters engraved with labels and with vines and flowers; (left and right) club shaped with spire stoppers; (centre) mallet shaped with a disc stopper. Circa 1760; heights 11¼ and 12 inches. (Delomosne & Son, Ltd.).*

Opposite, above, *Fig. 10: Decanter cut all over with flat diamonds, and with a disc stopper similarly cut. Circa 1760; height 9½ inches. (City Museum and Art Gallery, Plymouth.)*

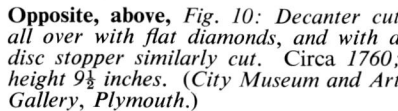

Opposite, *Fig. 11: Six pairs of cut decanters with mushroom stoppers. Average height, 10 inches. (Delomosne & Son, Ltd.)*

tively plain for sale at a lower price.

At about the same date square-based, straight-sided decanters were made, sometimes in sets in metal frames of the type used for sauce and condiment bottles. They were generally in coloured glass with cut and gilt decoration, and have always been supposed to be of Bristol origin. The shape did not reach the height of fashion until Victorian times, when sets of three or four in heavily-cut clear glass were enclosed in a lockable open wood container. Known as a 'Tantalus', it was a uniform feature of the average home, where it stood in splendour on the dining-room sideboard with its liquor-filled contents invitingly, but inaccessibly, displayed.

While most decanters have an average capacity in the region of 1¼ pints (about 750 c.c.), it varied and there was no set standard. A large number were undoubtedly sold singly, but many were made in pairs and sets; in the latter instance with other tableware, such as drinking-glasses and finger-bowls to match (see Fig. 3). In such cases, the stopper was sometimes scratched with a tiny numeral to correspond with one on the decanter itself. This was an obvious precaution to ensure they would be kept together after washing, as they were very seldom interchangeable.

The rarest and most sought-after decanters are probably those with bases of extra-large diameter and steeply-sloping sides rising from them. They are known as 'Rodney' or 'Ship's' decanters; the former after the renowned Admiral of the name who died in 1792. They continued to be manufactured for some years after that date, and have, incidentally, been reproduced in the present century. The example shown in Fig. 13 is engraved with the coat of arms of George, Prince of Wales, later George IV, and was made between 1801 and 1820. He was not a man particularly addicted to nautical life (this was more the sphere of his brother, William IV, known as the 'Sailor King'), so perhaps these decanters were not taken to sea. Their shape, of course, was devised to keep them upright while a vessel was in motion, but they are equally attractive in appearance on land.

A variation that falls between the decanter and the jug is the claret jug. It was sometimes made to match, in both general outline and ornament, a decanter, and sets of both articles are not unknown (Fig. 3). The claret jug is quite rare in its Georgian form, but increased in popularity during the nineteenth century.

Decanters, too, were made in large numbers during the reign of Victoria. The exuberant cutting of specimens in about 1820 was followed by plain facets running from base to neck, and an occasional return to the long-necked bulbous style of a century or so earlier. Later still, the neck was shortened and the whole raised on a low circular foot, but no one pattern prevailed. The buyer had a wide choice and might select according to his taste from clear or coloured, and cut or plain. More recently, especially since about 1920, revival of interest in eighteenth century design has resulted in the making of large numbers of reproduction Georgian decanters. They were not invariably produced to deceive, and when new have a garish glitter about them that betrays their recent manufacture. However, some have suffered sufficient everyday wear-and-tear to give them a spurious air of greater age than they really possess.

Above, *Fig. 13: Set of three decanters with faceted sides and spire stoppers, in a plated stand; circa 1840; overall height 16 inches. (City Museum and Art Gallery, Plymouth.)* **Opposite,** *Fig. 14: Ship's decanter, engraved with the coat of arms of George, Prince of Wales. Made between 1801 and 1820, when the Prince succeeded to the throne as George IV. Height 8⅜ inches. (Howard Phillips.)*

F INALLY, mention must be made of the decanter stopper; an important artistic and functional feature of the whole, and no less subject to changes in fashion. The earliest stoppers, those of the loose-fitting type were similar to the one shown in

Fig. 15: Decanter with a moulded stopper, made at a Tyneside glass-house. Circa 1830. Height 11½ inches.

Fig. 8, which is hollow and domed with a ribbed top and a button finial. From the middle of the eighteenth century, when cutting had become general, a sequence of styles can be discerned, but many of them overlapped in date and it is not possible to be emphatic as to exactly when they came and went. Variations of the basic types are not infrequently found, and many were possibly featured by particular makers or cutters who can no longer be identified.

The pointed 'spire' cut with facets all over was in use about 1750, and was followed by a partially-cut flattened ball. This last type was further flattened and cut either at the edges or all over its surface, and was current during the years 1760 to 1770.

A plain upright disc was often used on stoppers of the late eighteenth and early nineteenth centuries, sometimes with a hollow centre and shallow radiating cuts on the broad sloping edge. About 1820 came the flat-topped hollow 'mushroom', almost always ornamented with complex cutting. Twenty years later, the spire returned, but it now appeared as if emerging from the preceding mushroom, and was cut with simple facets to match its decanter (Fig. 13). Alternatively, some of the 'revived spire' type were moulded, and are attributed to a glass-house in the Newcastle area (Fig. 15). In the second half of the nineteenth century the hollow ball was introduced, and this was either left completely plain or was heavily cut, according to taste or pocket.

Odd stoppers can sometimes be bought, but it is important to match them to a decanter for both style and colour. They seldom make a good fit, which would be too much to expect, but can be ground-in by a glass merchant.

© *Geoffrey Wills, 1968.*

5

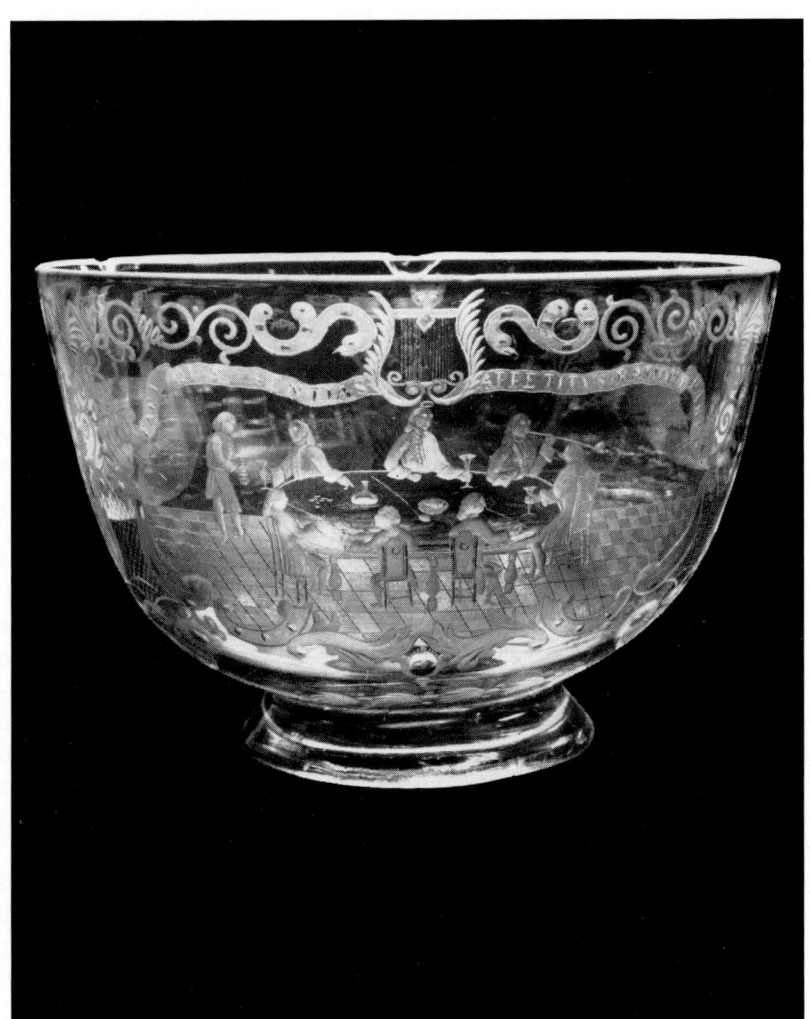

Table Wares

THE score or so of pieces of glass bearing George Ravenscroft's seal include the two bowls illustrated in Figs. 1 and 2. Both of them are transparent, and free from the fine web of interior cracks, "crisselling", that disfigured much of his earlier output. It was early in 1674 that he petitioned for a patent for making "a particular sort of crystalline glass resembling rock crystal", which was granted to him in May of the same year.

Ravenscroft was visited in about 1675 at his Henley glass-house by Dr. Robert Plot, who was busily gathering material for his book, *A Natural History of Oxfordshire*, published in the following year. In it, he described how the glass was first made from burnt black flints and white sand to which were added nitre, tartar and borax to assist their melting. However, he wrote, it was "subject to that unpardonable fault called crizelling caused by the too great quantities of the salts in the mixture, which . . . induce a scabrites or dull roughness irrecoverably clouding the transparency of the glass". Plot then stated that the quantity of salts (nitre, tartar and borax) was subsequently lessened, and as a result "they now make a sort of pebble glass which are hard durable and whiter than any from Venice and will not crizel, but under the severest trials whatever, to be known from the former by a seal set purposely on them".

It would seem that Ravenscroft wisely kept his secret to himself during Plot's visit. His action is understandable when it is recalled that he was not his own master but an employee of the Glass Sellers' Company, and therefore not free to divulge anything even if he had

Opposite, *An oval shallow bowl with a shaped and serrated rim, the sides cut with relief diamonds and the base with radiating and transverse prisms. Circa 1820. Length 9 inches.* **Below,** *Fig. 1: Bowl marked with the raven's head seal of George Ravenscroft. Circa 1680. Diameter 7 inches.*

Fig. 2: Bowl with a ribbed base and folded rim, marked with the Ravenscroft seal. Circa 1680. Diameter $8\frac{7}{8}$ inches. (Cecil Higgins Art Gallery, Bedford.)

wanted to do so. There is little doubt that the proportion of salts was reduced, as Plot related, but he did not tell his readers (even if he may have known of it), that at the same time a quantity of lead oxide, in the form of red lead, was added. It was this last important ingredient that rectified the earlier instability, and enabled the Company to "certify and attest that the defect of the flint glasses (which were formerly observed to crissel and decay) hath been redressed severall months agoe and the glasses since made have all proved durable and lasting as any glasses whatsoever".

In order to still any doubts in the minds of the public, the Company permitted Ravenscroft to mark all the new-style, "glass-of-lead" wares with a personal seal, and for this he chose the punning device of a raven's head. In addition, to prove the truth of the statement, an advertisement in the *London Gazette* made a promise of money being returned if any seal-marked piece should crissel or decay. Whereas crisselling affected the appearance of an article and it lost it transparency, it could also be affected by a more serious type of decay. In this, the surface became moist and ran with "tears"; no sooner were they wiped away than they re-appeared, and finally the piece might disintegrate completely. As this would seem to have occurred with some of Ravenscroft's earliest pieces it is quite understandable that the public was apprehensive and needed assurances from the Company.

In spite of the "satisfaction or money back" guarantee and the strenuous attempts to sell only perfect goods, the unsightly crisselling was not always kept at bay. The bowl shown in Fig. 3 demonstrates the fact all too obviously, and as it is a sealed one it must have been made after the autumn of 1676 when such marking was begun. It is of similar pattern to the bowl in Fig. 2, with a series of ribs round the base, but it is of larger diameter.

There was one important further item that went into the clay pot in which the ingredients were placed in the furnace. It was an ingredient that not only assisted materially in the manufacturing process but also saved money, and it was none other than broken glass; known as "cullet". In the glass-works itself, all waste and broken material was carefully saved, and in the outside world a man might avoid starvation or the workhouse by collecting

Fig. 3: Bowl of similar pattern to that in Fig. 2, but affected by crisselling. Circa 1675. Diameter 11¾ inches. (The London Museum.)

it. In 1697 it was stated that "Many hundreds of poor families keep themselves from the Parish by picking up broken glass of all sorts to sell to the Maker".

Cullet was added because it helped the other constituents to fuse more completely. It became of increased importance when the Duty of 1745 was laid on glass, for it not only saved the high cost of fresh materials but a proportion was allowed to be included in the mixture free of tax.

The use of cullet certainly assisted the glass-maker, but it has had the effect of making the task of the historian extremely difficult. In the case of pottery and porcelain, once a site has been located it is often possible to excavate it. The finding of fragments and discarded pieces can be of considerable assistance in identifying the work of a particular manufactory. This has occurred in recent years; notably in Staffordshire, where the Longton Hall porcelain factory site was successfully investigated prior to the erection over it of a housing estate. Alas, the same thing does not apply to glass-houses, where almost all waste material was re-used and there is little or no evidence to assist later research. Equally, waste-pits in town and country have yielded only a minute proportion of glass as compared with the great quantity of ceramic ware, whole or smashed, brought to light.

The history of English glass wares has had to be built up largely from contemporaneous mentions, which are few in number and liable to be misinterpreted, and from such actual pieces as have been preserved by chance. We have no knowledge of the appearance of many types of articles that we know existed and have vanished completely; broken, discarded and re-melted as cullet. Only during the past seventy years has there been any real interest in old glass, but a remarkable amount of research has been done in the time, and we now seem to have a fairly accurate idea of what was made. However, there is no finality in such research, and much more remains to be discovered.

While the original use of such bowls as those in Figs. 1, 2 and 3 cannot now be decided, it was not long afterwards that some for an identifiable purpose were being made. Glass punch bowls, similar in outline and ornament to silver ones of the time, have survived from

Left, *Fig. 4: Punch bowl with "nipt diamond waies" decoration round the upper part of the foot and the base of the bowl. Circa 1690. Height 10¼ inches. (The London Museum.)* **Left, above,** *Fig. 5: Punch bowl engraved with sailing ships and inscribed 1*TILLY STEYNING. Circa 1760. Diameter 11¼ inches. (Howard Phillips.)* **Opposite,** *Fig. 6: Punch bowl of pale green glass with an opaque-white rim, decorated with engraving. Circa 1760. Diameter 8⅛ inches. (Sotheby's.)*

the last quarter of the seventeenth century. The hazards of handling such easily breakable articles, and the use in them of heated liquid has meant that most were broken and thrown away long ago. It is probable that they were once far from uncommon.

The early examples resemble that illustrated in Fig. 4. The base of the bowl and the dome of the folded foot are ornamented with a raised trellis-pattern (named by Ravenscroft as "nipt diamond waies" and sometimes abbreviated in print to NDW) and there is a sturdy bulge or "knop" forming the stem. Another punch bowl, of similar late seventeeth century date, is in the Victoria and Albert Museum, and differs from the preceding one by having the hollow foot rising directly up to the bowl. Thus there is no real stem, but instead the maker has placed a scalloped canopy round the junction of the two parts. Again, "nipt diamond waies" ornament appears on the lower half of the bowl, and is found also on the cover; a rare feature to be found intact. The cover has a finial in the form of a crown with frilled edges, formed by nipping the hot metal with a pair of pincers.

Pincers were also used in making the trellis ornament. The half-completed article was given a further coating or "gather" of molten glass, and this was pincered at intervals to produce diamond-shaped enclosures. The band of decoration round the middle of the bowl was made by trailing round it a couple of strands of molten glass, which were similarly treated with the pincers.

By the middle years of the eighteenth century the punch bowl was made to rest on a low foot, or on a mere shallow base. Fig. 5 shows a bowl of the first-named type, with a broad foot and a stem shaped as a flattened disc; a feature found in wine glasses and then known as a "merese". The bowl is engraved with two scenes of ships sailing between headlands upon which are Oriental buildings and figures, and is inscribed I. TILLY STEYNING. I. Tilly has not been traced, but it may be assumed he was connected in some way with one or more of the ships depicted and that they had perhaps returned successfully from a distant

trading voyage. Steyning is a Sussex village that once returned two members to Parliament, and was described in the eighteenth century as "a mean, contemptible place, with hardly a building fit to put a horse in".

The third punch bowl illustrated (Fig. 6) is raised on a shallow circular foot, and in this respect, and in its general outline, resembles those made at the time of pottery and porcelain. The decoration, too, is not dissimilar to that on ceramic specimens, and takes the form of a scene with seven gentlemen seated round a table drinking and smoking, on the right a servant replenishing the glass of one of the drinkers. Elsewhere on the bowl is engraved a staghunt, and a view of the façade of a seventeenth century mansion. It is inscribed with two legends: *Fari Quae Sentias* (Speak what you think), which is the motto of the Walpole family, and *Apetitus Rationi Pareat* (Let the appetite be obedient to reason), motto of the Fitzwilliam family.

This bowl is made of glass of a light bottle-green colour, and the rim is embellished with opaque white. It is conjectured that the house depicted on it might be Milton, Northamptonshire, which was once the home of the Fitzwilliams, and that the bowl was made at a glasshouse in the north of England.

SALVERS. The salver is a flat-topped dish, usually with a rim, raised on a central foot (Fig. 7). Known sometimes as a tazza (apparently from the Arab words *tass*, or *tassah*, meaning a bowl), it is paralleled in silver of the late seventeenth and early eighteenth centuries. In a book published in 1661 the salver is described as

. . . a new fashioned peece of wrought plate, broad and flat, with a foot underneath, and is used in giving Beer, or other liquid thing to save the Carpit or Cloathes from drops . . .

It would seem possible that the salver illustrated was once complete with a matching tankard or perhaps a cup and cover.

A later version of the salver, of greater diameter than the earlier ones, came into use during the second quarter of the eighteenth century. In appearance very like a Victorian cake stand, it has a number of features that differentiate it. As seen in the example shown in Fig. 8, the rim is moulded on the outside, the stem is hollow and the domed foot has a

Left, *Fig. 7: Salver or tazza. Circa 1680. Diameter 13¼ inches. (Sotheby's.)*
Below, *Fig. 8: Salver for sweetmeat-glasses, with a ribbed edge, hollow stem and domed folded foot. Circa 1750. Diameter 11¼ inches.* **Right,** *Fig. 9: "Captain", "Orange" or "Master" glass for sweetmeats, with a short bucket-shaped bowl on an opaque-twist stem. Circa 1760. Height 7½ inches.*
(L. G. G. Ramsey, Esq., F.S.A.)

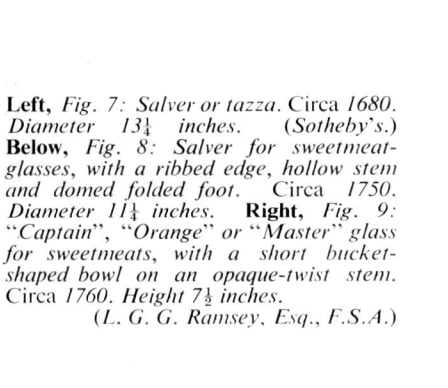

folded edge. Most or all of these would not be present in a nineteenth century piece, especially the folded foot.

The purpose of these salvers is described in a diary entry made by Lady Grizell Baillie, who noted all she encountered in her daily round between 1692 and 1733. They were used for holding custards, jellies and sweetmeats, which formed the dessert course of a dinner. The variety of good things noted on one occasion by Lady Grizell included French figs and plums, apricots, dried fruits, almond biscuits, fruit jellies, apples in syrup, sliced oranges, almonds and raisins and pistachio nuts. Most of which might be found on a well-laden table in the present century.

Slightly later, in 1753, Mrs. Hannah Glasse, who is always misquoted as writing in her *Art of Cookery* "First catch your hare" in a recipe for cooking that animal, wrote of the use of salvers:

> A high pyramid of one salver above another, the bottom one large, the next smaller, and the top one less; these salvers are to be filled with all kinds of wet and dry sweetmeats in glass, or little plates, colour'd jellies, creams, etc., biscuits, crisp'd almonds and little knicknacks, and bottles of flowers prettily intermix'd, and the little top salver must have a large preserved fruit in the centre.

The "large preserved fruit in the centre" would have been placed in a taller glass than the others surrounding it. It is referred to sometimes as a "Captain" glass, a "Master" glass or an "Orange" glass, and its pattern followed that of its smaller fellows (Fig. 9). Some of the tazzas were made in two separate parts, top and base, fitting neatly one into the other. When assembled, the top could be revolved at will to bring any particular glass within reach. Similar stands made of wood, and also dating from the middle of the eighteenth century, are known as "Lazy Susans".

Vying in effect with the pyramid of salvers was the epergne. It is an elaborate and fragile table ornament that has survived in greater numbers made of silver than of glass. Standing up to two feet or so in height, the epergne has a central pillar from which radiate shaped arms holding removable small baskets. The whole article was constructed in parts that can be fitted together in a simple manner for use, and stored safely when taken apart. The baskets were used for sweetmeats, and some of the earlier columns were surmounted by a small bowl for the "preserved fruit". About 1770, when cut ornament was highly fashionable the epergne was decorated in that manner. It was then sometimes hung with glittering drops of the kind used on chandeliers, and fitted with candle-holders (Fig. 10).

Many other table appointments were made of glass, and one dealer's advertisement of the 1750's announced the sale of saltcellars, dishes, plates, bowls, basins, cruets and castors, as well as less obviously recognisable things such as "large Glasses for Cool-Tankards" and "glass plates for china dishes". The former would not appear to have been identified yet, but the latter are probably circular discs with folded edges, and with a small-sized pontil-mark on the rather convex underside. Presumably they were used to enhance and protect painted porcelain plates and dishes, but must have been impractical if they were used for anything other than display.

CRUETS: From about 1760 glass cruets and castors were frequently made in sets and fitted in silver frames. Usually they were given lids of the same metal, which can occasionally be dated by means of the hall-marks on them and provide a useful means of studying what was fashionable at a certain time. The marking, and exemption from its necessity, varied from time to time between 1738 and 1790. In the former year Parliament laid down that gold and silver "Mounts, Screws, or Stoppers to Stone or Glass Bottles or Phials" did not have to be assayed to test their quality and therefore need not bear a hall-mark.

A duty of 6d. an ounce on new silver ware was imposed in 1784, and to prove that it had been paid a mark in the form of the sovereign's head was stamped on the article. It was in addition to the usual marks denoting the purity of the metal, the date of stamping, the location of the assay office, and the initials of the maker. The exemptions allowed earlier, including those noted above in respect of glass bottles, etc., remained unchanged.

Six years later a further Act, while leaving gold items unaffected, repealed the 1738 silver

Opposite, *Fig. 10: Epergne and candelabrum with cut decoration. Circa 1780. Height 26¾ inches. (Cecil Davis Ltd.)*

exemptions and altered the list of articles that did not have to pay duty or be marked by the assay office. This changed list of 1790 included:

Tippings, Swages, or Mounts not weighing 10 dwt. of Silver each, except Necks and Collars for Castors, Cruets, or Glasses, appertaining to any sort of Stands or Frames.

Another section of the Act stated that, amongst other items, "Necks, and Collars" weighing under 5 dwt. of silver each were also liable for assay and payment of the duty.

To sum up: it was not until 1790 that it became obligatory for a maker to send these small items to the assay office, and it was not until that year that they were fully stamped. Earlier, they would be given only the maker's personal mark, and could be dated solely by such signs of fashion that they showed or from knowing the years during which the maker was active. In either case, this could only give an approximate year, whereas the hall-marking does give the exact one in which the marking took place; which is normally very close to the date of manufacture.

Glass was a most practical material for the making of salt cellars, because, unlike metals, it was unaffected by its contents. A silver cellar had to have its interior gilded or be fitted with a removable glass lining, and even then there was a risk of stray grains of salt doing damage. The earliest glass ones, dating perhaps from the start of the eighteenth century, were of bowl shape raised on a low circular foot, and were double-blown with a space in-between the outside and the interior. As the century advanced, the bowl was given a short stem between it and the foot, and was decorated with cutting (Fig. 11).

Silver salt cellars were the models for circular glass ones, each raised on three short curved legs with lion-masks at the knees. They date from about the middle of the century, and as an alternative to the lion, whose mask was so commonly seen at the time on all forms of applied art, the knees of the legs are found with simple raspberry-pattern prunts. Only rarely were salts of this type given cut ornament, and the decorator relied on the use of moulding in its place.

About 1800, the stem shrank once again, the foot disappeared and a simple bowl resulted. It was almost always cut and given a serrated rim, which served not only as decoration but prevented the small salt-spoon from sliding about. Many salt cellars of the time were sold complete with Sheffield Plate stands, and some had small dishes of glass cut to match.

Fig. 11: Two boat-shaped salt-cellars decorated with cut ornament, and possibly of Irish make. Circa 1790. Height 3⅜ inches. (City Museum and Art Gallery, Plymouth.)

WATER GLASSES AND FINGER BOWLS: Old advertisements speak of "water glasses", finger bowls and glass coolers. All three of them varied less in their form than in their uses. The first-named, water glasses, were the subject of references in literature of the last third of the eighteenth century, which tells that their use was not universally approved. A mention of them was made by Tobias Smollett, author of *Roderick Random* and other novels, who wrote in 1766:

> I know of no custom more beastly than that of using water glasses in which polite company spirt and squirt and spue the filthy scourings of their gums.

Ten years later William Twiss remarked on a similar habit he had noticed in Ireland, and added that "no well-bred persons would touch their victuals with their fingers, and such ablutions ought to be unnecessary".

We have no means of knowing how widespread were such unseemly habits, and it might possibly be thought that both Smollett and Twiss were being satirical or were generalising from isolated incidents. However, François de la Rochefoucauld, a Frenchman who visited this country in the early 1780's, noted:

> Dinner is one of the most wearisome of English experiences, lasting, as it does, for four or five hours. The first two are spent in eating ... After the sweets you are given water in small bowls of very clear glass in order to rinse out your mouth—a custom that strikes me as extremely unfortunate. The more fashionable folk do not rinse out their mouths but that seems to me even worse; for, if you use the water to wash your hands, it becomes dirty and quite disgusting.

It has been suggested that the earlier water glasses were of the shape of the modern tumbler, but by the time de la Rochefoucauld published his reminiscences (1784) they were small-sized bowls; at least they were where he visited.

Bucket-shaped tumblers were made in the eighteenth century, but are usually found in small sizes about 4 inches in height. They are now rare, and are usually found decorated; plain ones were not highly regarded in the past and have now vanished. Examples dating from about 1800 and decorated with cutting were made in quantity, and are often of a capacity in the region of half-a-pint. Some with the distinctive ornament of a series of slightly raised horizontal ribs, attributed to the King's Lynn glass-house, have been recorded. As an alternative to the popular outward-sloping bucket-shaped, small-sized glasses of waisted form were also made. It would seem they were on the market in about 1770, and may have been the product of a particular glass-house perhaps in the Newcastle district.

In about 1780 the finger-bowl began to be advertised as a "finger glass", "finger cup" or "finger basin". Its function was obvious and it was used at table to hold water in which diners might politely rinse their fingers (Fig. 15).

The wine-glass cooler was a miniature individual Monteith: the latter being a seventeenth century introduction, a large bowl with a notched rim, named after a Scotsman who wore a cloak with a scalloped hem. The cooler is in appearance very similar to a finger-bowl, but with the addition of one or two notches in the rim. As with the full-sized Monteith, wine-glasses were set in the notches with their feet outermost and their bowls resting in water in the vessel (Fig. 15). The purpose was to cool the glasses in readiness for the wine they would hold, and for rinsing them between courses.

Dishes for use at the dining-table certainly existed during the middle years of the eighteenth century, and probably at an earlier date. They would have been easily damaged when in use, and the majority of surviving specimens date from about the year 1800, and later. They are usually heavily-made and elaborately cut in the fashion of the period, and the majority are oval in shape (frontispiece). We do not know if they were made in very large numbers, but it is probable that less breakable materials were found more practical. Silver, and the

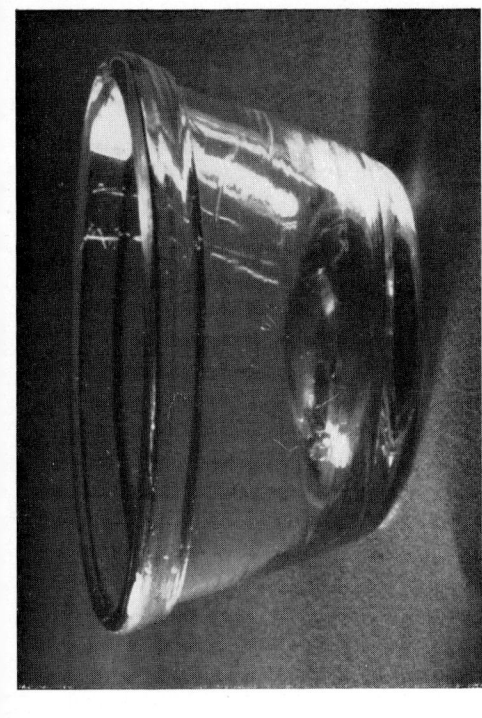

Above, Fig. 12: Five sweetmeat-glasses; (left to right) funnel-shaped bowl with serrated rim, cut with diamonds and fluting, c. 1790, height 7¾ inches; the bowl "nipt diamond waies", the double-knopped stem with elongated tear, c. 1710, 5½ inches; double-ogee bowl on spherical tear knop above inverted stem and terraced foot, c. 1710, 6½ inches; oval bowl with contracted mouth on "bobbin-turned" stem of graduated knops, c. 1710, 6¼ inches; ogee bowl with flared, scalloped rim matching the foot, c. 1790, 7⅝ inches. (Sotheby's). **Right,** Fig. 13: Small bowl with folded rim, 18th Century, diameter 2⅝ inches. **Below,** Fig. 14: Five sweetmeat-glasses; (left to right) bowl with everted, shaped rim on opaque-twist stem, height 6¾ inches; double-ogee bowl on air-twist stem, 6¾ inches; ogee bowl on opaque-twist stem, 6 inches; bowl patterned with reticulations on opaque-twist stem, 6⅜ inches; double-ogee bowl on opaque-twist stem, 6¾ inches. Air-twist, c. 1750; opaque-twists, c. 1760. (Sotheby's).

Page 15

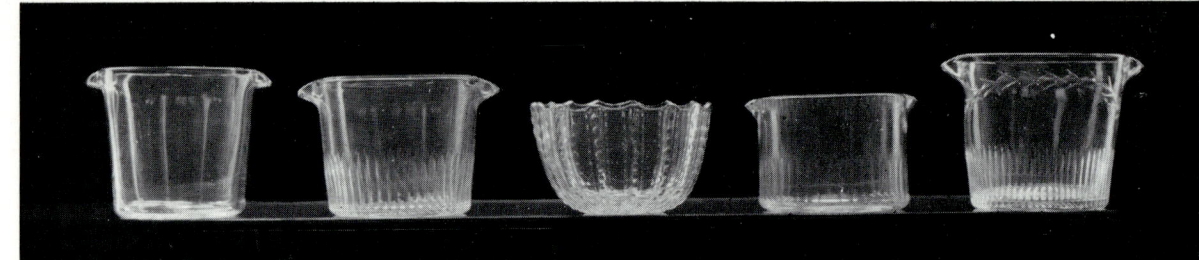

Fig. 15: Fingerbowl (centre) and four wine-glass coolers. Circa 1790-1810. Average diameter 4 inches. (Cecil Davis Ltd.)

newly-devised Sheffield Plate, may well have been more popular at the time. Also, metal would have had a wider range of uses, as old glass is limited to holding cool or cold foods and is no substitute for the covered entrée dish.

SWEETMEAT GLASSES: Sweetmeat glasses is the term applied generally to glasses used for the dessert course of a meal. They were intended to contain sweetmeats of two types: "wet", which are comparable to present-day sweets like ice-cream, trifles, and so forth, and "dry", which were such things as preserved fruits, nuts, and the delicacies noted above by Lady Grizell Baillie.

Many of the surviving examples of the glasses are of comparable design to the wine glasses of their time, and each followed fashion in the same manner. Thus, the earliest and rarest examples, dating from the end of the seventeenth century, show a similar variety of stem forms with multiple knops and balusters. The bowl did not have to have a plain rim, as in the case of a drinking glass, and it was quite often ornamented.

Three of the sweetmeats in Fig. 12 have plain-rimmed bowls, one of them "nipt diamond waies", but their stems exhibit wide divergences of design. That on the left is double-knopped and contains an elongated "tear" of air, in the centre is a large spherical tear-filled knop above an inverted baluster, and on the right are seven graduated knops forming what is known in woodwork as bobbin-turning. In addition, the last glass has an oval bowl.

An equally wide selection of stem patterns is seen in the group of sweetmeats dating from 1750-60, shown in Fig. 14. The earliest of them, the second from the left, has an air-twist in contrast to the other four of 1760 which have interior twists of opaque white glass. The bowls are all of similar outline, but one of them is moulded with a reticulated pattern, and another has a flared and shaped rim.

The second half of the century saw cutting applied to sweetmeat glasses just as much as to everything else. Two typical examples are shown in Fig. 12 (outer left and right), and although it is likely that these were made in Ireland they differ little from English ones of the time. Some of the glasses were reversible: the domed foot seen in so many specimens was deepened and cut in the same manner as the upper bowl, and the resulting two bowls were sometimes of differing sizes. The finished products resemble dumb-bells in appearance, and no doubt were bought eagerly by hostesses in search of a novelty.

Small stemless and footless bowls were also possibly used for sweetmeats or pickles at the table. It has been thought that they were mortar-glasses: for holding a night light. Equally they may have been used for salt, and one is illustrated in Fig. 13, leaving a decision to the reader.

© *Geoffrey Wills, 1968.*

Candlesticks and Lustres

During the seventeenth and eighteenth centuries those who wished to work or play during the hours of darkness relied on the candle. If poor, the simple rushlight was used: a rush, stripped and dipped in tallow saved from cooking mutton or bacon. Candles were of tallow or wax, each made by men who belonged to one of two Companies: the Tallow Chandlers, who were incorporated in 1461, or the Wax Chandlers, incorporated just over twenty years later. The latter made their wares from beeswax, but in the 1750's spermacetti, obtained from sperm whales, came into use. The wax candle was burned in churches and in those homes where its cost could be afforded; whereas the humbler tallow did duty for the average household. A writer in 1764 noted:

> A tallow candle, to be good, must be half sheeps, and half bullocks tallow; for hogs tallow makes the candle gutter, and always gives an offensive smell, with a thick black smoke.

All candles were made with a wick of twisted cotton, which bent over as it burned. If this state of affairs was left unremedied, the candle started to melt rapidly where the wick rested and the molten material ran to waste. To prevent this occurring it was necessary to trim or "snuff" the wick, and candles of best London tallow were stated to need such attention every half hour. This may have been a true claim with regard to those of good quality, but others were much more demanding on the time of the user. If attention was not given as regularly as it was required, the result was a stream of molten fat, objectionable black and evil-smelling smoke, and diminished illumination.

Altogether the use of tallow candles demanded skilled and constant service, for trimming the wicks was an operation needing care. It was no difficult

Opposite, *Pair of candlesticks, each with cut ornament and hung with icicle drops, the drum-shaped bases of blue jasperware with reliefs in white in the manner of Josiah Wedgwood, mounted in gilt metal. Early 19th century. Height 11¼ inches. (Cecil Davis Ltd.)* **Above,** *Fig. 1: Hollow candlestick with a large central knop. Circa 1685. Height 8 inches.*

matter to misjudge the undertaking and extinguish the light; hence the double meaning of the term to "snuff it": to trim a flame and to lose a life. Wax candles were far more reliable and gave a better and steadier light, but their cost was several times greater than that of tallow.

The earliest surviving English glass candlesticks are conjectured to be a number dating from about the year 1685. Although each is composed conventionally of a series of variously-shaped knops rising from a domed foot, they are unusual in both manufacture and appearance because they are completely hollow. Had they not been found to be of glass-of-lead it might be supposed they were foreign work, but in that case they would certainly have been made of soda glass. However, in explanation of their uncustomary aspect it has been suggested that they were made in this country by immigrant glass-workers from Lorraine, in northern France (Fig. 1).

The aforementioned pieces fail to be successful on two grounds: their shape, and their technique of manufacture. The shaping of the individual components is passable, but their assembly into the stem of a candlestick has resulted in an ungainly appearance unlike that of almost all other English glass of the time. The blown construction has employed a minimum of material, and the beauty of it, its "light-dispersing character that gave it a remarkable interior fire", remains completely unrealised.

Above, left, *Fig. 2: Three candlesticks of about 1700; (left and right) a pair, each stem composed of an inverted acorn knop, a ball knop containing air bubbles and, at the base, an annular knop, height 8¾ inches; and (centre) the stem composed of a ball knop containing air bubbles above an inverted baluster, height 7½ inches. (Photograph:* The Connoisseur.*)* **Above,** *Fig. 3: Candlestick with a Silesian stem and a removable shaped nozzle. Circa 1720. Height 9¾ inches. (Howard Phillips.)*

Above, *Fig. 4: Pair of candlesticks with scalloped nozzles and feet, decorated with cutting. Circa 1770. Height 14 inches. (Photograph:* The Connoisseur.)
Above right, *Fig. 5: Pair of candlesticks, each with an air-twist stem and domed, ridged foot. Circa 1750. Height 7½ inches.*
(Delomosne & Son Ltd.)

At about the same date as the preceding type were being made, other makers were employing the technique of building-up the stems in the manner of those of wine-glasses. From using solid and not hollow members there is an immediate improvement in the appearance of finished candlesticks. The enclosing of air bubbles in some of the knops heightens the natural brilliance of the shining glass; a shine enhanced a hundredfold when a lighted candle is reflected from the curved surfaces.

The styles of candlesticks were based largely on silver ones and on wine-glasses. Thus, balusters, ball-knops, and flattened rings (annular knops) were employed in forming innumerable combinations. Many of the stems enclose one or more bubbles of air, round or tear-shaped, and all rise to a simple candle-holder with an out-turned rim. Bases usually have a pronounced dome, and are of a width to provide maximum stability; the feet are folded. In most instances the candle-socket is of plain outline, but rare variants are ribbed. Ribbing is less scarce on the upper surface of the base, where it may have been inspired by a sight of turned wood specimens (Fig. 2).

About 1715 the Silesian stem, of faceted section with an expanded shoulder, made an appearance on candlesticks in the same way as it did on wine-glasses. The foot remained domed and of a large diameter, and the everted rim of the socket was sometimes folded at the top for strength and

Fig. 6: Candlestick hung with two tiers of cut icicle drops. Circa 1815. Height about 8 inches. (Delomosne & Son Ltd.)

appearance. In some instances the candle-holder was made with a shaped rim and is removable, features which are found on silver prototypes of the time. This treatment of the candle-holder is seen in the example illustrated in Fig. 3, where the ornament on the base, ribs rising to shaped knops, is matched at the corners of the Silesian stem.

Cutting first began to appear on candlesticks from about 1740. They were ideal recipients for that type of ornament; the cut sections glittered by day, and at night they amplified the candle light. At the same time air-twist, and occasionally opaque-twist, stems were made; a further example of slavish following of drinking-glass fashions (Fig. 5). They were not apparently made in large numbers, as few have survived, and apart from being a novel ornament they could not have competed seriously with the more practical cutting. A pair of cut candlesticks of exceptional size is illustrated in Fig. 4. From the style of their tall straight stems with flat faceted surfaces, and with feet and sockets similarly cut, they can be dated to 1760-70.

Towards the end of the eighteenth century there appeared a different pattern of candlestick, of which the most noticeable feature is a pendant fringe of cut-glass drops. These usually hang from a shaped grease-pan fitted below the candle socket, the pan being ostensibly to catch dripping wax. Probably it serves a more real function as an anchorage for the strings of shining drops. In conformity with the prevailing neo-Classical style, the circular foot is no longer present and a square stepped one replaces it.

The heavy cutting familiar on so many glass objects from the early years of the nineteenth century was applied to candlesticks of this last type. Gradually the central greasepan diminished until it was no longer present, and the rim of the socket broadened. At the same time, the strings of round and pear-shaped drops were supplanted by "icicles" hanging from single buttons so that the central stem was almost obscured (Fig. 6). Once again the foot is circular, and is usually cut on the underside with radiating lines to give a star-like effect.

A final modification was to substitute for the icicles long drops of "finger" shape: oval or oblong in section and with vertical facets the length of each side. They formed an even closer screen round the supporting vase than had the preceding type, and gave the candlestick an unbroken and uninteresting straight line from base to top. The supporting vase continued to be painstakingly cut, but remained closely hidden unless the drops were removed for any reason.

Josiah Wedgwood, ever seeking fresh uses for his jasperware, introduced it as being suitable for forming candlestick bases in the 1780's. The ware was supplied in a number of colours, most often in the familiar "Wedgwood Blue", and with reliefs of various designs applied in white. It was made in the form of a drum with holes at top and bottom so that a metal rod could be fitted through it. The rod was threaded at each end, and the component parts of the whole article were thus securely held together and might be taken apart for cleaning without difficulty. The drums were fixed on gilt metal bases and given tops to match, usually ornamented with fluting and round or oval paterae. Typical of the earlier Wedgwood-based candlesticks is a pair in the British Museum, with black and white jasperware drums mounted in gilt metal; the greasepans have deep scallops and the sockets have scalloped upturned rims. Both pans and sockets are hung with pear-shaped drops, in this instance of an unusual topaz colour. One of a pair of similar pattern, but with clear glass throughout, is illustrated in Fig. 7.

A few decades later in date than the preceding is the pair of candlesticks shown in the frontispiece. The blue-ground drums are unmarked, so are probably the work of one of Wedgwood's numerous imitators: men who plagued Josiah and his successors, and whose output was sometimes up to the high standard of the original. The metal mounts are quite plain, although of similar outline to the earlier ones. The glass drops are of "icicle" shape suspended from gilt balls, and the surface of pans and sockets is cut with small diamonds in relief.

Fig. 7: One of a pair of candlesticks, the base composed of a drum of marked Wedgwood jasperware ornamented with reliefs in white and mounted in gilt metal, the candle-sockets and grease-pans of cut glass. Circa 1790. Height 11 inches. (Josiah Wedgwood & Sons Ltd.)

TAPERSTICKS: The small-sized taperstick followed the design of its full-sized relative, and examples are known dating from 1690 to 1770 (Fig. 9). Various suggestions have been put forward as to its original use: that it had a place at the tea table, where a light was required only for a short period and a small-sized candle would have suitably provided it. Also, that a taperstick would have provided a handy source of flame from which other, bigger, candles might be lighted. More credibly, its place was the writing-desk and its function was to provide heat by which to melt sealing-wax. Silver and porcelain examples are frequently found forming a part of a complete inkstand, with inkwell and pounce-pot to match, which seems to settle the question.

Tapersticks vary in height from five to seven inches, and the candle-socket is about the diameter of an ordinary lead pencil. They are pretty little objects, and have attracted the attention of makers of reproductions.

OIL-LAMPS: The use of oil for lighting was not widespread in England before the 1780's, and was confined in the main to those who performed close work. Various kinds of oil might be used: fish, mineral or vegetable, and all smelled more or less according to their quality and the extent to which they had been purified. Its advantage was that the burning flame remained in a constant position, whereas the candle flame lowered as the candle itself was consumed. This defect was eventually overcome by the use of spring-loaded candle-holders, but most existing examples of these devices do not possess much age.

Lace-making and engraving were probably the crafts most dependent on bright illumination within a small area, so that operatives could do their extremely delicate work. The lamp was placed beyond a glass globe, water-filled so that it formed a condenser, and the comparatively small light was thereby concentrated and magnified. By arranging the apparatus suitably, the bright disc of light could be made to shine exactly where it was wanted. A glass oil-lamp of the type generally termed a lace-maker's lamp is illustrated in Fig. 8.

An important advance in artificial lighting came after 1782, when a Swiss, Ami Argand, invented an improved lamp. He used a circular wick working between two tubes, of which the inner one permitted air to reach the inside of the flame, and a shaped

Left, *Fig. 8: Lace-maker's oil lamp, 18th century. Height 5½ inches. (County Museum, Truro.)*

Left, *Fig. 9: Taperstick with an inverted acorn knop at the top of the stem. Circa 1710. Height 7 inches. (County Museum, Truro.)*

glass shade above the latter additionally helped combustion. Argand came to London in 1784 and patented his invention, but litigation followed and the patent was declared invalid. Lamps made to his pattern were soon put on the market in large numbers, and quickly became popular.

A visitor to London from Germany, Sophie von La Roche, wrote of a visit she paid to Oxford Street in 1786:

> Most of all we admired a stall with Argand and other lamps, situated in a corner-house, and forming a really dazzling spectacle; every variety of lamp, crystal, lacquer and metal ones, silver and brass in every possible shade: large and small lamps arranged so artistically that each was visible as in broad daylight. There were reflecting lamps inside, which intensified the glare to such an extent that my eye could scarce stand it a moment: large pewter oil-vessels, gleaming like silver, were ranged there, and oil of every description, so that the lamp and the oil can be bought and taken home together if one likes, the oil in a beautiful glass flask, and the wick, too, in a dainty box. The highest lord and the humblest labourer may purchase here lamps of immense beauty and price or at a very reasonable figure, and both receive equally rapid and courteous attention.

Sophie's graphic description makes it plain that glass played its part in Argand's lamps. Not only was it used for the shades, but the main supports and the oil-reservoirs were sometimes of the same material. We may wonder what type of bottle containing the necessary oil caused her to use the phrase "a beautiful glass flask".

It was not long after this date that the Cornish-domiciled Scot, William Murdock, began experimenting with coal-gas as a possible illuminant. In 1802 he lighted the outside of Boulton and Watt's Soho, Birmingham, engineering factory in celebration of the Treaty of Amiens, and in the next year gas-light was used inside the building. By 1807, a London street, Pall Mall, was being lighted, and within a few years of that date a public company had been launched.

The humble and long-serving candle was not completely neglected during this time. Between

Above, *Fig. 10: Candelabrum for four lights, constructed in two parts. Circa 1695. Height 13½ inches. (Victoria and Albert Museum.)* **Opposite, below,** *Fig. 11: Pair of candelabra, each for three lights, with notched spires rising to crescents. Circa 1780. Height about 25 inches. (Delomosne & Son Ltd.)* **Opposite, above,** *Fig. 12: Two-light candelabra with curled ornamental arms and a spire surmounted by a star. Circa 1785. Height 24½ inches. (Howard Phillips.)*

1815 and 1820 experiments led to the manufacture of stearine, and in the latter year a Frenchman, named Cambacères, invented a plaited wick that was self-consuming and did not require snuffing. Finally, in the 1860's came paraffin wax, and the modern constituents of the candle, still an indispensable source of light in an emergency, had all been discovered.

The candle managed to retain its popularity for some years in competition with the Argand lamp. For the general lighting of a room, a number of small points of light was probably preferable to a few very bright areas from Argands. These were superior for close work, as each gave the equivalent light of numerous candles and were unbeatable for the purpose. Like the candle, the oil-lamp required attention; the wick had to be trimmed carefully before lighting, and the heavy Colza oil or Train oil (obtained from cole or rape seeds and from whale blubber, respectively) were probable sources of mess if all did not function perfectly. Gas did not become generally available as an illuminant in the home until the third quarter of the nineteenth century, but once its use became widespread the supremacy of the candle was ended and the oil-lamp slowly fell into disuse.

The rising competition of gas from the time of the forming of the Chartered Gas Light & Coke Company in 1812 led to a number of improvements taking place in other spheres. The candle benefited from the plaited wick and stearine wax, and Argand's oil-lamp also received attention. One of its drawbacks was that the flame often burned much more of the oil than the wick could draw up to it; capillary attraction was unable to overcome either the basic lack of fluidity or the proportion of impurities it contained. To assist combustion, the reservoir was invariably placed at a higher level than the flame, and gravity was able to play what part it could. However, it was not enough, and further inventions took the form of a small clockwork-driven pump to ensure the oil flowed in sufficient quantity. It was patented by G. B. Carcel, and the resulting article was known as a "Carcel" lamp. Later, a variation known as the "Moderator" lamp employed a spring-loaded piston within the oil reservoir.

During the nineteenth century many new fuels

came and went. Camphine (sometimes spelled Kamphine), a mixture of turpentine and alcohol achieved a temporary popularity, but caused so many violent explosions on account of its low flash-point that its use ceased. Finally, after minor sources of oil had been experimented with in various parts of the world for many centuries, came the discovery of petroleum in the United States. The result was a near-endless supply of paraffin, or kerosene as it is called in the land where it was found.

It was in Pennsylvania on 28th August 1859 that E. L. Drake, the first man to drill deliberately in search of oil, got down as far as a crevice that engulfed his tools. On the next day, the oil was discovered at a depth of 69 feet, and thenceforth an output of 25 barrels a day was produced. The total for the year for the whole country was officially given as 2,000 barrels, in 1869 it was 4,215,000 barrels, and ten years later it was just short of 20,000,000 barrels.

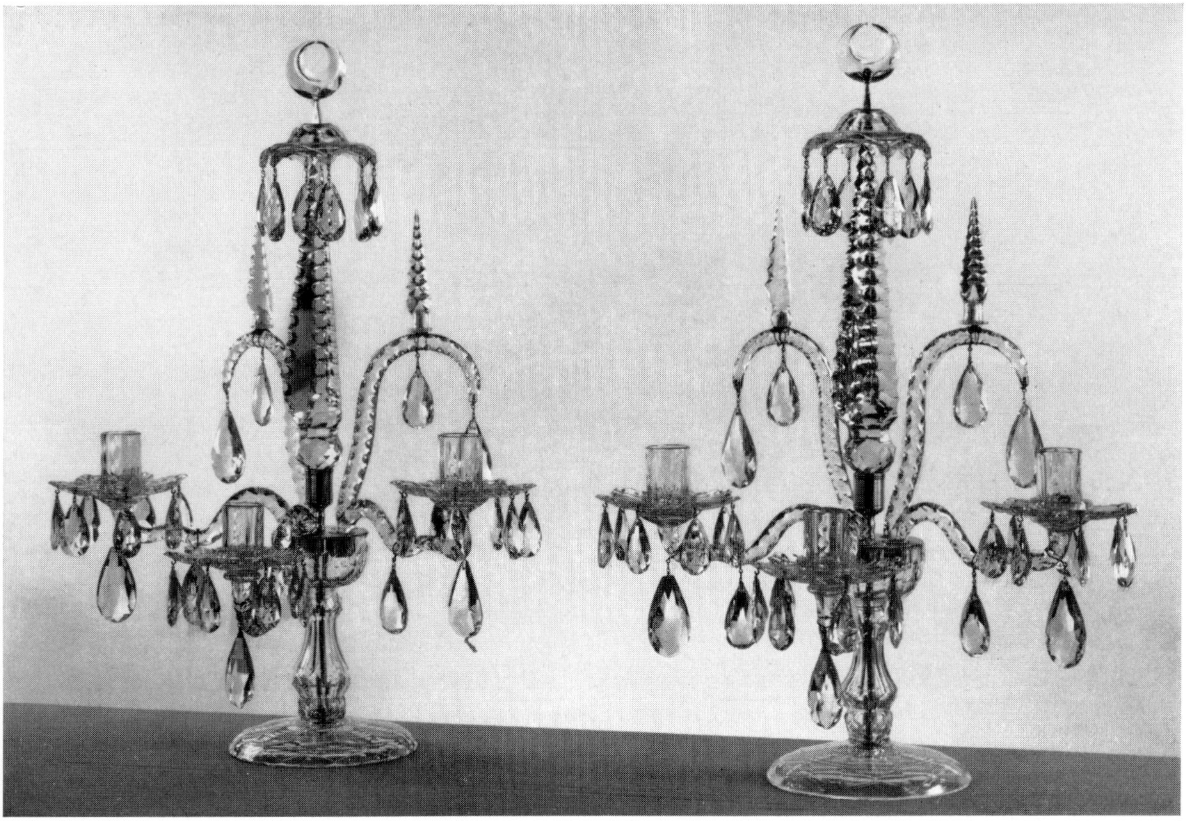

Paraffin oil was a vast improvement on any used earlier, and the ingenious devices of Argand's followers became superflous overnight. It was not only less costly in comparison with the old vegetable oils, but it could be made to burn without smell and was altogether pleasanter to handle. Lamps for its use were manufactured in enormous numbers, very many of them incorporating glass for their stems and other parts.

CANDELABRA: The term candelabra is of comparatively modern usage. In the late seventeenth and early eighteenth centuries there were "lustres", "branches", and "girandoles" which were, more or less, interchangeable. All of them would appear to have been applied at the will of the writer or speaker, to chandeliers, branched candlesticks or ornamental single candlesticks, and wall-lights. The confusion lasted until the early 1790's, and by then the word candelabrum was applied, as it is to-day, to a candlestick for two or more lights.

Fig. 13: Pair of candelabra, each for two lights, with vase-shaped bases, curled ornamental arms, and tall spires surmounted by gadrooned urns. Circa 1785. Height about 27 inches. (Delomosne & Son Ltd.)

The earliest recorded English glass candelabrum is the one illustrated in Fig. 10. It exhibits most of the features to be found in other glass wares of the early eighteenth century: a domed and terraced foot, an annular knop in the stem, and knops enclosing air-bubbles above and below the arms. It will be seen that the ribs round the foot are echoed in the finial, and that the whole is made in two parts so that the lower section forms a candlestick on its own. Such a method of construction is usual in silver and brass, and this glass one would seem to owe its inspiration to an example in one of those metals.

From about 1740 one of the London glass-dealers, Jerom Johnson, was actively advertising his wares in the newspapers of his day. In February 1752 one of his announcements was as follows:

> For Glass Engraving or Flow'ring, Cutting Scolloping, and finest Polishing upon Glass in general, *At the intire* GLASS-SHOP, *over-against the New Exchange, in the Strand,*
> IS to be sold all sorts of fine Flint Glasses, brilliant Lustres, Branches, Candlesticks, Dishes, Plates, Bowls, Basons, Cups and

Fig. 14: Candelabra supported on a base of Wedgwood jasperware mounted in gilt metal. Circa 1790. Height 19 inches. (Delomosne & Son Ltd.)

Covers, Saucers, Saltcellars, cut Bottles, Decanters, Rummers, cut and flowered, Desart Glasses of all sorts; Scollop'd or engraved Salvers, large Glasses for Cool-Tankards; Cruets and Castors; curious Lamps, Wash-hand Glasses, most curiously engraved new-fashion'd or scollop'd; and finest polish'd Mugs, and Pitchers, Turkish-fashion Diamond-cut, and Brilliant polish'd, Wholesale and Retail, at the most reasonable Rates, and before no where else cheaper, in London, being the first Inventor,

JEROM JOHNSON.

Johnson dealt in glass exclusively in his "Intire Glass-Shop", whereas many others of the time combined trading in glass with other commodities. His premises were situated a few doors to the east of Bedford Street, on the north side of the Strand. Opposite was the New Exchange, a row of a dozen or so shops with living-quarters above, erected in 1737 and demolished in 1923. The shop was later occupied by successive sellers of wallpaper: Pope and Mclellan from 1754 to 1756, and Richard Masefield until 1788.

Johnson's "Lustres, Branches and Candlesticks" would be identifiable nowadays as chandeliers, candelabra and candlesticks. Beyond that, we have only guesswork on which to base any idea of their appearance, as no surviving examples of cut candelabra are considered as having been made before about 1770. As it is agreed that the earlier cutting comprised mostly flat facets and that deep work was not done until later in the century, it is probable that Johnson's stock-in-trade glittered only discreetly and was duly discarded in favour of more splendid later fashions.

We are at rather a loss, also, to imagine the appearance of cutting in "Turkish-fashion". The vogue for *turquerie* began in Europe following the visit to Paris early in the eighteenth century of an embassy from the Porte. It left behind it a liking for costume and much else *à la Turque* that remained current for many years afterwards, and was a small-scale companion to *chinoiserie*. Not only did this occur in France but it spread across the Channel to England, where several of the newly-founded porcelain manufactories filled a public demand for figures of Turks and Sultanas. Possibly the so-called Turkish glass-cutting was little more than the addition of a crescent moon to the top of a spire, as seen in the candelabra in Fig. 11.

Candelabra were made in pairs, like so much else of the period. They would have stood nobly, for instance, on each of the two tables placed against the piers of a room. The piers are the narrow upright walls between the windows of a room, and it was fashionable to place matching sets of tables in front of them. In most instances, each stood beneath a tall looking-glass, reaching from table-top to just below the ceiling. On such tables, suitably reflected in the looking-glass, would have stood cut-glass candelabra of the types illustrated in Figs. 11, 12, 13 and 14.

A decade or so later, Wedgwood was supplying bases for similar candelabra. They were square in section, but larger at the foot than at the top and with reliefs in white on each of the four sides. As with the candlesticks, they were mounted in gilt metal and the sockets were hung with glass drops. The example in Fig. 14 shows a relief modelled

Fig. 15: Pair of three-light candelabra, the bases, candle-holders and grease-pans cut with small diamonds in relief and the latter hung with icicle and button drops. Circa 1820. Height about 10 inches. (Cecil Davis Ltd.)

Fig. 16: Lustre of ruby glass overlaid with white, painted and gilt, and hung with long cut drops. Circa 1845. Height 8½ inches.

with *Domestic Employment*, a girl spinning, designed by Lady Templetown in the early 1780's. Of somewhat similar form are other candelabra with bases, also square in plan, of coloured glass.

Soon after the turn of the century a further change took place, and in place of arms made of glass to support the candle-holders it became usual to have them of gilt metal. The glass portions were cut all over with small diamonds in relief and the hanging drops were of icicle shape, each suspended from one or more buttons (Fig. 15). The flowing curves of earlier designs were replaced by a severity of line that formed a complete contrast.

LUSTRES: With the fierce competition between the various forms of illumination that developed during the early part of the nineteenth century, the candle lost its place. For almost the entire eighteenth century it had been the principal medium of artificial light, but with the advent of Argand's oil-lamp and then of gas it could no longer retain its eminence. This is not to say that it ceased entirely to be used, but it was relegated to purely functional purposes in the homes of the less well-to-do.

The candlestick by 1820 had acquired a rim to the candle-socket that was almost as broad as its circular base, and it was fringed round with long cut drops. Soon, it began to expand in size while losing its original identity, and the Lustre came into being. Few homes were without a pair as the century progressed, and few of their owners would realize that their mantelpieces were adorned by what were in effect direct descendants of the out-moded candlestick.

The quality of Victorian Lustres varied so that they might appeal to all buyers. The cheapest were of single-colour glass, including a strong pink, with heavy drops which sometimes had faceted spherical ends. Others were of superior craftsmanship, like the example in Fig. 16, made of red or green glass overlaid with opaque white. The latter was cut away as required to reveal the lower surface, which was usually given a gilded pattern and the panels of white were painted in colours.

© *Geoffrey Wills, 1968.*

7

Opposite, *one of a pair of early nineteenth century chandeliers hanging in the Saloon at Saltram, Devonshire; the decoration of the room was designed by Robert Adam in 1768. (The National Trust.)* **Right,** *Fig. 1: For twelve lights, the stem cut with flat diamonds. Circa 1740. Height 4 ft. 2 ins. (Delomosne & Son, Ltd.)*

Chandeliers

THE particular beauties of English glass-of-lead, its brilliant surface and its reflective power, are nowhere more evident than in the chandelier. These magnificent articles commemorate both the skill of George Ravenscroft, who created the glass, and the many anonymous men who cut it. Their efforts resulted in the making of numbers of glittering cascades of glass, which as much as any other relics of the time evoke a picture of eighteenth and nineteenth century splendour.

The general use of the term chandelier for a hanging free-standing light is comparatively modern. Early eighteenth century advertisements note such things as lustres and branches, which were employed as alternative names. They were also interchangeable with candelabra, girandole and wall-light, so the few references in literature to any of them are liable to be misconstrued unless studied carefully.

The use of a chandelier in the home does not seem to have been at all widespread until the first decades of the eighteenth century. Prior to that time, they had been used in churches and public buildings, but were made from iron or brass. Of the latter, many remain to be seen in England; they hang in the naves where they were first placed two or more centuries ago, and are often engraved with the name of a donor. Some of the great houses of the wealthy boasted chandeliers of silver, but few have

Opposite, *Fig. 2: For eight lights, the stem, arms and grease-pans decorated with cutting. Circa 1760. Height about 3ft. 6in. (Delomosne & Son, Ltd.)* **Right,** *Fig. 3: For eight lights, the arms cut with facets. About 1755. Height 3 ft. 4 ins. (Cecil Davis, Ltd.)*

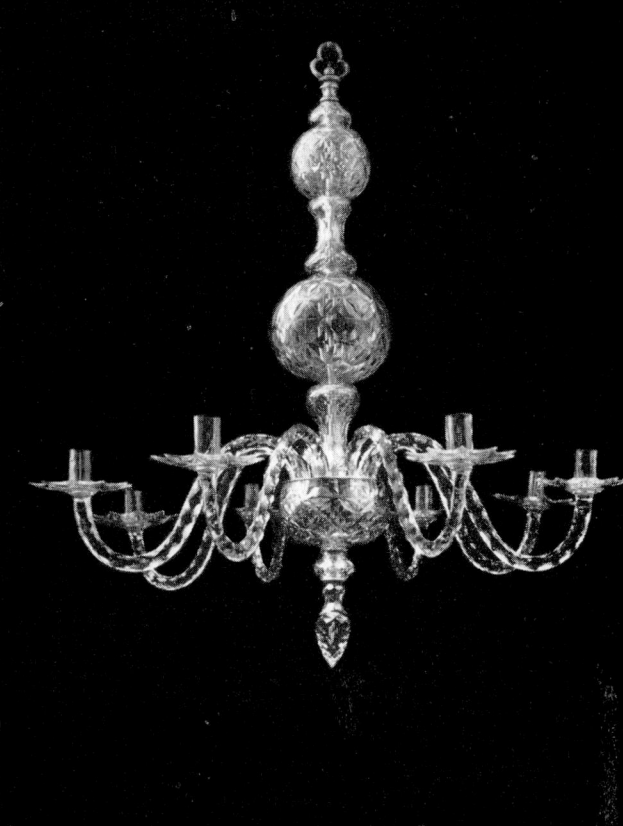

survived the melting-pot which eagerly swallowed the unfashionable.

A mention of chandeliers, but apparently not of glass, was made by Mrs. Pendarves, better-known by her later name of Mrs. Delany. In a letter to her sister she recorded her visit to Westminster Hall in October 1727, when she witnessed the coronation of King George II. Part of the letter reads:

> The room was finely illuminated, and though there was 1800 candles, besides what were on the tables, they were all lighted in less than three minutes by an invention of Mr. Heidegger's, which succeeded to the admiration of all spectators; the branches that held the candles were all gilt and in the form of pyramids.

John James Heidegger was called the "Swiss Count", and renowned in his lifetime for his ugliness. In spite of such a physical misfortune, which, not unexpectedly, was caricatured by William Hogarth, he had a successful career as a manager of operas at the Haymarket theatre. No doubt this experience as an impresario proved valuable on such an occasion as a coronation.

The feat of lighting the chandeliers more or less simultaneously was probably performed by means of a fuse. This would have been a length of cotton treated with sulphur that ran from one set of lights to another. It is not a surprise to see instantaneous light in the twentieth century, but nearly

Right, *Fig. 4: For four lights, the stem with diamonds in relief and the candle-holders interspersed with notched spires. Circa 1775. Height 3 ft. 6 ins. (Cecil Davis, Ltd.)*

Right, *Fig. 5: Drawing of a "Lustre for Lady Derby's Dressing Room", 1775. (By courtesy of the Trustees of Sir John Sloane's Museum.)*

two and a half centuries ago, when neither gas nor electricity had been harnessed, the effect must have been an unforgettable experience.

The first mention of glass chandeliers in England so far recorded appeared in print in 1727. In that year John Gumley advertised that he had for sale "Looking Glasses, Coach Glasses and Glass Schandeliers". Gumley was a prominent cabinet-maker with premises in the Strand, London, who established a glass-house at Lambeth in 1705. He made plates for looking-glasses, and one which bears his name on the frame is at Hampton Court Palace, while a pair supplied to the Duke of Devonshire at a cost of £200 is still at Chatsworth, Derbyshire. Unfortunately, none of his chandeliers is known, and we have no means at present of learning what they may have looked like.

The earliest type of light that has been preserved is exemplified in Fig. 1. The central supporting shaft is built up from spherical and cushion-shaped pieces threaded on an iron rod, the bowl at the base concealing a pierced metal disc into which the arms are fitted. It will be noticed that the arms are uncut and have broad grease-pans, while the remainder of the chandelier is cut with shallow facets.

Within a decade or so, cutting had spread to the arms, and their glitter was added to that of the shaft (Fig. 2). The spherical members of the central shaft became

Right, *Fig. 6: For eight lights, the gilt metal framework designed with honeysuckle flowers and hung with glass drops. Late 18th century. Height 3 ft. 6 ins. (Howard Phillips.)*

changed in form, and the earlier strict adherence to a series of globes was no longer always in evidence. In the specimen illustrated in Fig. 3 the dish from which the arms spring is placed almost half-way up the stem, and the arms themselves are longer than in the past. The lower section of the shaft is occupied by a sphere, while above the arms is an inverted baluster surmounted by a series of flattened globes in diminishing sizes. The grease-pans remain of large diameter, although they are now shaped in place of being a plain circle.

The use of a source of light hung high and centrally in a room was recognised as being an uneconomical source of illumination. In 1746 Isaac Ware, the architect, suggested that a room "if wainscoted [*panelled in oak*] will take six candles to light it, will in stucco require eight or if hung ten". Most lighting of living-rooms was by means of candlesticks or candelabra on tables, and the ceiling light was a luxury confined to the wealthy throughout the eighteenth century and during much of the succeeding one. When installed, it was confined to the largest rooms of big houses, or to public rooms, and was lighted only on important occasions when numerous people were present.

The increased use of cutting to be seen on other forms of glass is noticeable on chandeliers from about 1765. By that date the rococo, conveniently summarised as regards furnishings in the designs of Thomas Chippendale, was on the wane. Chairs, tables and other articles had been incorporating in their ornamentation motifs of Chinese, French and Gothic origin, either singly or in rather uneasy concert. By 1765 such themes were rapidly growing out of date, and were being replaced by the neo-classical of Robert Adam.

The rococo style had its greatest exponents on the Continent, where they followed the concept that it should exhibit the utmost contortion and, above all, be asymmetrical. When it crossed the Channel, a native caution deemed it more in conformity to national taste to water-down its more extravagant features. The resulting English rococo is seen to be a seemly version of the French audacities: one that rarely rises to the daring of asymmetry, but gives designer and craftsman a chance to show their skills within restrained limits.

Left, *Fig. 7: For eight lights, with a vase-shaped stem feature, plain spires and festoons of cut drops. Circa 1790. Height 4 ft. 8 ins. (Cecil Davis, Ltd.)*
Right, *Figs. 8 and 8a: For twelve lights, the "bag" or "tent" composed of hundreds of cut drops, and the base lowering to reveal six interior lights. Circa 1810. Height 5 ft. 7 ins. (Delomosne & Son, Ltd.)*

Chandeliers made in the second half of the century appear to have set their own timing for conforming to fashion. This may well have been because they were placed in a room high and remote from other decorative features, and did not have to blend with them. In addition, being made of glass their general form was less definite to the vision than if they had been made in a solid material. Thus the chandelier of more or less rococo type was in fashion when the style was dying, and for quite a time afterwards.

The curves and carving on furniture of 1750-60 duly had their effect on chandelier design, and this is observed in an increase of glitter. It was achieved with the aid of facet-cut drops, copied from earlier ones that had been made of natural rock-crystal, which were hung from the grease-pans. Additionally, canopies of glass were added at the top of the stem and towards the base, and from their edges more drops were suspended.

Hitherto, the chandelier had been of the most simple pattern: it was little more than a device for holding candles at a height, and the sole concessions to decoration had been to curve the arms and disguise the straight iron shaft by clothing it in glass spheres. Even the cutting was functional in that it increased the output of light, and the fact that it gave the object added grace was a subsidiary point.

Under the influence of rococo design it was permissible to elaborate the slight ornamentation hitherto exhibited. The cutting of the arms was made more complicated in pattern, as was the cutting of the canopies and stem, and more drops were added. In addition, extra arms were interspersed with the candle-holders, and these held tall glass spires. Some, indeed, were themselves surmounted by crescents and surrounded by drops cut into the shape of stars.

Fig. 4 shows a chandelier dating from about 1780. The upper portion of the stem forms an inverted baluster, and is cut with relief diamonds. The spires are of elongated pyramid shape, with notches cut along each of their three edges. Unlike the earlier

examples illustrated, the candle sockets have shaped and cut out-turned rims.

LATER in the century, about 1790, there came the final type of rococo chandelier. By that date the style had long since passed out of fashion in favour of the neo-classical of Robert Adam; which, in turn, was itself almost out-moded. However, the chandelier of the day was a mixture of the two styles, combining the abandon of rococo with the severity of Adam. The former is seen in the adding of further drops, strung together in lengths and festooned from arm to arm: the drops not confined to the old pear shape, but also round, oval or diamond-shaped. The influence of Adam is plainly visible in the stem, which has its upper section in the shape of a vase and cover of contemporary form (Fig. 7).

Up to about this date, the candle-nozzle and curved arm had left the manufactory in a single piece. Now, a change took place, and the base of the nozzle terminated in a short stem to which a threaded metal cap was affixed with plaster. The top end of the arm was similarly mounted to receive it, and when the two were screwed together the junction was masked by the lower grease-pan.

Robert Adam designed many of the magnificent suites of apartments that were decorated and furnished between the years

1760 to 1790. His work is recognisable from its delicate patterning of classical motifs, notably the honeysuckle flower, and its reliance to a large degree on pastel-toned colour schemes. A stern critic wrote at the time of "Mr. Adam's gingerbread and sippets of embroidery", alluding to the tenuous meanderings in pale colours, but the architect provided a background for social life that has never been excelled in this country.

It might be thought that the grace of a glass chandelier would have taken its place fittingly and unobtrusively in such surroundings. In fact Adam's saloons, eating-rooms and libraries were probably completed without any such illuminant. They relied for their lighting on girandoles affixed to the walls, or candelabra and candlesticks standing on tables and stands made to his designs.

Saltram, Devonshire, for instance, formerly seat of the Earls of Morley, which belongs now to the National Trust, has a superb suite of rooms designed by Adam in about 1770. The fine double-cube Saloon, some 50 feet in length, now boasts a pair of fine glass chandeliers (*frontispiece*), but their date is some 40-50 years later than that of the decoration of the room. Although it has been suggested they were installed in place of earlier ones, there is no proof that this took place. It is indeed probable that the room was completed without any lighting arrangement of the kind at all.

Chandeliers that have survived from the years 1790-1800 certainly show signs of having been influenced by the style closely associated with Adam's name. However, as far as is known they owe nothing whatsoever to him personally. While there are many hundreds of drawings by Robert Adam in Sir John Soane's Museum, London, only one of them depicts a chandelier. It cannot even be stated with certainty that it is from his hand, but its presence among so much else of Adam's work suggests that at least he must have seen it.

The drawing in question is dated 14th November 1775, and is of a "Lustre" for the Dressing-room of Lady Derby in Grosvenor Square; a mansion decorated by Adam. As can be seen in the illustration (Fig. 5), little glass is included in the design. There is no indication, either, of whether it was ever made, and if so whether of wood or metal. Unfortunately the house was demolished in 1862, and we will never have answers to these queries.

The probability that the principal rooms of Adam's private houses, and those designed by his contemporaries, did not include chandeliers may be attributed to a number of reasons. In the main it was probably due to the inconvenience of lighting and attending to them, and the difficulty likely to arise if anything went amiss. However reliable a wax candle might be in ordinary circumstances, a steady draught, or a sudden one, would play havoc with it. It has to be considered, too, what standard of lighting was accepted as reasonable in the past, and this is hard to appreciate nowadays. The general level of illumination in a room would almost certainly have been low, and have consisted of a series of "pools" of light wherever candles burned. Elsewhere there would have been a contrasting gloom.

Even when the Argand oil-lamp came

Fig. 9: In the Banqueting Room, the Royal Pavilion, Brighton, for which it was made in 1817. (By courtesy of the Committee, Brighton Royal Pavilion.)

into use in the early 1780's there was only an improvement *locally*, and the overall half-light stayed unrelieved. With the introduction of gas, and more especially of electricity, it became possible for the first time to fill a large space evenly with light. Then the chandelier became a practical proposition, and not only shed its rays all about but formed a decorative eye-catching centrepiece in a room.

In public places it was usual for chandeliers to provide light during events held after daylight. The best-known of such chandeliers is the set supplied to the Bath Assembly Rooms by William Parker in 1771. At that date Parker had premises at 69 Fleet Street, London, and he and his successors supplied many fine examples over the years. They had the habit of engraving their name on one or all of a set, and this evidence together with surviving bills has proved they were manufacturers of considerable importance.

By about the turn of the century there came a change in the design of chandeliers. The earlier curved glass arms, which had been a striking feature, had been for some years becoming hidden amongst a welter of drops, spires and crescents, and they now disappeared altogether. Long strings of drops were suspended from a canopy at ceiling height and fixed to a large-diameter metal ring some feet below, while from the underside of the ring were more drops leading to a central boss. At intervals around the ring, which was made of gilt metal, appeared short arms, often also of metal, which were usually given glass nozzles, grease-pans and the inevitable fringes of faceted drops.

The drops used were round, oval or pear shaped, often accompanied by larger ones in the form of thin "icicles". A splendid example of this type of chandelier is illustrated in Fig. 8. It is remarkable for the feature of six candles burning within the upper curtain of drops. They are fitted in cut-glass nozzles arranged on a counter-weighted platform concealed in the base, and which can be lowered in order to light the candles. The chandelier is composed of no fewer than 4,300 separate pieces of glass; an impressive number, but one that is eclipsed by an example in the Victoria and Albert Museum which boasts a total of two hundred more.

The firm of Parker, mentioned above, was responsible for making the unique chandelier in the Royal Pavilion, Brighton, illustrated in Fig. 9. It hangs in the Banqueting Room, suspended from a large silver dragon which is itself placed beneath a group of lotus leaves. When it was placed in position in 1817 it cost a total sum of £5,613 9s. It was said that one of Queen Adelaide's ladies-in-waiting dreamed that the chandelier, which weighs one ton, suddenly fell and killed the King, William IV. The event happily did not occur, but for some reason it was removed in about 1834. Some years later Queen Victoria had the chandelier replaced, and after some further adventures it is in its original position today.

The Brighton chandelier was created especially for the room in which it was to hang, a room noteworthy for its most exotic ornament. Other houses being furnished at about the same date were

Fig. 10: For six lights, hung with round drops and long "fingers". Circa 1825. Height 3ft. 4ins. (Delomosne & Son, Ltd.)

decorated in less costly and homelier styles. Chandeliers for them were modified examples of the "bag-shaped" style just noticed, but with the multitude of small-sized drops replaced by fewer and larger ones. The neat, slim "icicles" became out-dated and their places were taken by longer and thicker drops of prism-shaped or of oval section with chamfered sides.

Round and oval buttons were supplanted by squares and oblongs joined end-to-end. The latter were devised by a well-known architect and designer of the time, John Buonarotti Papworth, whose biographer wrote that they "were so appreciated by the public that the fashion for the small and long oval or diamond-shaped drops was discarded". Papworth's chandeliers were made by John Blades, a prominent glass-dealer of Ludgate Hill, who also supplied to his designs a sherbet service for the Pasha of Egypt and a glass throne for the Shah of Persia.

By about 1835 the design of chandeliers came round almost to a full circle. The earliest of them (Fig. 1) with its well-defined central shaft from which sprang a series of curved arms, was to be seen again in a modified form. No longer was it fashionable to have a glittering bag-shaped object suspended from the ceiling, with the candle-arms only just emerging at the lower end. Instead the general outline was made to resemble an inverted "T": the re-discovered stem was represented by the upright, and the arms by the cross-piece (Fig. 10). Fringes of cut drops remained and were hung from the canopy, the nozzles and, in rows of diminishing diameter, at the base.

WALL-LIGHTS

GIRANDOLES, sconces or wall-lights, were made during the same years as were chandeliers, and they followed the latter in style. They were fitted to take from one to four candles, and designed to be screwed

Opposite, *Fig. 11: Wall-light for five candles, with cut arms and a notched spire. Circa 1780. Height about 30 ins. (Delomosne & Son, Ltd.)* **Below,** *Fig. 12: Wall-light for two candles, the vase and canopy above supported on a curved and cut arm. Circa 1780. Height 22½ ins. (Cecil Davis, Ltd.)*

Fig. 13: Wall-light for three candles, hung with round and "finger" drops. Circa *1830. Width about 15 ins.*
(Delomosne & Son, Ltd.)

firmly to the wall. For this purpose, a decorative metal plate was provided and from it sprang an arm supporting the glass portion. Being more accessible when requiring attention it is possible that they enjoyed greater popularity than the chandelier, but for the same reason were more vulnerable and it is probable that many have been destroyed in the past.

A short sequence of wall-light styles is shown in the examples illustrated in Figs. 11 to 13. It may be noticed that they closely resemble chandeliers in most details, although on a small scale.

It should be realised that the drops suspended on both chandeliers and wall-lights (and candlesticks, too) are easily damaged. The tiny holes drilled in them are easily split away if carelessly handled, and once they have been broken they are useless. The most frequent cause of such damage is the use of iron wire or common pins for threading them together, and they should never be used for the purpose. All worn or broken wires should be replaced by using the soft brass pins manufactured especially for the task, which bend very easily while being of sufficient strength to do all that is required of them.

© *Geoffrey Wills, 1968.*

8

Irish Glass

No country has had its glasswares more bedevilled by fiction than Ireland. During the past half century, reams of paper have been covered by numerous writers who have added legend to legend, and obscured the history of the industry and its manufactures under a flood of questionable statements. They add nothing to understanding the subject, and only impede the enthusiast in search of knowledge. Typical of such assertions are the three following ones referring to cut pieces of the late eighteenth century:

"Irish glass does not feel harsh or cold like most English or foreign, but gives a sense of soft warmth to the touch".
"Irish glass is far tougher and stronger than any other, hence its wonderful survival even when in constant use".

Opposite, *A set of four boat-shaped salt-cellars and an oval tea caddy of Irish blue glass with cut ornament; salts, circa 1780, height 2¾ ins.; caddy, circa 1800. (Cecil Davis Ltd.)* **Below, Fig. 1:** *An oval bowl with "turnover" rim, the body decorated with cutting and the spreading foot moulded with radiating ribs; sometimes termed a "lemon-squeezer" foot. Circa 1780. Width 13 ins. (Delomosne & Son, Ltd.)*

"All British glass has a clear, definite, bright ring, but to anyone with a musical ear it will be interesting to listen to the peculiar throb of Irish glass . . . I do not say that you get this in all Irish glass, only in the greater part of it".

In fact, glass-making in Ireland followed much the same pattern in early times as it did in England. There is a record of a man named "William the Glassmaker" in 1258, and it is thought he was probably an emigrant from northern France who crossed the Irish Channel after a stay in Sussex. Succeeding centuries provide similar brief glimpses of minor activity, and it was not until the accession of Queen Elizabeth that something more tangible emerged. In 1586 a retired army officer, Thomas Woodhouse, was granted a patent giving him a monopoly for eight years in these words:

Her Majesty considering that the making of glass might prove commodious to both realms and that Woodhouse was the first that with any success had begun the art in Ireland is pleased to condescend to his petition and therefore orders that a grant be made to him of the privilege of making glass for glazing and drinking or otherwise, and to build convenient houses, for the term of eight years, the glass to be sold as cheepe or rather better cheepe than the similar glass in foreign parts.

Three years later, in 1589, Woodhouse sold the unexpired portion of the patent, to a man named George Longe. Longe was already concerned in the running of several glass-houses in England, and in his petition to Lord Burghley, Lord Treasurer at the time, made some telling points:

At no tyme to contynue above 4 glashouses in England, whereas there are now 14 or 15, to the greate spoile of woodes. But to erect the rest in Ireland,

Fig. 2: A "canoe-shaped" bowl, the body cut with a lozenge pattern within circular medallions, and the moulded foot similar to that of the bowl in Fig. 1. Circa 1790. Width 15¼ ins. (Christie's.)

wheare every glashouse wilbe so good as 20 men in garison, for proof I wilbe bounde to fynd 12 men at every glashouse sufficiently furnished, ready to serve her majestie within 20 myles of their aboude. And whereas it maye be thought by such a graunte, many poore strangers which now live by making of glass in England should for want of worke lacke maintenaunce, I wilbe bounde to set them all on worke, some in England & some in Ireland & to give them wages for wages, they doing worke for worke as at this present they have.

In a further document addressed to Burghley, Longe added that to permit him to manufacture in Ireland would lead to a worthwhile reduction in consumption of English timber for the furnaces. On the other hand, the plentiful woods of Ireland would be used, "then which in tyme of rebellion Her Majestie hath no greater enemy theare". Finally, he added that trade and civility would increase in the country from using the woods and the passage to and fro of ships for transporting the glass.

Longe was granted his patent, and established a glass-house in county Cork, at Curryglas, near the Drumfenning Woods. Nothing has been identified as having been made by him, but at least the surviving documents give a clear picture of conditions at the time on the far side of the Irish Sea.

LIKE that of Longe, other glass-houses came and went over the years, but details of their activities are few. Soon after 1690, following George Ravenscroft's successful introduction in England of glass-of-lead, "flint" or "lead" glass was being made in Ireland. It was produced under the partnership of Captain Philip Roche and two brothers, Richard and Christopher Fitzsimons, at an establishment named the Round Glasshouse, in St. Mary's Lane, Dublin. Successive members of the Fitzsimons family carried on the business from the same premises until about 1760. In January 1752 *Faulkner's Dublin Journal* printed an advertisement detailing goods which the Round Glasshouse was pleased to sell. It covered most types for house and garden use then in vogue in England, and ran:

drinking-glasses, water-bottles, claret and Burgundy ditto, decanters, jugs, water-glasses with and without feet

Page 5

Above, *Fig. 3: Pair of vases with covers and a bowl with "turnover" rim, cut with flat diamonds. Circa 1780. Vases, height 10½ ins.; bowl, diameter 10½ ins. (Cecil Davis Ltd.)* **Right,** *Fig. 4: Pair of vases and covers, with scalloped rims and flat diamond cutting. Late 18th century. Height 14½ ins. (Howard Phillips.)*

and saucers, plain, ribbed, and diamond-moulded jelly-glasses of all sorts and sizes, sillybub-glasses, comfit- and sweetmeat-glasses for desserts, salvers, glass plates for china dishes, toort [*retort*] covers, pine- and orange-glasses, bells and shades, hall lanthornes, glass branches, etc., all in the newest-fashioned mounting now used in London.

It may be queried whether all the goods on offer were actually made on the premises, or whether a proportion was imported from London. This was a common practice in the china trade, where a manufacturer did not always restrict his showroom to supplying only his own productions, and it is not at all improbable under the circumstances that the same trading custom was followed by the Round Glasshouse. In fact, a rival concern, started in Fleet Street, Dublin, in 1734 had ceased operating by 1750, and for the next few years the owners were occupied solely in the sale of ware imported from England. (For a possible connection between the Round Glasshouse and engraved Williamite glasses, see *Signature* No. 11.)

Other, minor, glass-houses came and went in various parts of Ireland during the eighteenth century. Many of them employed workers from England, but few flourished for more than a decade or so and there is little evidence of their existence other than in writing or print. Most of those in operation in the later 1750's suffered from a trade depression that afflicted the whole country, and had great difficulty in continuing in business. To assist both commerce and agriculture, a Dublin counterpart of the London Society for the Encouragement of Arts and Manufactures (now The Royal Society of Arts) was set up. It was founded in the first instance in 1731, 23 years before the London Society, but languished, was re-started, and in 1748 was incorporated as the Royal Dublin Society. Unlike the English one, it was aided by the Government, and

between 1761 and 1767 disbursed £42,000 in grants to promote agriculture and manufactures.

One of the grants, for the sum of £1,600 was awarded to Richard Williams and Company, a firm of which the founders were of Welsh origin, with a glass-house at Marlborough Green, Dublin. It is assumed that their grant, which was made in 1764, enabled them to start the business; they prospered, and by 1773 advertised that they "had brought the manufacture to as great perfection as carried on abroad". Four years later they built a new glass-house in Marlborough Street, and there seems no doubt they were the most successful manufacturers at work in Ireland during the third quarter of the eighteenth century. The firm continued in business until 1829.

THE Excise Act passed in 1745 laid a duty upon all glass made in England and Scotland, and at the same time completely prohibited the export of any such ware manufactured in Ireland. As the industry in the latter country was then of a very limited nature, this would seem to have been hardly worth doing. Whatever the reason, and it was perhaps no more than to give a sop in the shape of a small captive export market to English makers, the deed was done. The struggling Irish glass-makers were thenceforward limited to supplying their insignificant home demand in competition with goods brought in from England.

Later in the century, conditions were very different; England was engaged in fighting the War of Independence with

America, and Irish commerce was severely depressed with no sign of relief ahead. The American Declaration of Independence of 4th July 1776 was followed by the French allying themselves with the newly-formed United States, and the imminent possibility of the former invading Ireland to attack the British. To counteract the situation a volunteer force was raised, and within a few weeks 40,000 Irishmen had been enrolled. Inevitably, a threat of war united those who were normally divided, and with one voice the volunteers clamoured for freedom to trade wherever they pleased. Aided by the eloquence of Henry Grattan, their case, which was well-nigh irresistible under the circumstances, was accepted.

In 1780 Parliament at Westminster passed an Act permitting a wide range of goods to

Below, *Fig. 5: Pair of vases and covers cut with swirling flutes and raised on square plinths. Late 18th century. Height 11 ins. (Delomosne & Son, Ltd.)* **Opposite, below,** *Fig. 6: Set of dishes and saltcellars with serrated edges, the bodies step-cut and centred on stars. Circa 1815. (Cecil Davis Ltd.)*

be exported from Ireland. It is relevant here to notice that the prohibition of 1745 was repealed, and the new Act allowed:

> the exportation of glass, glass bottles, and other articles of glass manufacture from the kingdom of Ireland, to any part of Europe, the British Colonies in America, the West Indies, and the British settlements on the coast of Africa.

The Duty imposed on glass in England in 1745 was raised in 1777, and again in 1781. This last turn of the screw brought Ireland into the forefront of the picture, for the glass products of that country were completely tax-free and might now be sent anywhere in the world without hindrance. The Irish glass-makers suddenly found themselves working to capacity, with a possibility of prosperity ahead of them for the first time. Demand for glassware was sufficiently high and trading conditions were attractive enough to stimulate an invasion of English managers and craftsmen. They joined the few who had come during the past twenty years or so, and set up glass-houses to supply their own countrymen as well as eager buyers from farther afield.

With no Duty on the weight of materials to consider, the glass-makers were able to disregard the economies they had practised in England; not only could they use as much red lead in the mixture as they required, but there was nothing to stop them making vessels with good thick walls to withstand deep cut ornament. This they did, and the term Irish Glass is commonly applied to pieces of heavy weight which are decorated with skilfully cut decoration. It is not

Above, *Fig. 7:* Three decanters; (left and right) a pair, each engraved with a crowned Irish harp, a thistle, and other plants. Probably Cork Glass Co., about 1800. (Centre), a piece engraved with a crowned Irish harp and banners inscribed "Liberty" and "Free Trade", the reverse with a soldier and "Pro Patria", dated 1783. Heights 10 ins. and 10¼ ins. (*Christie's.*) **Left,** *Fig. 8:* Water jug with moulded flutes round the lower part of the body, which is engraved with a pattern and initials. Marked CORK GLASS CO under the base. Circa 1810. (*Cecil Davis Ltd.*)

possible to state definitely whether a piece was made at a particular factory, although pundits have from time to time suggested that such distinctions can be made.

The most frequently repeated statement is that Waterford glass has a grey-blue tint to be found in no other. In fact, much glass from all factories of the later eighteenth century shares this feature, in spite of the assertion that Waterford's "steel or grey-blue tone stands alone". The dark shade of a proportion of the glass of the time was due to accident or inexperience: the addition of overmuch manganese in the mixture.

Without manganese the glass is of a greenish tint, due to minute quantities of iron in the silica (sand). The careful adding of a decolouriser cures the fault, but the exact amount required has to be gauged with great care. Otherwise the pendulum swings too far; it goes past clarity and into the vaunted dark tone.

Alternatively, it has been suggested that the colouring of the glass was due to an impurity present in the lead oxide employed at the time. One of the last of the glass-workers, named Richard Pugh, is reported as having made a statement to that effect, and it has subsequently been said that the lead responsible came from mines in Derbyshire. Only a proportion of it apparently contained the blueing ingredient, which is proffered in explanation as to why not all Irish glass was tinted.

Authoritative words were penned on the subject of "grey-blue Waterford" by Mr. Dudley Westropp, for many years Curator of the National Museum of Ireland and writer of the standard work on Irish glass. He attempted to kill the legend as long ago as 1920, but with little effect. More recently he reiterated his conclusion: "all genuine marked pieces of Waterford glass I have seen and others of which I have traced their origin to Waterford, are of a clear white metal, though other Irish glass-houses produced metal with a bluish tint".

Within a few years of the passing of the Act allowing freedom of trade to Irish-based glass-makers, a number of new establishments had been set up. They flourished until 1825, the year in which the Irish themselves placed a tax on their products. From about 1830 machine-made pressed glass from England was being made in increasing quantities, and no hand-finished articles could compete with it in price. Some of the glass-houses managed to keep going for a further period, but most had disappeared by 1840. Particulars of the majority of the manufactories established after 1780 are as follows:

WATERFORD

IN its issue of 4th October 1783 the *Dublin Evening Post* printed a brief announcement reading:

> Waterford Glass House. George and William Penrose have established an extensive glass manufacture in this city; their friends and the public may be supplied with all kinds of plain and flint glass, useful and ornamental.

The Penrose brothers were merchants who had had no previous connection with glass manufacturing, but who foresaw possibilities in its future under the new conditions of trade. They took into their employ a manager, John Hill, who came over from Stourbridge and who, it was later reported, brought with him "the best set of workmen that he could get in the county of Worcester". So with a staff of skilled craftsmen, a glass-house and a warehouse, production commenced and business was invited "for ready money only".

Within a month the owners presented a petition to Parliament in Dublin requesting a subsidy. The grounds were that their success had been sufficient to put a stop to imports of flint glass from England, and therefore they were preventing the loss of Irish currency and deserved official support for so doing. In spite of what would appear to be economic ambiguity their claim was allowed, and a further petition followed in 1786. This second attempt was possibly received with scepticism, at any rate there is no record of whether or not it succeeded.

John Hill brought with him his knowledge of Stourbridge formulas and methods, and evidently knew what he was about. Unfortunately it would seem that in 1786 he had a serious disagreement with one of the owners, allegedly through offending one of the brothers' wives, and hurriedly left Ireland. Before he went he had time in which to write a letter to his friend, Jonathan Gatchell, a clerk at the glass-house, in which he wrote:

> For heaven's sake do not reproach me but put the best construction on my conduct. I wish it was in my power to pay thee and all my creditors but if ever fortune should put it in my power depend upon it I will satisfy every one. My mind is so hurt that I scarcely know what I write.

To the same man he communicated the secrets of manufacture which he had learned at Stourbridge, and hitherto had applied so successfully at Waterford.

Gatchell was duly promoted to take Hill's place as manager of the glass-house, and a few years later, following the replacement of the Penroses by other financiers, became a partner in the firm. After further changes, the sole proprietor eventually was a descendant of the original Jonathan Gatchell. This man, George Gatchell, carried on the business until 1851, when the making of flint glass ceased at Waterford.

The productions of the factory were mainly of clear glass of excellent quality, but some coloured pieces were made. Marked blue and green specimens have been recorded but are very rare. A formula for making opaque white glass was found amongst the factory documents, although it is not known if it was ever put to the test.

The majority of ware resembled closely that from other manufactories on both sides of the Irish Sea. Cutting was the most

Fig. 9: Jug of similar design to the one illustrated in Fig. 8; marked WATER-LOO CO. CORK. Circa 1810. (Delomosne & Son, Ltd.)

popular method of ornamenting, and has earned Waterford in particular, and Irish glass in general, its long-lasting fame. It cannot be said that any special type of cut was peculiar to Waterford, and the lack of marked cut examples has meant that the style of workmanship cannot be studied.

Decanters, water jugs and finger bowls are known with the words *PENROSE WATERFORD* in raised letters running round beneath the base. All were made by blowing into a mould which had the lettering incised, and the sides fluted vertically for about two inches. Re-heating to finish the article usually resulted in the inscription becoming blurred and sometimes indecipherable; in extreme instances it can easily be overlooked altogether. The decanters mostly have stoppers of the flat mushroom type, but the upright disc variety was also used.

George Gatchell was an exhibitor at the Great Exhibition, held in London in 1851. Giving the address Anne Street, Waterford, Ireland, and his category as "Manufacturer", the catalogue entry is:

> Etagère, or ornamental centre stand for a banqueting table; consisting of forty pieces of cut glass, so fitted to each other as to require no connecting sockets of any other material. Quart and pint decanters, cut in hollow prisms. Centre vase, or bowl, on detached tripod stand. Vases with covers. Designed and executed at the Waterford glass works.

The Exhibition closed to the public on 11th October 1851, but a month before that the *Waterford News* had printed an announcement of a sale of "the entire stock of glass". On 23rd December of the same year Gatchell left Waterford for Bristol, and soon afterwards the machinery and fittings of the glass-house and cutting-shop were sold up.

Fig. 10: Pair of decanters marked WATERLOO CO. CORK. Circa 1800. Height 10½ ins. (Delomosne & Son, Ltd.)

CORK GLASS COMPANY

In the same year that saw the start of operations at Waterford, 1783, a glass-house was established in Hanover Street, Cork. The partners in the enterprise were Atwell Hayes, Thomas Burnett and Francis Richard Rowe, but there were continual changes until 1787 when business was temporarily suspended. In the same year Parliament was petitioned for a grant and an award of £1,600 made as a result, and in 1793 a further petition gained a grant from the same source by way of the Dublin Society. With further changes in partnership taking place from time to time the company managed to keep its head above water until 1818, when it finally closed its premises.

Decanters made by the Cork Glass Company are similar in appearance to those of Waterford and other Irish glass-houses. Beneath the base is the inscription in raised letters, which are more or less legible, *CORK GLASS Co.*, and the same short vertical flutes ornament the lower part of the body. Three neck rings are usually present, and the mushroom-shaped stopper was evidently the favourite type.

Page 13

WATERLOO GLASS HOUSE COMPANY, CORK

THE company was started by a glass dealer, Daniel Foley, and received its first mention in 1815. A year later, the *Cork Overseer* printed the following paragraph:

> Foley's workmen are well selected, from whose superior skill the most beautiful glass will shortly make its appearance to dazzle the eyes of the public, and to outshine those of any competitor. He is to treat his men at Christmas with a whole roasted ox and everything adequate. They have a new band of music with glass instruments with bassoon serpents, horns, trumpets, etc., and they have a glass pleasure boat, a cot and a glass set which when seen will astonish the world.

In 1825 Foley took a partner, Geoffrey O'Connell, and five years later retired. O'Connell continued the business on his own, but went bankrupt in 1835 when the glass-house ceased to operate.

Again, marked decanters were produced, but inscribed *WATERLOO Co CORK*. They were similar in other respects to those made at Waterford and by the Cork Glass Company.

TERRACE GLASS WORKS, CORK

FOLLOWING the closure of the Cork Glass Company in 1818, two brothers, Edward and Richard Ronayne, established a glass-house in the city during the following year. They dissolved their partnership in 1838 and three years later the business was closed. It has been remarked, possibly with some truth, that as the factory was founded at such a late date its products probably had little artistic merit. Whatever they may have been like, none of the wares has been identified. At the date of closure it was stated that the company had equipment for forty glass-cutters.

Altogether the city of Cork, with three firms operating at one time or another, must have given employment to a considerable number of skilled glass-cutters. There were enough of them to support a Union for the regulation of their affairs, and to provide assistance to each other in adversity. The membership card is engraved with the title *CORK Glass Cutters New Union Society* above a pair of clasped hands, and with rococo scrollwork framing a claret jug and two goblets. The motto is perhaps unexpected, but as so many of the craftsmen were immigrants is not entirely inappropriate: "A pleasant road and cheerful welcome to every tramp".

LONG BRIDGE GLASS-HOUSE, BELFAST

IN 1771 the proprietors of the Tyrone Collieries brought over from Bristol a skilled glass-maker, Benjamin Edwards, to make use of local supplies of coal and sand. Edwards stayed for four or five years and then went to Belfast, where he started a manufactory of his own. It seems that his prices were more reasonable than those of his competitors because he did his own retailing, and had got his business so well established by 1787 that he was then able to lower his charges. Benjamin Edwards died in 1812, and his son of the same name carried on in his stead. The Irish glass tax of 1825 must have affected the fortunes of the firm seriously, because it was sold by Edwards junior in the following year. It never recovered its former prosperity, and apparently closed in about 1829.

Decanters of tall tapering form are known with *B. EDWARDS BELFAST* in raised letters beneath the base. They are fluted vertically round the lower part of the body, and have two neck rings in place of the more usual three. Stoppers are of the upright disc type, sometimes with a central depression within a border of short radiating

Fig. 11: Pouring glass decorated with cut facets and small diamonds and inscribed CORK CORPORATION. Circa 1820. Height 5 ins. (Howard Phillips.)

Fig. 12: Decanter marked CORK GLASS CO. Circa 1800. Height 10 ins.

cuts: a variety referred to by some writers as a target stopper.

BELFAST GLASS-WORKS

Another of Benjamin Edwards's sons, John, established a glass-house at Peter's Hill, Belfast, in 1803. Three years later he sold it to a company, and successive owners kept the business in operation until 1850. Nothing, so far, has been recorded about the types of ware produced.

CHARLES MULVANY, DUBLIN

Charles Mulvany, an Irishman, built a glass-house in Dublin in 1785. Three years later he advertised for sale a large variety of goods which included: glass lustres, girandoles, epergnes, lamps, decanters, goblets, bowls, and so forth. It is not unlikely that a proportion was made elsewhere, and as, like Benjamin Edwards, he did his own retailing, it would not be surprising if Mulvany built up his stock from other sources.

In 1801 he stated in an advertisement that his business was "confessedly the most extensive in Ireland", and in the same year he began to manufacture window-glass. In 1815 he built a new glass-house, but three years later he was bankrupt. Undaunted, a further glass-house was built by him in 1820, and in 1829 he transferred his business to the premises formerly occupied by Richard Williams & Co., at Marlborough Green. Mulvany took a partner in about 1830, and himself left the firm in 1835.

Although so much is recorded about his activities over the years, very little indeed is known about the wares he made and sold. The only positive evidence is to be found in some decanters, which are marked beneath the base in raised letters *C.M. Co.*, and were produced in Mulvany's glass-house.

THOMAS AND JOHN CHEBSEY, DUBLIN

During 1786 and 1787 Thomas and John Chebsey converted an iron foundry near Ballybough Bridge, Dublin, into a glass-house. They remained in business for only eleven years, during which time they received several grants from the Dublin Society. Soon after the Chebseys started, in 1788, "they executed a set of lustres for St. Patrick's Hall to the order of the Lord-Lieutenant".

A few prominent and publicity-conscious Dublin glass-dealers had their names put on decanters in the same manner as the makers at Waterford, Cork and Belfast, noted above. The articles were of similar pattern to the others, and were doubtless made to order by one or more of the firms named. The retailers concerned are:
FRANCIS COLLINS, DUBLIN
ARMSTRONG, ORMOND QUAY and
J. D. AYCKBOWM, DUBLIN.

© *Geoffrey Wills, 1968*

9

Bottles: to 1720

In preceding *Signatures*, Nos. 1 to 8, attention was directed towards clear glass, and no mention was made of the variety known as "green" or "bottle" glass. This unsophisticated material has a lengthy history, and its manufacture was carried on in later years alongside that of the superior variety.

At least as far back as the thirteenth century, glass of the coarser kind was being made in England wherever suitable sand and plentiful timber were available. The makers came from Normandy, and settled in Kent, Surrey and Sussex, where there existed large areas of woodland. Excavations carried out on some of the sites of former furnaces have revealed traces of drinking-vessels, lamps and bottles, but the principal output was of window-glass.

In the second half of the sixteenth century came a further wave of immigrants from France, this time from Lorraine. Again, they were mostly makers of window-glass, but there is no doubt they extended their activities into other fields as the Normandy settlers had done before. Many of this fresh group of arrivals moved westwards and northwards as supplies of timber in the south diminished, and made use of the sand and fuel they found in Hampshire, Gloucestershire and Staffordshire. Later, some of them penetrated even farther to the north, and their descendants are traceable in Newcastle and elsewhere for many subsequent generations. Lorraine names like Thisac, Hennezel and Thiétry were duly anglicised, so that their bearers were recorded as Tyzack, Henzey or Ensell, and Tittery.

Opposite, *bottle sealed with a merchant's mark and dated 1698. (Detail of seal illustrated in Fig. 15, page 16.) Height 5½ inches.* **Above,** *Fig. 1: Tin-glazed earthenware ("delftware") serving bottle inscribed in blue* WHIT, *for white wine, and dated 1646. Height 5 inches.*

The metal used by all these men was of a green hue and coarse appearance, and the alkali constituent was the ash resulting from burned wood or bracken. The process gave its name to the product in Germany, where it was called *Waldglas*, and in France, *verre de fougère*. Interest in early glass of this type is restricted mainly to archaeologists, but in the mid-seventeenth century it began to be employed for making bottles for wine and other liquids. In recent years the bottles have received a considerable amount of study, and an increasing number of collectors on both sides of the Atlantic confine their interest in glass to this particular variety.

Above left, *Fig. 2: Serving bottle of pale green glass, sealed Philip Sergeant, 1717. Height 9 inches. (Victoria and Albert Museum.)* **Above right,** *Fig. 3: Bottle sealed with initials RW. Circa 1650. (Ivor Noël Hume.)*

Bottles for holding liquids of one kind and another had been known from antiquity, and continued to be made down the centuries. Documents list the ownership of such things as "a lyttle bottel", "a glasse bottel" and "an ewrynall"; the latter recorded by a writer in 1688 as

a cleare and thyn glasse bottle, with a long

neck and round body: it is used by doctors, Apothicaries, and such as follow physick, to put in the water of diseased bodyes for them to looke at, and to give their judgement of the distemper.

Bottles of numerous shapes and sizes have been excavated in London and elsewhere, but it is rarely, if ever, possible to determine their original purpose. In many instances they would have been provided for medicinal use, but a large number could have held other liquids and drinks of various kinds. No examples bearing labels, or of a shape that proclaims an especial use, have been found, so they will probably remain forever in the realm of conjecture.

Sir Robert Mansell acquired in the 1670's a monopoly of glass-making in England which allowed him to manufacture, amongst much else, "... bottles violls [phials] or vessels whatsoever, made of glass of any fashion, stuff, matter or metal". No doubt some of the glass-houses under his control supplied the demands of the ensuing thirty years, but none of them would appear to have borne any identification mark and they cannot now be allocated to a particular place of origin.

Next to appear upon the scene were Henry Holden and John Colenet, who were granted a patent in 1662 in view of their claim to have "invented and attained unto perfection of making glass bottles". They were allowed a monopoly lasting fourteen years, but the products had to be suitable for containing full measures of liquids in gallons and other quantities, and "shall be marked with Colnett's particular stamp or mark".

A month after the granting of the patent it was alleged by two London dealers in bottles that Colenet (or Colnett) had not been responsible for the invention. It was stated that he had merely manufactured some of the articles about 30 years earlier, and it had been done to the order of Sir Kenelm Digby, a naval commander, author and diplomatist: a gentleman named "the Ornament of England". The patent was thereupon withdrawn, and it has been suggested that what Sir Kenelm introduced was the idea of using English glass bottles for holding wine.

It is difficult to believe to-day that anyone could have laid claim to inventing such a commonplace

Above, *Fig. 4: Bottle sealed with a king's head, the initials* R P M *, and the date 1657. Height $8\frac{4}{5}$ inches. (Central Museum, Northampton.)*

Fig. 5: Bottle initialled E.S and dated 1688. Height 6½ inches. (Sotheby's.)

as a bottle; an object which had been in everyday use in Roman times. However, since then there had been an interval, the several hundred years known as the Dark Ages, during which so much that was familiar in the third and fourth centuries A.D. was completely forgotten. In England, these lost arts may have included bottle-making, and the needs of the inhabitants would have had to have been supplied from abroad.

Wine, ale and beer were certainly known and enjoyed during this apparently bottleless period, for there are ample records to prove the fact. They would have been transported and stored in wood casks, and served in vessels of pottery or pewter. The wealthier people used cups of silver or, from the fifteenth century, Venetian glass.

As the activities of the forest-based glass-makers were confined mainly to window-glass, it is likely that their output of domestic articles was small. No doubt some of them made bottles, but the primitive working-conditions and limited skill of the time must have ensured they were only small in size. It would have been no easy matter, if at all possible, to anneal wine-bottles in quantity with the resources available. The treatment comprised a very slow cooling of the articles over a period of many hours, and unless carried out the products would be useless. Unannealed glass fractures at a touch and is generally unstable in its properties. With the introduction of well-organized glass-houses, the annealing-oven (or *leer*) was incorporated in the building, and the process could be effected without any difficulty.

The immediate forerunners of glass wine-bottles were made of pottery, possibly at Lambeth where an extensive industry was based. The pottery articles are small in size, fat-bellied and with handles, and lettered in blue with the name of their contents: *Claret*, *Whit* (for White Wine), *Sack* and *Rhenish Wine* (Fig. 1). They bear dates between 1637 and 1672, and some have initials or, very rarely, coats of arms on them. They were outnumbered by others made of hard stoneware, which were imported from the Rhineland and may have been brought here either full or empty. Exactly how these ceramics types were used is not quite certain; the general opinion is that they were too decorative to have been purely for storage purposes, and they were placed on the table in the manner of the later decanter.

A few glass bottles have been preserved that show a direct link with the early pottery ones. Like the latter they have handles but, as in the example illustrated in Fig. 2, some of them bear seals. They are usually referred to as serving bottles.

Further confirmation of the descent of glass bottles from those of pottery is to be found in the arms and regulations of the Glass Sellers' Company. The arms show "a Venetian glass cup between a laverpot [ewer] of white ware on the dexter and a looking glass on the sinister". The by-laws made following the charter of incorporation, granted on 25th July 1664, specify commerce in "glasses, looking-glasses, hourglasses, stone pots [made of stoneware, a type of hard pottery], or earthen bottles". From these references it is clear that the two sorts of vessel were bought and sold by the same men, and not improbable that their functions were interchangeable.

Just as the pottery bottle bore a date, so also did many of its glass successors. The date, sometimes with initials, a crest or some other insignia, was stamped on a pad of about one-inch in diameter on the shoulder; the pad being a drop of molten glass impressed with a stamp cut in intaglio exactly as if it was to be used with sealing-wax. Like the bottle itself, this was no novelty, as a comparable device had been used as a trade mark by a glass-maker in the second century A.D.

The placing of an exact date on a bottle in this way has enabled a sequence of styles to be compiled. Again, the seals themselves have proved far more durable than the articles on which they were placed, and it is not uncommon for one to be recovered when all other trace has vanished. In many instances they have proved invaluable to historians in locating long-vanished homes and in confirming written records.

Possibly the earliest known English wine-bottles are two that were found in London, and although undated bear a seal with the initials *R.W.* (Fig. 3). An identical seal was excavated in Jamestown, Virginia, the first permanent English settlement in the New World. One of the colonists

Fig. 6: The seal inscribed Cha. Turnor *and dated 1690. Height* $5\frac{9}{10}$ *inches. (Central Museum, Northampton.)*

Left, *Fig. 7: Base of a bottle of about 1700, showing the deep "kick". The seal depicts a crest in the form of an elephant's head couped. (County Museum, Truro, Cornwall.)*

in the first half of the seventeenth century was a man name Ralph Wormeley, upon whose property the *R.W.* seal was discovered. As he died in 1651, and the two bottles are of the earliest known shape, it is not unreasonable on the strength of the available information to suppose that the bottles were made not later than that year.

The first dated evidence is provided by a seal of 1652, which has outlasted the bottle it once embellished and is now in the London Museum. It bears a coat of arms and the name JOHN JEFFERSON. Next in chronological order is a complete bottle dated 1657, with the initials R P M and a representation of a king's head; doubtless made to the order of the owner of a King's Head tavern. It was found at Wellingborough, Northamptonshire, and is now in the Central Museum, Northampton (Fig. 4).

As can be seen, the bottle has a tall neck in relation to its body, and near the mouth is a narrow rim. This latter is known as the string-rim, and was provided in the first instance to retain the string which held a cork in place. Later, when the cork was driven flush with the top and stringing became unnecessary, the string-rim was retained but raised level with the orifice.

The base of this early bottle shows the mark where the iron rod, the "pontil" or "puntee",

Right, *Fig. 8: Seal showing the coat of arms of Lucius Henry Cary, 6th Viscount Falkland (1687-1730). Diameter 1⅜ inches.*

had been attached during manufacture. The "kick" or indentation, where the pontil mark was pushed up, is not a deep one in this early bottle, but is sufficient to allow the object to stand firmly. The rough mark, if left in its natural position would protrude unevenly, and not only make the bottle unsteady but would scratch a surface on which it stood.

The interior of an eighteenth century bottle-making glass-house is seen in the engraving reproduced in Fig. 9. The artist has made the scene of work very much tidier than it would have been in real life, and there is no indication of the great heat in which the men worked. It was noted by a writer that the men at the furnace-mouths "receive these scorching heats, sallying directly into their faces, mouths and lungs; whence they are forc'd to work in their shirts, with a straw brim'd hat on their heads, to defend their eyes from the excessive heat and light".

There is scant information about where the bottles were being made between about 1650 and 1690. Later, in 1696 a list of the then-existing glass-houses was published. It was compiled by John Houghton, a Fellow of the Royal Society, who wrote a series of "letters" dealing with "Husbandry and Trade" of the time, which were printed between 1681 and 1703. Houghton's *Letter CXCVIII* is dated 15th May 1696, and opens as follows:

An account of all the glasshouses in England and Wales.	The several counties they are in.	The No. of houses.	And the sorts of glass each house makes.
In and about London, and Southwark,		9	For bottles.
		2	Looking-glass plates.
		4	Crown-glass and plates.
		9	Flint, green and ordinary.
Woolwich,	Kent,	1	Crown-glass and plates.
		1	Fint, green and ordinary.
Isle of Wight,	Hampshire,	1	Flint, green and ordinary.
Topsham near Exon.	Devonshire,	1	Bottles.
Oddam near Bath,	Sommersetsh.	1	Bottles.
Chellwood,		2	Bottles and window-glass.
In and about Bristol,		5	Bottles.
		1	Bottles and window-glass.
		3	Flint, green and ordinary.
Glocester,	Glocestersh.	3	Bottles.
Newnham,		2	Bottle-houses.
Swansey in Wales,	Glamorgan.	1	Bottles.
Oaken-Yate,	Shropshire,	1	Bottles and window-glass.
Worcester,	Worcestersh.	1	Flint, green and ordinary.
Coventry,	Warwicksh.	1	Flint, green and ordinary.
Stowerbridge,	Worcestersh.	7	Window-glass.
		5	Bottles.
		5	Flint, green and ordinary.
Near Leverpool,	Lancashire,	1	Flint, green and ordinary.
Warrington,		1	Window-glass.
Nottingham,	Nottingham.	1	Bottles.
		1	Flint, green and ordinary.
Answorth,		1	Bottles.
Custom-more, near Answorth,		1	Flint, green and ordinary.
		1	Bottles.
Near Silkstone,	Yorkshire,	1	Bottles.
Near Ferry-bridge,		1	Flint, green and ordinary.
		1	Bottles, flint, green and ordinary.
Kings-Lynn,	Norfolk,	1	Bottles.
Yarmouth,		1	Flint, green and ordinary.
		1	Bottles.
New-Castle upon Tine,	Northumberland	6	Window-glass.
		4	Bottles.
		1	Flint, green and ordinary.
		90	

Note, Some of these houses are not at work.

Opposite, Fig. 9: Bottle-making in an eighteenth century glass-house. The man on the left is blowing molten glass on his blowing-iron, while his neighbour (centre) is flattening the base of his blown 'bubble' on a slab of iron (a marver) prior to attaching the pontil and forming the neck. In the background is a man helping to take goods to the leer to be annealed, and above his head are shelves of finished bottles. (Glass Manufacturers' Federation.)

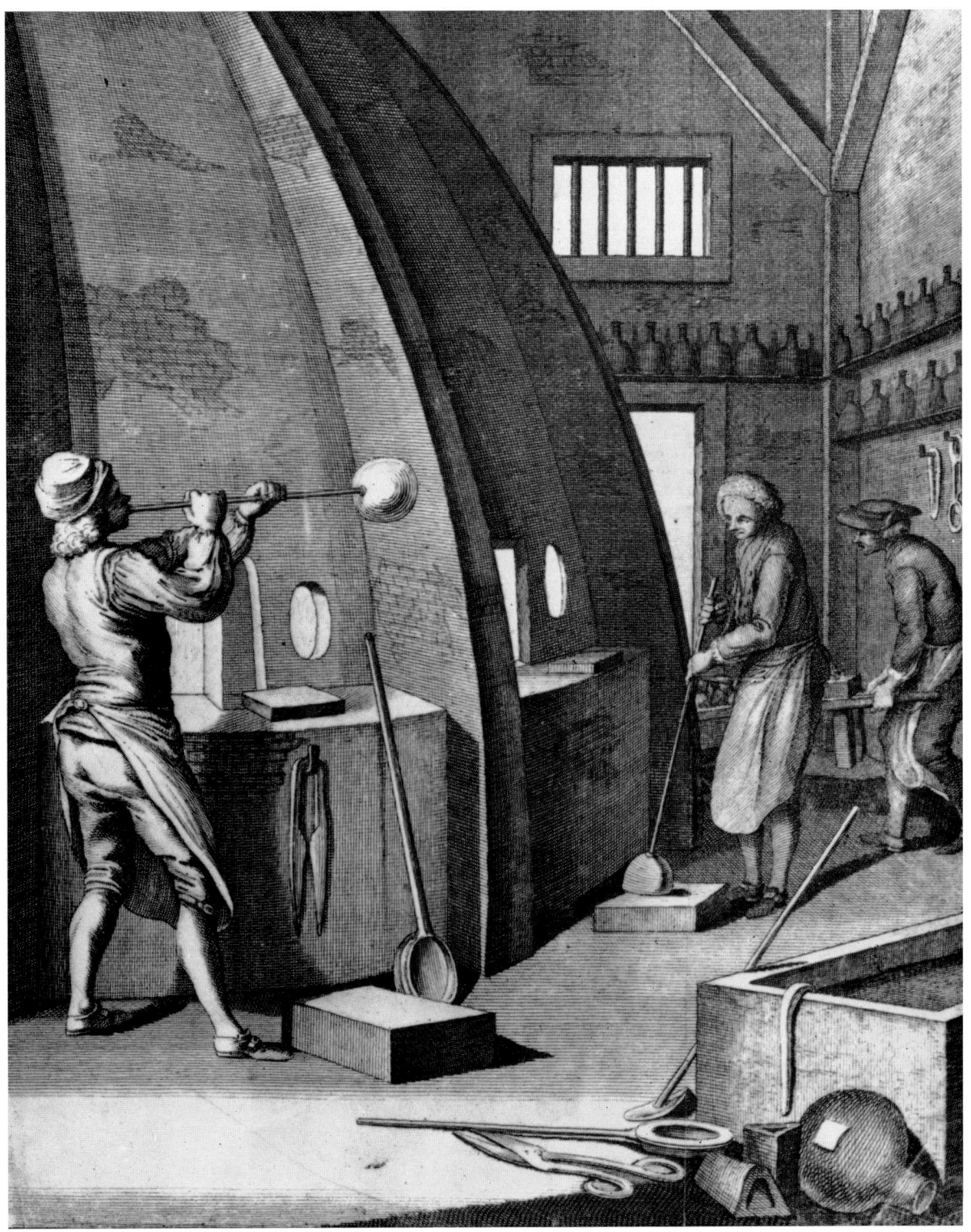

Above, *Fig. 10: Bottle sealed with a plume of feathers and a name, the latter now indecipherable with only* FR . . . PH *remaining. Circa 1650-65. Height 8½ inches. Of three complete bottles excavated on the site of Jamestown, Virginia, this is the only sealed example. (U.S. Dept. of the Interior, National Park Service.)*

HOUGHTON continues by pointing out that London and Bristol were the places with the greatest number of glass-houses, the others being divided between fourteen counties: "and all the other counties have none at all, and how much it is to their honour and advantage, I wish this may make them consider". He noted that whereas twenty-eight houses made flint, green and ordinary glass, no fewer than forty-two produced bottles. They were able to make sufficient to supply almost the entire needs of the home market, for Houghton recorded that imports of glass bottles in 1694 totalled a mere eight dozen from Sweden: "I presume their importation we have quite spoiled".

A final quotation from Houghton reveals the composition of bottle-glass at the time:

> Our green glass, or glass for bottles is made of any sort of ashes well powder'd, and ordinary sea-sand from Woolwich, &c. This is what at present occurs on this subject.
>
> By another [informant] I understand they use kelp and pulverine, which are still but a finer sort of pot-ash.

With so many glass-houses at work making bottles, it is to be expected that there was considerable variation in design. Each one was blown individually, and the size of the finished object judged by the eye. There was no such thing as a legal standard content, and no means by which a bottle could be made to conform to one. Thus, no two are exactly alike.

The sequence of styles has been charted and is roughly reliable, but many exceptions have been recorded and unless a bottle is actually dated it is always safer to describe it as "*circa*".

The very first bottles have been described above; later in the seventeenth century came the following:

- 1670: the neck is shorter than in the preceding type, but the body remains bulbous.
- 1680: the neck is again shorter, and the body still has a base smaller in diameter than the shoulder.
- 1690: the neck expands gradually along its brief length, and is so very short that the bottle is difficult to grip satisfactorily. The kick is deep. (Figs. 5 and 6).

The last of the types endured with minor variations until about 1720, so an unmarked bottle of the shape can have been made at anytime during a period of thirty years or so. In spite of the drawback that it was far from easy to grip while pouring, buyers of the time must have found it serviceable or the pattern would not have remained current for so long.

In addition to dates on the seals, armorial bearings can be almost as useful as a guide to the year of manufacture. When traced, they sometimes prove a latest year in which a certain coat was borne, and with a newly-conferred title the dates can often be narrowed. Unfortunately, few give a positive answer; a coat was not always changed whenever a title passed from one member of a family to another, and the strict rules of heraldry were not always followed rigidly.

The seal illustrated in Fig. 8 would appear to be identifiable with reasonable certainty. It is on a bottle of the shape current in 1690-1720, and the coat of arms is that of the Cary family who were created Viscounts Falkland in 1620. The original owner of the bottle can be decided without much doubt to have been the 6th Viscount Falkland, Lucius Henry Cary, who was born in 1687 and died in 1730. He succeeded to the title in 1694, following the death of his cousin. The career of the 6th Viscount calls for little comment (unlike that of his ancestor, the famous Cavalier, killed at the battle of Newbury in 1643), but it may be mentioned that he was created an Earl by the "Old Pretender".

CAREFUL excavation by trained archaeologists in the United States has resulted in considerable and worthwhile additions to our knowledge of old English wine-bottles. The site of the former town of Jamestown, Virginia, has yielded no fewer than 20,000 fragments of bottles, and three that were brought from the mud complete (see Fig. 10). A total of 104 seals has been found in the course of two separate sessions of digging, which took place in 1934-41 and 1954-56.

The first colonists left the port of London in 1606, and consisted of a party of 144 men and women with their supplies. Their three ships were named the *Susan Constant* and, appropriately, the *Godspeed* and the *Discovery*. Eventually the coast of

Above, *Figs. 11 and 12: Seals from bottles probably belonging to Sir Francis Nicholson, Lieutenant-Governor of Virginia, 1690-1705. Excavated on the site of Jamestown, Va. Diameters about 1¾ inches. (U.S. Dept. of the Interior, National Park Service.)*

Above, *Fig. 13: Early eighteenth century bottle with seal inscribed* THOMAS GREAT COLCHESTER, *and the sign of* The Old Twisted Posts and Pots. (*Mr. James Wharton, Weems, Va.*)

America was reached, by which time their numbers had fallen to 105, and the spot chosen for settling was named Jamestown, after their king, James I.

The party suffered all the privations of disease and death inseparable from their lot, and duly were led to something approaching stability by Captain James Smith. Smith was later captured by Indians, and is alleged to have been set free through the intervention of Pocahontas, daughter of their chief. John Rolfe, one of the colonists, earned a lasting fame on two counts: he initiated the cultivation of tobacco, and he married the aforementioned Pocahontas.

By 1642 the colony had a population of 8,000, but Jamestown itself, although the administrative centre, showed little sign of advancement. A period of political unrest culminated in a series of fires started by dissatisfied colonists, and following the burning of the fourth statehouse in 1698 the centre of government was removed to Williamsburg.

Although it is known that two attempts were made to start a local glass-house, no bottles were apparently made there and all the excavated glass is accepted as having been made in England. The more successful of the colonists sent home for bottles, many of which they had ornamented fashionably with their marks in the form of seals.

One such seal bears the legend THE KING'S BAGNIO encircling the initials *H A*. It is conjectured to have been made for Henry Ames, keeper of a public bagnio, or baths, built in Long Acre, London, in about 1682. There is no answer to the query as to how it reached Virginia, but no doubt it was among the few wordly goods of a settler from the Old World.

Probably with a strong local tie are the seals illustrated in Figs. 11 and 12. Both bear the initials *F N*, one with a small cross above the letters and the other with a star (or heraldic mullet) in the same position. They are thought to have been on bottles belonging to Sir Francis Nicholson, who was Lieutenant-Governor of Virginia between 1690 and 1705. It was he who made the recommendation that the move be made from Jamestown to Middle Plantation, then the name of Williamsburg. The seals thus date from the last quarter of the seventeenth century.

Similar excavations to those systematically

carried out at Jamestown have taken place elsewhere in Virginia. The ruins of a mansion named Corotoman, in Lancaster County, consumed in a fire in 1729, yielded the bottle illustrated in Fig. 13. The seal is inscribed THOMAS GREAT COLCHESTER. Charles Great, no doubt a relative, is known to have lived at *The Old Twisted Posts and Pots* in the same town, and these are shown on the seal. A similar bottle was found in Priory Street, Colchester in 1934, and has been described as "containing an evil-smelling liquid that was presumably once wine".

Farther to the south-west in the State, at Tutter's Neck, James City County, excavations revealed the two bottles illustrated in Fig. 14. Both have been badly smashed and portions of them are missing, but the general outline of each is plain

Below, *Fig. 14:* (*Left*) *sealed with the initials* F.I. *for Frederick Jones, and* (*right*) *with the name* Richard Burbydge *and dated 1701.* (*Smithsonian Institution, Washington, D.C.*)

Fig. 15. Seal showing a merchant's mark and dated 1698; see frontispiece. Diameter 1 inch.

and their seals are intact. One bears the initials of Frederick Jones, and the other the names in full of Richard Burbydge with the date 1701. Little has been recorded about the latter, but Jones is known to have arrived in Virginia in 1702. He died twenty years later.

Many of the bottles sent from England to the order of American settlers were sealed with names or initials, with or without a date. Some, however, bore a special sign known as a merchants' mark: a personal device used by traders and others from about the year 1400. When it was placed on goods it not only readily proclaimed their ownership, but could be interpreted as a guarantee of quality in the manner of a modern trade-mark. Their use spread from business to the home, and they formed what has been termed a commercial heraldry. One of the Verzelini glass goblets was marked in this manner (*Signature* 1, page 7 and Fig. 2), and the marks have been found on woodwork, stonework, memorial brasses, silver and stained glass, as well as on signet rings and as a watermark on paper.

A few glass bottle-seals bearing merchants' marks, dating from the last quarter of the seventeenth century, have been excavated at Jamestown, Virginia. None has yet been identified with a particular colonist, and it is probable that the marks were used by growers on their tobacco and other exports. It would have been a natural step for a trader to employ his business sign on his private property, and this is what occurred. Such merchants' marks were rarely used at all in Europe by that date, so these American examples are in the nature of a survival.

A bottle sealed with a merchants' mark and dated 1698 is illustrated in the *frontispiece* and Fig. 15. It was purchased in Devonshire in about 1957, and is so far the sole recorded bottle thus marked to have been found in England. Also, it may be added, none of the American seals bears a date. The bottle in question may have returned across the Atlantic at some time to the country where it was made, or was it one that for some reason did not make the trip in the first instance? The answer will probably never be known.

© *Geoffrey Wills, 1968.*

Figs. 3, 13 and 14 are reproduced by permission of the author, Ivor Noël Hume, from Here Lies Virginia *published by Alfred Knopf, New York, 1963.*

10

Bottles: from 1720

About 1725 a change in the design of the wine-bottle is discernible. For the preceding thirty or so years it had had a stumpy neck sloping outwards to join the body, and then the slope became less pronounced while the body sides followed a straight line from shoulder to base. The deep kick remained to do its duty of keeping the pontil-mark out of the way and not, as cynics have observed, of allowing the vintner to supply short measure to his clients.

The well-defined shoulder and straight sides of the new type of bottle are the first clear signs of the shape that eventually evolved into the familiar wine-bottle of today. It has been suggested that the Methuen Treaty with Portugal, concluded in 1703 by the British Ambassador, John Methuen, encouraged the change from the earlier "onion" shape. The Treaty allowed English woollen goods to be imported into the country at a preferential rate, while in return Portuguese wines were admitted into England at a lower duty than was levied on French wines.

The result was that Portuguese wine, and Port in particular, soon began to oust French on the English market. In time, the benefits of allowing the wine to mature in the bottle called for the containers to be of a shape requiring a minimum of storage space. In addition, the use of the corkscrew had become general, and instead of tying a cork in place with wire or strong thread it was driven in flush with the top of the bottle-neck. To ensure it remained airtight, the cork had to be kept moist and swollen, and the bottle was laid on its side so that the contents remained in contact with the cork. A flat-sided bottle provided the answer: it could be laid down without trouble and was easy to store.

By 1740 the majority of bottles had acquired a body that was more or less square in outline, while the neck and shoulder together were of about the same height as the body. Gradually the proportions changed, until by the last quarter of the century the body had become taller and slimmer. The neck remained of much the same length as before. Hitherto the string-rim at the top of the neck had been applied in the form of separate threads of glass, but from this time onwards the lip was thickened to become the upper edge of the string-rim.

Opposite, (*back*) *inscribed in diamond-point on the shoulder* Richard Robartes his hand July 5th 1785, *height 13½ inches;* (*left*) M. Bradford 1723, *height 7¾ inches;* (*centre*) I. Knill 1781, *height 9 inches;* (*right*) Wm. Taylor Bossiney 1836, *height 10½ inches.* (*County Museum, Truro, Cornwall.*)

Fig. 1: Bottle sealed Saml. Archer *(see Fig. 2), the word* **PATENT** *on the shoulder at the back, and the maker's name under the base (see Fig. 10). Height 10½ inches.*

The custom of a gentleman having his name or some other indication of ownership placed on his bottles continued throughout the eighteenth century. Wine merchants and tavern keepers did the same, in part to ensure their bottles were not used by competitors and in part as an advertisement. By the time Victoria succeeded to the throne the use of such marks was becoming rare, and soon afterwards it more or less died out. From then onwards, the buyer of wine purchased it ready-bottled, and no longer had it put in his own containers. The vintner seldom marked his bottles, although a few of the larger suppliers continue the practice to the present day. In such instances, however, a careful examination will show that the seal is moulded in one with the bottle, and not applied separately as on earlier examples.

ANOTHER type of eighteenth century bottle was oval in section. Of the two examples illustrated in the *frontispiece*, the wine-bottle on the left is sealed with the name *M. BRADFORD* and dated 1723. Such bottles are much rarer than round-based ones, although they seem to have enjoyed a moderately lengthy popularity. Examples have been recorded bearing dates between 1710 and 1758, but it may be supposed they were made especially to suit the buyers' preference. A number of them bearing the name of a west-country family, the Bastards, have survived, and this has led some writers to term them "bastard bottles".

The larger of the oval bottles illustrated is not sealed, but has a name and date scratched on it in diamond-point. The inscription, which is on the shoulder, reads: *Richard Robartes his hand July 5th* 1785. The appearance of the bottle suggests it was made at about that date, and it is interesting that the fact is confirmed in writing. Whether such a large vessel was used for wine is debatable.

A variety of bottle in use from the late nineteenth century is unusual enough in appearance and usage to provoke numerous inquiries. It is the type stoppered ingeniously by means of a glass marble or "alley", and that continued to be employed until at least the early 1930's. The thick-walled body bears the name of the drink-supplier in raised letters, and the glass itself is of a pale green tint (Fig. 3).

Fig. 2: Seal on the bottle in Fig. 1, enlarged to show the guide-lines used by the engraver.

The bottles were used solely for "soft" drinks, of which the gassy content kept the marble inside the neck in tight contact with a rubber washer at the top. The neck was pinched in such a manner that the marble could not fall down into the body of the bottle. To release the liquid it was only necessary to press the marble inwards from the top, and a wood cap was supplied for the purpose. Alternatively, an eager young finger could be used, but was not always strong enough. After being emptied, many of the bottles were smashed to extract the glass ball, which acquired another lease of life in the hand of a marbles player.

Yet another, and older, shape of bottle is that known as a "case bottle", which is of a square section widening from the base to the shoulder. A distinctive feature is that it invariably has a very short neck with the top of the mouth everted and thickened for strength, and it is usually much more thinly blown than the cylindrical wine-bottle. The earlier examples, dating from the seventeenth century, are thinner-walled than later examples, and they tend to be of a paler coloured metal.

Some eighteenth century case bottles survive in their original wood cases or "cellars", but their actual use in the past is not always certain. A very few are labelled, but the majority are devoid of any indication of what they may have contained. Some twentieth century writers refer to them as "Dutch gin bottles", but this is perhaps no more than a notion that they are somehow connected with a modern square-faced bottle peculiar to a brand of the spirit from Holland. They could have been used in the past to contain a multiplicity of liquids, ranging from the alcoholic to the non-alcoholic, not omitting the strange mixtures blended by alchemists.

The examples illustrated on page 15 date from the eighteenth century, the largest of them having a capacity measureable in gallons rather than pints. The smallest of the three is better described as a square bottle than as a case bottle, and is made of a pale green glass containing innumerable small bubbles. It is of an unusual shape, and has the additional distinction of being marked on one corner with a seal. The latter is imperfect, but was damaged during manufacture as the broken side is partially melted. An initial *N* is legible, but there are traces of some further markings above it which cannot be deciphered.

Case bottles were made by blowing the molten metal on the end of the blowing-iron into a shaped mould. When it had cooled a little and contracted, the bottle was lifted from the mould and a pontil (or *puntee:* a plain iron rod) affixed with a small blob of glass to the base. The blowing-iron at the mouth was then cut off, and the article held by the pontil in the furnace-mouth so that the neck was re-heated for finishing. Thus, beneath the base these bottles have a mark remaining from where the pontil was finally removed. The sloping sides of the bottles enabled them to be taken out of the moulds easily, but once they had been removed the thin walls usually sagged inwards and most of them are concave-sided instead of flat.

There exist a few contemporary accounts of eighteenth and nineteenth century wine-bottle-making that give a good idea of the process. One, published in 1735, relates how the maker blows into

the lump of molten metal on the end of his iron, and then "whirls the iron many times round his head to lengthen and cool the glass". Then he flattens the base and gives it to the master workman to break off the neck.

> The collet or neck is the narrow part which clove to the iron: to set the glass at liberty they put a drop of cold water on the collet, which by its coldness cuts or cracks a quarter of an inch; after which by giving it a slight knock, the fracture is communicated all round the collet and it drops off.

At this stage a pontil is affixed to the base, as noted above with reference to case bottles, and the mouth is finished off. If the bottle is to be sealed, a blob of molten glass is put on the shoulder and then stamped with a seal cut in intaglio in just the same manner as with sealing-wax. The seals were occasionally composed of individual letters held in a small frame, but usually they were cut especially in a piece of metal. Some examples show clearly the guide-lines scratched lightly into the surface to assist the engraver (Fig. 2).

John Houghton's list compiled in about 1696 (see *Signature* 9) showed that the majority of bottles were made in London. At that time nine glasshouses were in operation there; Bristol boasted five, while the remainder of the country had a further twenty-eight. Writing in 1725 Daniel Defoe recorded a changed position:

> There are no less than fifteen Glass-Houses in Bristol, which is more than there are in the City of London. They have indeed a very great Expence of Glass Bottles, by sending them fill'd with Beer, Cyder, and Wine to the West Indies, much more than goes from London; also great Numbers of Bottles, even such as is almost incredible, are now used for sending the Waters of St. Vincent's Rock away, which are now carry'd, not only all over England only, but, we may say, all over the world.

A couple of years prior an advertisement in the *Freeholders' Journal* had announced:

> Bristol water for sale in Bottles. The empty Bottles at 2s. per dozen. N.B.—The Bottles are large and London-shaped.

Fig. 3: "Soft" drink bottle sealed with a glass ball, seen here in the neck. Inscribed: W. Dubbin, Mineral Waters, Devonport. Made by Dan Rylands, Barnsley, Yorkshire. Early 20th century. Length 9 inches. (Mr. and Mrs. F. W. May.)

Fig. 4, illustrating the wine-bottle from 1721 to 1793: height 9 inches; Cha. Pugh 1765, *height 9¼ inches;*

While seventy years later the trade was still in being, as an Annual published in 1792 noted:

> The returns made here in the glass-manufactory are prodigious; great numbers of bottles are used for sending the water of St. Vincent rocks to all parts of England and the world.

The waters of St. Vincent's Rock, or the Hotwells as it was called alternatively, were famed as a cure for diabetes, but were no doubt taken for many other ailments as well. Medicinal waters from other sources were also packed in containers for use in the homes of those unable or unwilling to travel. In the British Museum is a large-sized stoneware jar inscribed *Iron Peartree Water, near Godstone, Surrey*, which dates from the mid-eighteenth century. It once held an allegedly successful cure for the gout.

A Williamsburg, Virginia, apothecary advertised in 1745 that he supplied "Hungary Water, Spaw and Pyrmont Waters", and seals with the words *Piermont Water* and *Pyrmont Water* on them have been excavated in the state. Others have been found in England, together with bottles sealed *Pouhon-in-Spa*, a watering-place in Belgium that was popular in the eighteenth century.

E. Herbert 1721, *height 7 inches;* G. H. 1733, *height 7¾ inches;* A. F. Sampson 1746, *height 8¾ inches;* W. & M. Law 1756, *height 11 inches;* N. Tredcroft 1784, *height 10½ inches;* C. Ellis 1793, *height 11 inches. (Findlater, Mackie, Todd & Co. Ltd.)*

MANY fragments of bottles dating from before 1700 have been excavated on the site of the earliest English settlement in Virginia (see *Signature* 9). Following a series of conflagrations, the capital, Jamestown, was removed to a place called Middle Plantation, re-named Williamsburg after the English king, William III. In recent years the long-neglected centre has been reconstructed and given a change of name once more. Now it is known as Colonial Williamsburg, and successive explorations there have resulted in the salvage of many traces of the eighteenth century inhabitants. Not least of the articles disinterred are wine-bottles and seals, which in earlier times had been imported from England (Figs. 5 and 7).

In some instances these finds have posed problems, for it is not always apparent why a particular bottle should have arrived in Virginia. The name of the person whose insignia it bears does not seem to have had any obvious connection with the area, and its location there defies explanation.

An example is the seal illustrated in Fig. 6,

Fig. 5: Octagonal bottle sealed Jno. Greenhow, Wms.burg 1770. (*Colonial Williamsburg, Va.*)

which was found during excavations at the Anthony Hay Cabinet Shop in Williamsburg. It depicts a coat of arms encircled by the Garter motto, *Honi soit qui mal y pense*, surmounted by an earl's coronet. The arms are those of John, first Earl Poulett, created an earl by Queen Anne in 1706. For a brief period, from 1710-1711, he was First Lord of the Treasury and Prime Minister of Great Britain, and from 1711 to 1714 Lord Steward of the Household. He married in 1702 the daughter of the Hon. Peregrine Bertie, and the arms of his wife are on the inescutcheon: the small shield superimposed on the arms of Poulett. As Lord Poulett was given the Garter in 1712 and died in 1743, the bottle which once bore the seal, and the seal itself, must have been made between those years.

What it was doing in a joiner's shop in America is not known, but bottles are useful portable objects and their wanderings cannot always be accounted for. Their final resting places are often utterly unpredictable, for who would expect a late seventeenth century bottle to be discovered in the grave of a Red Indian? One was found in those circumstances on Rhode Island, and the undated seal bore the name of a London tavern: *The Whit Beare at the Bridge Foot*.

In addition to wines, spirits and spa-waters, medicines also were sold in glass bottles. The majority of them have disappeared completely, but among the survivors is an early nineteenth century example inscribed in raised letters *TRUE DAFFY'S MIXTURE*. This was a concoction first compounded by a man named Anthony Daffy in the late seventeenth century, which remained on sale until at least 1931.

A recipe for Daffy's Elixir printed in 1742 included: elecampane root, liquorice, aniseed, coriander seeds, carraway seeds, senna, guaiacum, rhubarb, saffron and raisins. The correct amount of each had to be infused for four days, stirred, strained and bottled. The writer concluded:

> This elixir is excellent good for the colic, the gravel in the kidneys, the dropsy, the griping of the guts, or any obstruction in the bowels; it purgeth two or three times a day.

It must have had a reputation for being somewhat unpalatable, for Mrs. Mann, in Charles Dickens's

Oliver Twist, excused the presence of a bottle of gin in her house by a glib reference to the Elixir. Producing the spirits, she remarked to her visitor, Mr. Bumble: "Why, it's what I'm obliged to keep a little of in the house, to put into the blessed infants' Daffy, when they ain't well".

*   *   *

Fig. 6: *Seal with the coat of arms of the first Earl Poulett (1663-1743) excavated at the Anthony Hay Cabinet Shop, Williamsburg. (Colonial Williamsburg, Va.)*

ON the whole there is surprisingly little detailed information about the bottle-industry in the past. Prior to 1845, when the Excise duty was removed, it was an entirely separate part of glass-making. The reason for the division was because the various types of glass were taxed at different rates; flint being charged much more than green or bottle glass. In addition, it was laid down in the Act imposing the tax in 1745 that the industry should be split into five distinct and closely-regulated parts. Each was permitted to manufacture only the type of glass for which it was licensed, and no overlapping was permitted. As Excise officers were permanently on the premises of every glass-house, there was little chance of the rules being broken.

While Bristol was certainly a busy centre of bottle-making, London continued to be of some importance during most of the eighteenth century. Ratcliff, in the east of the city, was a centre of the trade, and another group of makers was located across the river in Southwark. There is a reference to one of the latter in a newspaper report in 1751:

> April 16. To New Gaol, Southwark.
> Samuel Dodd, charged with buying and receiving four Dozen of Glass Bottles, the property of Mr. Gerard Van Horn, knowing the same to be stolen.
> John Phillips, charged on the Oath of John Ford, with stealing Four Dozen of Glass Bottles, from the Glasshouse of the said Mr. Vanhorn, in the Parish of St. Saviour, Southwark.

It is from random references like the foregoing that what little knowledge we possess of most bottle-houses has been gained. Some of the men who protested in 1695 against the imposition of a tax on their products stated they were bottle makers, but gave no other particulars. The names of districts and streets sometimes keep alive the

memory of former occupants, and may reveal a little. A minor street situated beside where Regent Street joins Piccadilly Circus, in London, is a typical instance. It is named Glasshouse Street, was first built in the late seventeenth century, and although no one knows how it got its name there must certainly have been a good reason.

In the city of London were Glasshouse Alley and several places named Glasshouse Yard, which have been swept away during rebuilding operations. Towns in the provinces have similar traces of former occupations, that would otherwise be completely forgotten.

The histories of some of the Bristol glass-houses have been partially recorded by a few writers, but because of continual amalgamations, bankruptcies and changes of name and address the resulting chronicle is confusing. It is not until the nineteenth century that indisputable evidence of a Bristol origin can be claimed for wine-bottles.

As early as 1752 a paragraph in a newspaper referred to "one Brass Bottle-Mould value 18s., the property of Mr. Thomas Warren & Co., [stolen] from the Glasshouse in Temple Street". Presumably the mould was of the hinged type that came together for making the article, and then fell neatly apart to release it. The join where the halves of it met inevitably left a trace on the finished product, and this appears as a narrow ridge running up each side to the top of the shoulder.

A description of the manufacturing process written in 1852 tells how a man blew the body of a bottle in the mould, knocked it off the end of the blowing iron and handed it on a pontil to another worker. The latter re-heated it at the furnace, and formed the neck.

> This operation, which goes on continuously and regularly, occupies about half a minute. As soon as one workman has left a mould, another, with a similar lump of red-hot glass, takes his place; and so quickly is the whole process carried forward, that one workman can form the necks of the bottles which three others are employed in moulding.

One of the best-known Bristol firms owned a number of glass-houses near Temple Gate. After numerous changes in partnership the business became Ricketts, Evans and the Phoenix Glass

Fig. 7: Named and dated bottle seals excavated on the site of Williamsburg. (Colonial Williamsburg, Va.)

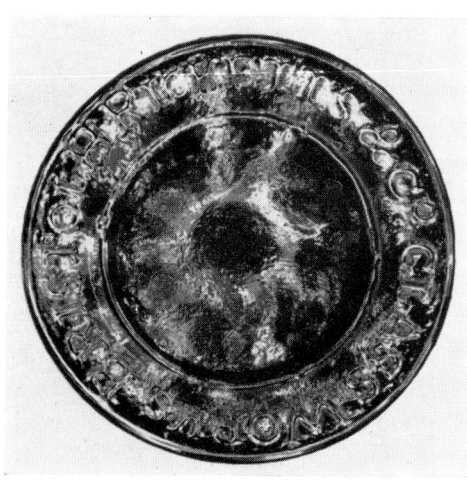

Fig. 8: Base of the bottle in Fig. 1, lettered H. RICKETTS & Co. GLASS-WORKS BRISTOL. *Circa 1830.*

Company. Then, about 1830, it was Henry Ricketts & Co., who put their name under the base of their bottles and the word *PATENT* in large letters on the shoulder (Figs. 1 and 8). In 1853 they amalgamated with an adjoining concern and became Powells, Ricketts and Filer, who used the same marking on the shoulder of their bottles but put their initials under the base (Fig. 9). Within a year of the start of the new partnership William Powell died, and the death of Edward Filer took place two years later. As a result, the company was re-formed with Powell's son, as Powell and Ricketts. Thus, the bottles marked *P R & F* were made only for the short period between 1853 and 1856.

By the last-mentioned date an instrument with a claw at the end had been introduced for handling the partly-made bottles. Instead of putting them on a pontil, the claw gripped the base and was used while the neck was being finished. Bottles made with its aid, therefore, do not have a pontil-mark.

Bristol was by no means the only provincial bottle-making centre. Houghton noted those active in or just before 1696, but as the goods they made were of little artistic or monetary value small notice was taken of them. Their comings and goings are at present largely unrecorded, or if noticed are known only locally.

A paragraph reprinted in 1832 mentions a Scottish bottle manufactory of the preceding century. It reads:

> In January, 1751, a globular bottle was blown at Leith, capable of holding two hogsheads. Its dimensions were forty inches by forty-two. This immense vessel was the largest ever produced at any glass work.

The bottle-making glass-house noted by Houghton at Exeter would seem not to have lasted for many years after 1696, when he wrote of it. The *London Gazette* for 22nd June 1702 noted that it was then for sale, but it is uncertain whether it was bought for continuing the business or put to some other use. The *Gazette* announcement makes it sound a very pleasant place:

Opposite, (*left and centre*) *Case bottles. Circa 1750. Heights 11 and 15½ inches. (County Museum, Truro, Cornwall.)*
(*Right*) *Square bottle sealed on the shoulder. 18th century. Height 8½ inches.*

Fig. 9: Bottle made by Powell, Ricketts & Filer, Bristol. Circa 1855. (Mrs. G. C. S. Coode.)

A Round Bottle-Glass-House 94 Foot high, and 60 Foot broad, with all Conveniences, a Pound House and Smith's Forge, a Quantity of Pot-Clay, and Working Tools for Bottles or Flint, with two Stone-built Dwelling-Houses, Two Gardens, and Three Large Orchards; also Eight Acres of Meadow-Ground, a large Kitchin-Garden and Nursery, with Barn, Stable and Outhouses, in Ware, between Topson [Topsham] and Exon [Exeter], near the River, fit to carry and recarry the Goods. 'Tis to be Set at 7, 14 or 21 years. Enquire of Eliz. Renell at the Glass-house near Exon, or of Isaac Barnard in Milk-Street, London.

During the nineteenth century the Bristol and other makers faced increasing competition from the north of England, where both fuel and labour were plentiful. By 1900, newly-invented machinery was beginning to oust the craftsman, and deliver an endless supply of bottles literally "untouched by human hand".

© *Geoffrey Wills, 1968.*

11

Enamelled and Engraved Glass

Opposite, *drinking-glass painted in enamels with a coat of arms, on the reverse a view of ruins, signed* Beilby pinxit; *by William and Mary Beilby, Newcastle upon Tyne. Circa 1770. Height 7½ inches. (Victoria and Albert Museum.)*
Below, *Fig. 1: The "Butler Buggin" bowls, of glass-of-lead decorated with diamond-point engraving. Circa 1676. Diameter 5 inches. The bowl on the left is now in the Corning Museum of Glass, Corning, N.Y., and that on the right is in the Victoria and Albert Museum, London. (Photograph:* The Connoisseur.*)*

GLASS can be transformed from the purely functional into the decorative, or a combination of both, in a number of ways. The simplest method is for the maker, while the metal is still in a molten state, to shape and twist it to suit his ideas. To a great extent he is limited in this by the nature of the glass itself, and the various styles into which it has been shaped owe much to this fact.

The slow-cooling Venetian soda-glass could be manipulated successfully into the most complicated and delicate forms, whereas the German potash-glass was more suitable for heavy-looking thick-walled articles. The latter were then passed on to lapidaries, who ornamented them with deep and shallow cutting. The resemblance to natural rock crystal was remarkably close, and the finished piece owed its appeal principally to the artistry of

the cutter. Ravenscroft's glass-of-lead, which was found to be comparatively quick in cooling, brought a further quality to specimens made from it.

The men using Ravenscroft's formula did their best to imitate the popular Venetian styles, but soon found that the new glass had a will of its own. Not only was it difficult to tease into the shapes of Muranese baroque forms, but its inherent virtues made any attempts to do it superfluous. The brilliant surface sheen and deep reflecting qualities of the material were seen at their best in simple shapes that required little or no further embellishment, but nevertheless sometimes received it.

Buyer and sellers in the late seventeenth century doubtless appreciated the unadorned beauty of the new product, but now and then had good reason for "gilding the lily". While this may not have been always to the artistic improvement of the piece, in most instances it has resulted in giving it added interest for later generations. An example

Fig. 2: Three Jacobite glasses engraved in diamond-point: (left and right) inscribed with a hymn and "Amen", height 7½ inches; (centre) inscribed "Send him soon home to Holyruood House/And that no Sooner than I do wish/Vive La Roy" [sic] with the crowned cypher J. R. and the figure 8, height 9½ inches. First half of the eighteenth century. (Photograph: The Connoisseur.)

Fig. 3: Five glasses wheel-engraved with Jacobite emblems: (left to right) with a six-petalled rose, an oak-leaf, and a Latin motto, height 7 inches; with a portrait of Prince Charles Edward and inscribed CAROLUS, height 7¾ inches; with an eight-petalled rose and two severed buds, and a Latin inscription "Tempora mudantur et nos mudantur in illis" [sic] signifying the decay of the movement, height 9½ inches; with a portrait of Prince Charles Edward and a toast, height 7⅝ inches; with a six-petalled rose and two buds, one opened and the other unopened, and the motto "Reddes Incolumen" ("Return unharmed"), height 6½ inches. Mid-eighteenth century. (Photograph: The Connoisseur.)

of this is seen in the pair of bowls illustrated in Fig. 1, which were probably decorated to commemorate a wedding that took place on 16th July 1676.

One of the bowls (right-hand of Fig. 1) bears the coat of arms of Butler Buggin, of North Cray, Kent, impaled with those of his wife, Winifred, one of the Burnett family, of Leys, co. Aberdeen. The other (left-hand), shows the arms of Buggin: sable, a cockatrice displayed argent, crested, membered and jelloped gules. Both bowls have on their reverse the Buggin crest, a cockatrice displayed above a helmet.

As the glass of which the bowls are made contains lead, they must have been produced after the date of Ravenscroft's successful experiments: 1675. Late in the following year it was announced that he was then marking all his ware with his personal seal of a raven's head. But the bowls are not sealed so they must have been made in the

Fig. 4: Goblet wheel-engraved with a six-petalled rose and two differing buds, an eight-rayed star, a lopped oak with two saplings at the roots, of which one has three leaves and an acorn, and inscribed Fiat*; the foot engraved with the Prince of Wales' feathers. Second quarter of the eighteenth century. Height 7⅛ inches. (Howard Phillips.)*

short period between the end of his researches and the start of sealing. The date of the Buggin-Burnett wedding is in that period and confirms the fact.

The twentieth-century continuation of the story is not unromantic. The bowls appeared completely unrecognised for what they really were and simply as two pieces of old glass, at a small auction sale held in Hitchin, Hertfordshire, in 1937. They were sold for a few shillings, but in November of the same year a magazine article with the title "A Find in 17th Century Glass" drew attention to them. In June 1963 they again came up for auction, this time in London, at Sotheby's and with the story catalogued competently. The two realised on this occasion the sum of £6,800, which fully justified the auctioneers' description of them as "Important". The bowls were offered in two separate lots, and as a result one of them is now in the Victoria and Albert Museum, London, and the other in the Corning Museum of Glass, Corning, N.Y.

Like the majority of the commemorative glass goblets made between 1577 and 1590 and attributed to Giacomo Verzelini (described and illustrated in *Signature* 1), the Butler-Buggin bowls were engraved with a diamond-point. No doubt the splinter of diamond was fixed to the end of a holder, and then used in much the same way as a pen or pencil. The surface of the glass was scratched as required, and many surviving examples of the work were probably done by amateurs. Equally, much was done to order by professionals, in England and abroad, but it is not always easy to tell into which category a piece falls.

The most noted of English diamond decoration of the eighteenth century is that on the so-called "Amen" glasses. These were made for supporters of the Old Pretender, James Francis Edward Stuart, son of James II, and his second wife, Mary of Modena. The child was born in 1688, and in the same year his father fled to France and the Queen took her son across the Channel in secret. On the death of James II in 1702 at St. Germain, near Paris, the boy, then aged 13, was declared King of England as James III and King of Scotland as James VIII. In the meantime, William III reigned in this country, and was succeeded on the throne by the half-sister of the Pretender, Queen Anne.

The matter was further complicated by the fact that Mary of Modena and James II had been Catholics, and that their child had been brought up in that faith. Further, it had been mooted from his very birth that the boy was a supposititious child, and this remained in the public mind as a possibility even after his father had made a formal declaration to the contrary soon after his birth. Anne was a Protestant, as had been her sister, Queen Mary III, and adherents of the two faiths ranged behind their respective leaders. The Catholic party, out of favour in English Court and Government circles, was encouraged by Louis XIV, who did all he could to embarrass his neighbours across the Channel.

The Old Pretender made an abortive attempt to lead a revolt from Scotland, but the English fleet in conjunction with English weather foiled the attempt. He fought with the French army against the British, and then made a slightly more successful expedition into Scotland. This time, in 1715, he landed, established his Court at Scone, but within a year he had fled back to France. He duly retired to Rome and married. His subsequent neglect of his wife displeased many of his followers, and in his career and behaviour generally he seems to have done his utmost to alienate all but the very staunchest of his adherents.

Glasses made and decorated in honour of the Pretender have been the subject of considerable argument for many decades. They are undoubtedly old with the exception, needless to say, of deliberate fakes, which are cunningly contrived and many in number! The query arises over the precise date of each, which can be at any time between 1720 and 1749.

The "Amen" glasses have gained their convenient name because of the hymn, running to two or more verses, that appears on them. A typical example is seen on the glass illustrated in Fig. 2, left-hand. It runs as follows:

God Save the King I pray
God bliss the King I pray,
God save the King;
Send Him Victorious
Happy and Glorious
Soon to Reign Over Us,
God Save the King

Fig. 5: Drinking-glass wheel-engraved with a portrait of Prince Charles Edward with rose, buds and thistle and inscribed Brittn^S Glory & Brittn^S Shame. Mid-eighteenth century. Height 7⅛ inches. (Howard Phillips.)

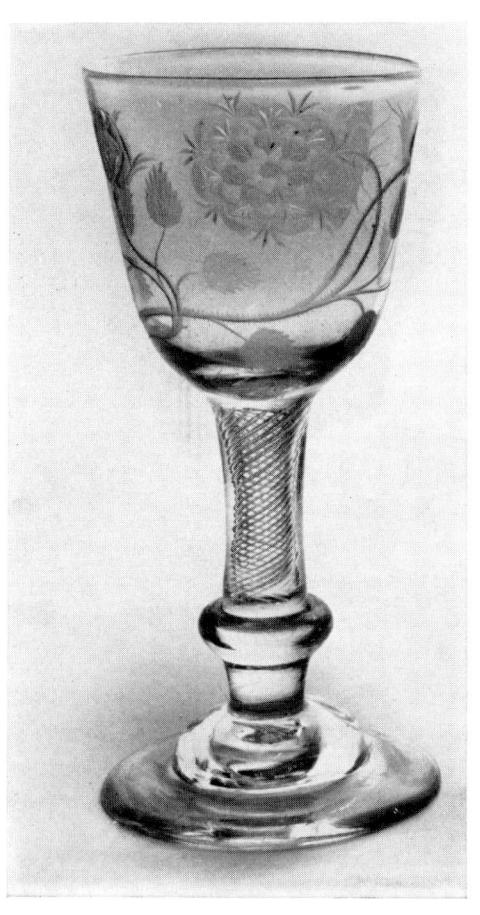

Below, *Fig. 6: Drinking-glass wheel-engraved with the Jacobite emblems of a seven-petalled rose with two buds, and a moth. Circa 1750. Height 7¾ inches. (Sotheby's.)* **Opposite,** *Fig. 7: Goblet wheel-engraved with an equestrian figure of King William III and an inscription (see page 11). First half of the eighteenth century, probably made and decorated in Ireland. Height 12½ inches. Now in the Ulster Museum, Stranmillis, Belfast. (Photograph:* The Connoisseur.*)*

God Bliss the PRINCE of Wales
The True Born Prince of Wales
Sent Us by Thee
Grant us one Favour more
The King for to Restore
As Thou hast done before
The Familie.

Additionally, there is the word "Amen" and the inscription "To the Increase of the Royal Family".

The Prince of Wales referred to was born in 1720, which gives the earliest possible year for the engraving. The glass itself, with a drawn stem containing a tear, dates from about the same time. The glass on the right-hand side in Fig. 2 is dated 1725 to commemorate the birth of Prince Henry, brother of the Prince of Wales, and other glasses of the same type are recorded which are dated as late as 1749.

Charles Edward Stuart, Prince of Wales and son of the Old Pretender, was known, in turn, as the Young Pretender. Like his father, he was the centre of much treasonable intrigue. It culminated in 1745, when he sailed from Nantes for Scotland and eventually landed there. Within a year, on 16th April 1746, his rapidly diminishing and disheartened army met the superior forces commanded by the Duke of Cumberland, brother of George III, and were beaten decisively at Culloden. Literally following in his father's footsteps he fled to France, and similarly his behaviour alienated his supporters. He died in 1788.

A<small>N</small> outline of the lives of the two Pretenders to the English throne may appear out of place in a history of glass, but they were indirectly responsible for many interesting pieces made in the eighteenth century. Their decoration was not confined to the diamond-point, but included the other main types of ornament: wheel-engraving and enamelling.

Wheel-engraving is almost self-descriptive: the work is done by the craftsman using small diameter wheels of copper with which the design is cut into the surface of the article. The abrasive used is a mixture of oil and emery, and wherever the wheel touches it leaves a greyish mark, varying in depth and width according to requirements, in contrast to the surrounding area.

Fig. 8: Drinking-glass wheel-engraved with an Oriental scene and with a facet-cut stem. Circa 1770. Height 6½ inches. (L. G. G. Ramsey, Esq., F.S.A.)

The collecting of glasses engraved with Jacobite emblems has been pursued actively since the late nineteenth century, and much time and ingenuity have been expended in unravelling the mystery attaching to many of them. The craftsmen of the time, and their patrons, contrived to disguise as far as possible the true significance of the decorative motifs on the glasses. Although the movement was looked upon officially as more or less harmless, it was doubtless wise for its followers to behave circumspectly. If they wished to toast "The King over the Water" it was wiser to do it in secret.

Many and various have been the theories put forward to account for the significance of the rose with from six to eight petals, with or without one or more buds, and of the other allegedly Jacobite flora (Fig. 4). They form quite a gardenful of blooms, and include: forget-me-nots, honeysuckle, daffodils, carnations, lily-of-the-valley, sun-flowers, and oak leaves. Accompanying them appropriately on occasion are moths, butterflies and other insects.

In no instance are all present on the same piece of glass, but many permutations are possible with the employment of a few at a time. The most popular of all is the full-blown rose, which was once taken to represent the Old Pretender himself, but is now accepted widely as standing for the English Crown (Fig. 5). The claimants are shown as buds: the small bud on the left being the Old Pretender and the smaller right-hand bud standing for his son. A star found occasionally is said also to represent the Young Pretender, and his unflattering portrait, with or without a framing of laurels, is on some rare and sought-after specimens (Fig. 6). Latin mottos appear sometimes in association with the foregoing, and amongst them are *Fiat* ("let it be so"), *Redeat* ("may he come back"), *Revirescit* ("he is renewed") and *Audentior Ibo* ("I will go boldly").

Jacobite emblems are found engraved on various types of drinking-glasses, but principally on wines. Most examples date from 1750-60, after the disaster of Culloden which one might have expected to have killed the "movement" completely. Decanters, tumblers and finger-bowls also exist with similar engraving (Fig. 7), but are scarce nowadays. Matching sets of decanters and glasses were made, but breakages have taken a heavy toll over the years and very few of them now exist.

While Jacobite adherents were catered for, the needs of the opposing loyalists were not forgotten by the glass-makers. An exceptionally fine goblet is illustrated in Fig. 7, and the inscription engraved round it proudly proclaims: THE GLORIOUS AND IMMORTAL MEMORY OF KING WILLIAM AND HIS QUEEN MARY AND PERPETUAL DISAPPOINTMENT TO THE POPE THE PRETENDER AND ALL THE ENEMIES OF THE PROTESTANT RELIGION. Glasses with comparable sentiments in their wording often refer also to the Battle of the Boyne, where on 1st July 1690 William's forces defeated those of James II. Such glasses date from the first half of the eighteenth century, and many of them may have been made and engraved, or only engraved, in Ireland. The Round Glasshouse, Dublin, advertised in 1752 that it could supply engraving "of any kind or pattern . . . toasts or any flourish whatsoever". This last being perhaps an allusion to their willingness to execute wording of a controversial nature.

Other loyalist glasses show representations of the rearing White Horse of Hanover, but engraving on glasses is not by any means confined to strictly political ends. Many were engraved with the coats of arms of their owners, and others commemorated national and local events (Fig. 9, and *Signature* 1, Figs. 9 to 14). A further group of glasses is ornamented with cutting that is purely decorative, like the example in Fig. 10.

Wheel-engraving continued to be employed throughout the eighteenth and nineteenth centuries, and is still used today; likewise, cutting is a type of decoration that has proved persistently popular. The technique was soon found to be admirably suited to glass-of-lead, from which it extracted the maximum of glittering reflection. Once this discovery had been made cut glass gained a place it has never lost. In the nineteenth century and later, it was attacked as barbaric, John Ruskin being among those who railed in vain against it, but it remains high in public esteem.

GLASS is cut in much the same manner as it is engraved: by using a series of revolving wheels. The wheels are, however, much larger in diameter,

Fig. 9: Decanter with a flat-topped stopper, the body cut with a pattern of small diamonds in relief and the shoulder step-cut. Circa 1820. Height 8 inches.

and instead of being made of copper are of iron and sandstone. The process can be divided into four distinct operations, namely: marking the article, preliminary cutting, final cutting and polishing. The first, marking, is done with a bright paint (often a mixture of red lead and turpentine), and the design is then given a first cutting by means of an iron wheel about 18 inches in diameter. A stream of wet sand falls on to the edge of the wheel, and does the actual work. Then comes further cutting by means of a wetted sandstone wheel, which deepens and widens the earlier cuts and removes much of their roughness. The work at this stage is still only in a crude state, and must be given a finish by means of wheels made of wood and fed with a series of powders of increasing smoothness.

The process relies on the hand and eye of the operator, and a false move can render preceding work completely useless. In the present century, much of the polishing is done chemically by dipping

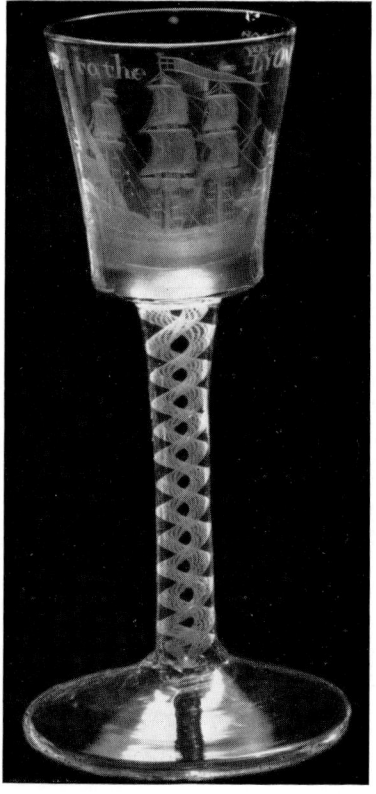

Opposite, left, *Fig. 10: Drinking-glass wheel-engraved with a ship in full sail and inscribed* "Success to the LYON Privateer". *Circa 1760. Height 6 inches.* **Centre,** *Fig. 11: Goblet enamelled in white with a rococo pattern, the bucket bowl suported on an opaque-twist stem. Circa 1760. Height 7 inches.* **Right,** *Fig. 12: Goblet enamelled in white with a vine-plant bearing grapes. Circa 1750. Height 7 inches. (All Sotheby's.)*

the semi-completed piece into a bath of hydrofluoric acid. This eats away a layer of the surface, a layer varying in depth according to the length of time the article remains immersed. Cutting when carefully examined always shows irregularities in design revealing the hand work entailed. Machine-made imitations (*Signature* 15) have a precision unattainable in any other way.

Cutting and engraving began to be known in England early in the eighteenth century, when an announcement in the *London Gazette* on 1st October 1709 stated:

> There is lately brought over a great parcel of very fine German Cut and Carved Glasses, viz. Jellies, Wine and Water Tumblers, Beer and Wine Glasses with Covers, and divers other sorts. The like hath not been exposed to public sale before.

A prominent glass-seller from a decade after that date was John Akerman, in due course holder of the office of Master of the Glass Sellers' Company. He announced in 1719 that he "continues to sell all sorts of tea, chinaware, plain and diamond-cut flint glasses"; the term "diamond-cut" referring to the polished facets being in the shape of diamonds. He is thought to have employed at least one craftsman of German origin, whose son, Christopher Haedy, was a glass-cutter later in the century. Akerman's son, Isaac, carried on his father's business and, in turn, was Master of the Company.

Two of Akerman's competitors in business in London were equally energetic in advertising their stocks of cut glass. Jerom Johnson (*Signature* 6) and Thomas Betts, the latter with premises named the King's Arms Glass Shop, situated opposite Pall Mall in Charing Cross. Betts's trade-card lists some of the goods he sold, which included:

> all sorts of Curious Cut Glass Such as Cruets, Castors, Salts, Lustres, Desarts, Dishes, Plates, Punch Bowles, Cream Bowles . . .

In addition, he called himself "the Real Workman", implying that he was manufacturer as well as retailer. Whether this was in fact the truth has not been proved, but it was a claim made or implied by others at the time.

Whether cut by their own employees or purchased wholesale from an independent cutter, the

Fig. 13: Drinking-glass enamelled in colours with a bust of Prince Charles Edward, the round funnel bowl raised on an opaque-twist stem. Circa 1760. Height 5⅞ inches. (Ashmolean Museum, Oxford.)

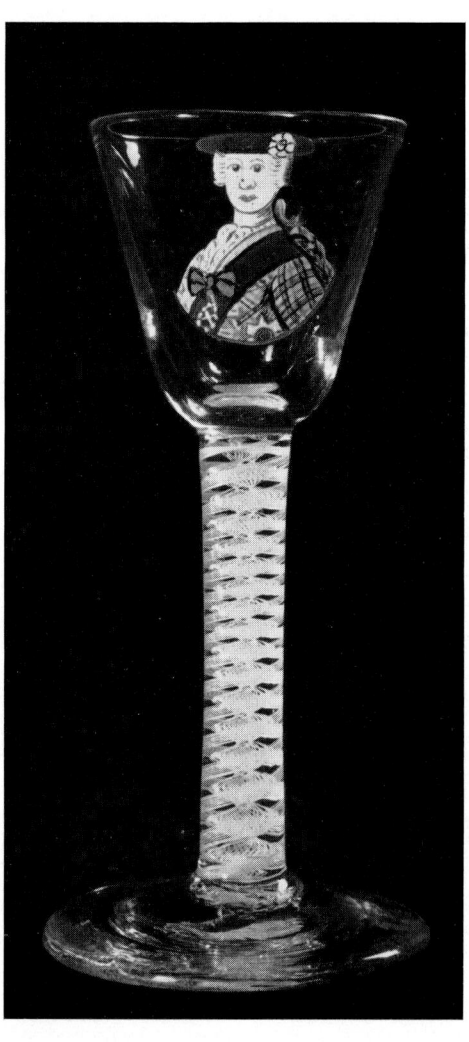

wares sold by Akerman and his fellow-traders cannot now be identified as to source. Nor is there any way by which we can distinguish the productions of the numerous other men whose names are now forgotten. Unlike some of the potters of the period, they did not mark their work and it must, perforce, remain anonymous.

A further method of decorating glass was to paint it with coloured enamels which were then heated to "fix" them, in much the same way as porcelain was treated. The art dated in England from the mid-eighteenth century, and its employment was perhaps limited by a shortage of craftsmen with the skill required for its execution. Of the types of ornament to be found, it is the one of which examples are today most scarce.

Probably the commonest variety of enamelled glass is that decorated in plain white, without the addition of any colour. The quality of the workmanship varies, but the contrast between the bright enamel and the clear glass surface can give it a brilliant crispness that conceals defects and enhances its merit. The wine-glass illustrated in Fig. 11, is an excellent example of its kind. The bucket bowl is supported on a straight stem containing opaque-white twists, and painted with a trellis or diaper pattern outlined with scrolls and formal leafage.

Another wine-glass, enamelled in white like the preceding example, but with a band of fruiting vine, is illustrated in Fig. 12. As the stem is a plain one, it can be dated rather earlier than examples with opaque twists. The latter type of stem is the most usual in conjunction with an enamelled bowl, and leads to a dating of examples to the years after 1755-60.

Made and decorated at about that date is the glass illustrated in Fig. 13. It shows the portrait of a rather surprised-looking Young Pretender, wearing Highland dress with a Star. Jacobite glasses painted in colours are very rare, and most of the few surviving examples of such pieces are decorated in plain white. They are of similar pattern to those with wheel-engraving on them, discussed above, and the same semi-obscure emblems were used.

The most celebrated enamelled work was done by members of the Beilby family of Newcastle

Fig. 14: (Left) decanter enamelled in colours with the Royal arms of George III, on the reverse the Prince of Wales' feathers; a piece perhaps made and decorated to celebrate the birth of the Prince in 1762. Height 9¼ inches. (Right) a goblet enamelled in colours with a landscape within foliate scrollwork, on the reverse a butterfly hovering over a leafy spray. Height 6⅞ inches. Both pieces painted by members of the Beilby family of Newcastle upon Tyne, 1760-70. The goblet is now in the Toledo Museum of Art, Toledo, Ohio. (Photograph: The Connoisseur.)

upon Tyne. Much of the information about them comes from an autobiography written by Thomas Bewick, the wood-engraver, who was apprenticed to Ralph Beilby for seven years from 1767. The father, William, was born at Scarborough, Yorkshire, and later established himself in business as a silversmith and jeweller at Durham. He is said to have had artistic talent, which was duly inherited by his seven children; five sons and two daughters. In 1760 they all moved to Newcastle, and there the father died five years later.

Fig. 15: Drinking-glass with an opaque-twist stem, the bowl gilt with a pattern of vine-leaves and grapes. Circa 1760. Height 6 inches. (*Photograph:* The Connoisseur.)

The son with whom Bewick learned his craft was principally an engraver, another was a drawing-master and the two others who received a mention in the autobiography were William, named after his father and born in 1740, and Mary, named after her mother and born nine years later. When Bewick went to live with them in 1767, they were 27 and 18 years of age respectively, and he recorded that they "had constant employment of enamel-painting on glass".

Fortunately some signed specimens of the Beilbys' work have been preserved, and it is possible to ascribe to them much else that would otherwise have to remain unattributed. The signed pieces are, with a single exception which bears the initial *W*, inscribed only with the surname (see *frontispiece*). A decanter in the Victoria and Albert Museum is signed *Beilby Junr. pinxit & invt. Ncastle*, and is painted with the arms of Newcastle and those of Sir Edward Blackett, Bt., member of Parliament for Northumberland from 1768 to 1774. A goblet painted with the Royal arms and similarly signed is also recorded.

The decanter illustrated in Fig. 14 is unsigned, but there can be no doubt of the authorship of the finely-painted arms upon it. They are those of George III with the Prince of Wales feathers on the reverse, and it is assumed it was decorated to commemorate the birth of the Prince, later George IV, in 1762. With the decanter is seen a drinking-glass enamelled in colours with a landscape scene within rococo framing. The design and execution of the latter may be compared with that on the glass in Fig. 11.

Mary Beilby, senior, died in 1778, after which the brother and sister left Newcastle and settled in Fife, Scotland. It is thought that they gave up their enamelling at that time.

One other style of decoration used during the eighteenth century remains to be mentioned: gilding. Like enamel, the gold was painted on with a brush, and fired at a suitable heat to make it adhere to the surface. It did not always do so, and many glasses show traces of what must once have been pleasing work. In a good state of preservation is the wine-glass illustrated in Fig. 15, which bears a pattern of fruiting vine and a deep rim-band in gold.

© *Geoffrey Wills, 1968.*

12

18th Century Coloured Glass

Opposite, *Pair of blue glass decanters, with decoration in gold by James Giles. Circa 1770. Height 11 inches. (Christie's.)* **Above,** *Fig. 1: Purple drinking-glass inscribed* God Bless King William & Queen Mary. *Late seventeenth century. Height 4⅞ inches. (Victoria and Albert Museum.)*

THE colours of natural stones have always been admired by man, and some of the earliest attempts at glass-making were efforts to imitate them. The ancient Egyptians successfully copied their favourite turquoise, and few stones, precious or semi-precious, have not been simulated in glass at one time or another.

The Venetians carried on the Egyptian tradition, and one of their achievements was the German-named *schmelzglas:* versions of agate, onyx, chalcedony and jasper, some of which have been accepted on occasion as the real thing. A further variety of the material resembles aventurine, a reddish-brown quartz shining with tiny gilt particles. The secret of its making is said to have been found by accident, when a worker in a Murano glasshouse carelessly knocked a quantity of copper filings into a pot of molten glass. The glass named from the Italian word *avventura* (chance) gave its name to the stone, but no one has ever explained why the copper filings were on the scene at all.

In addition to copying stones, the Venetians gave attention to making coloured glass in its own right, and the results were sent all over the world. They were esteemed no less in England than elsewhere, and an inventory taken in 1547 lists a number of unquestionably Venetian pieces in the possession of Henry VIII. Amongst them were the following:

    Thre Bottelles or Flagons of blewe glasse partely gilte.
    Two Bottelles or Flagons of glasse jasper colour.
    Two great Glasses like Bolles standing upon fete blewe and white partely gilte.
    Oone litle glasse Cuppe with a cover of blewe glasse.

Fyvetene Cruses [pots] of glasse with covers, xiiij [14] of them being grene and oone blewe.
Oone Cruse withoute a cover of glasse of many colours.

There follows a gap in English records of about a century and a half, but it cannot be doubted that coloured wares continued to be favoured as fashion demanded. The majority would have continued to have been imported, either from Venice or from some of the other glass-houses set up across the Channel. In England, the various documents relating to the activities of Sir Robert Mansell make no mention of coloured articles, and he may well have had sufficient difficulties in manufacturing clear glass without troubling about coloured.

Orders sent to their Venetian suppliers in 1668 by the London dealers, John Greene and Richard Measey, specified "calsedonia" and "speckled enamelled" drinking-glasses. None has been identified, and it must be assumed that all the glasses asked for, totalling about two hundred, have perished. This is not unexpected, for such articles would have had hard usage and the Venetian metal, while it was attractive in appearance, was most fragile.

Below, *Fig. 2: Green wine glasses with air-twist stems; (centre) the trumpet bowl with an engraved rim, height 7¼ inches; (left and right) with moulded bowls, height of each 7⅜ inches. 1750-60. (Sotheby's.)*

Ravenscroft's glass-of-lead proved not only to have better looks, but was considerably stronger than the imported ware with which it competed. A few coloured pieces were made in the early days of manufacture, and of them two purple decanters have been preserved. They are tall-necked and their flattened globular bodies have "nipt diamond waies" ornamentation. One of them is in the Victoria & Albert Museum, London, and the other in the Ashmolean Museum, Oxford; the latter illustrated in *Signature* 4, Fig. 7. They resemble in both form and decoration a clear glass decanter in the British Museum, which is marked with Ravenscroft's seal of a raven's head. All must date from about 1675.

Rather later in date is a drinking-glass, also purple in colour, in the Victoria & Albert Museum (Fig. 1). It bears the legend *God Bless King William & Queen Mary*, and was probably made at about the time of their coronation on 11th April 1689.

Glass of a green colour would seem to have been introduced during the first quarter of the eighteenth century, but examples that can be dated to before 1750 are very rare. This is not to say that the mid-century ones are plentiful, as genuine Georgian examples of any date are scarce and eagerly sought. Known specimens are similar in general shape to those of clear glass, and drinking-vessels show comparable varieties of stem formation. It is by such parallels that age can be assessed, as there is no reason to suppose that the coloured and the clear were not made at the same time.

Baluster and Silesian stems are known and can be dated to about 1720, but the majority of surviving specimens are later. Three of 1750-60 are illustrated in Fig. 2. The centre one, with a trumpet bowl, the rim engraved with a pattern of scrolls and swags, has a plain column stem containing an air-twist. It once formed part of a service that has been dispersed, and a matching glass to it is in the British Museum. The two other glasses illustrated each have moulded bowls and air-twist stems.

The colour of the glass in Fig. 3 is a most unusual shade of emerald-green, and in place of an air-twist stem it has one containing a pattern of opaque-twists. The variants in each colour are just as

Fig. 3: Emerald-green wine glass with an opaque-twist stem. Circa 1760. Height 5¾ inches. (Sotheby's.)

Above, *Fig. 5: Pair of green decanters with gilt labels, the stoppers initialled to correspond. Circa 1770. Height about 10 inches. (Cecil Davis, Ltd.)*

Opposite, *Fig. 4: Group of articles in "Bristol Blue" with gilt decoration. The cruet in a mahogany frame,* circa *1765; square decanter, covered basin and finger bowl, 1800-1810, the latter signed* I. Jacobs, Bristol *(see page 11). (Delomosne & Son, Ltd.)*

interesting to collectors as the shapes of bowls and stems. As in dyeing fabrics, the mixing of a particular colour with the aid of available ingredients and equipment was not a simple matter. To match one shade precisely with another tended to be well-nigh an impossibility. Each pot of metal would vary from the next, albeit only slightly, and age has often mellowed what might be thought permanent tints. One glass of a set, exposed over the years to more sunshine and air than the rest will gradually cease to match its fellows exactly.

JUDGING from the quantity still existing, the most popular colour for glass in the second half of the eighteenth century was blue (Fig. 4). This is invariably referred to as "Bristol Blue", although it is improbable that more than a small proportion of it was actually made there. As it is, we do know that several firms in the west country did manufacture it, so it is a matter of convenience to attribute it all to the same source.

One other type of glass has also been ascribed to Bristol, and although strictly speaking it is not coloured at all it is convenient to discuss it under that head. It is opaque-white or, as it was called in the past "enamel" glass.

The Bristol link with the two types of glass, blue and white, has rested largely on their connection with a man named Michael Edkins. He would perhaps have been forgotten had not his son, William, been a collector, and recorded for posterity some information about his father. His son, also named William, was a dealer in antiques. William Edkins, Senior, stated that his father had been apprenticed at an enamelling establishment in Birmingham, and had then come to Bristol where he painted for several of the pottery-makers. He decorated dishes and tiles, "which were all at that time painted by the hand with pencils made by the workmen themselves, of bristles from the noses and eyelids of oxen".

Edkins then took to decorating coaches, and "enamel and blue glass-ware, then much in vogue, at which he had no equal". He had a good voice and spent some time on the stage in both Bristol and London. He also painted scenery, and "he had a large family—thirty-three children".

William Edkins, Junior, owned a number of

articles which he averred had been painted by his grandfather, and they included a set of pottery plates. Each depicted an Oriental scene, in the fashion of the time, and on the backs were the initials M E B and the date 1760. The initials were arranged in the accepted eighteenth century manner with that of the surname at the top, and it was said that they stood for Michael Edkins and his wife, Betty. Other Edkins possessions were a number of opaque-white glass articles, including vases and tea-caddies.

Some further information about Michael Edkins is contained in a business ledger he once owned, which is now in the City Museum, Bristol. It gives details of some of the glass-houses for which he worked, and the dates of his employment by them. They are as follows:

    1762-1767   Little & Longman, Redcliffe Backs.
    1767-1787   Longman & Vigor,
    1765   William Dunbar & Co., Bristol and Chepstow.
    1775-1787   Vigor & Stevens, Thomas Street.
    1785-1787   Lazarus Jacobs, Temple Street.

Some of the items in the ledger are:

    1762 Apl. 26. To 5 long doz. Amell [enamel] Beakers, 10s. 0d.
             July 26. To 1 Pint Blue can ornamented with Gold and Letters, 8d.

Above left, *Fig. 6: "Bristol Blue"; a scent bottle and a patch box with painted decoration. Circa 1770. Height (bottle) 2⅞ inches, length (box) 2¼ inches. (Victoria and Albert Museum.)* **Above right,** *Fig. 7: Opaque-white cream jug with "cold" painted decoration. Late eighteenth century. Height 3½ inches. (County Museum, Truro, Cornwall.)*

1763	Aug. 18.	To 6 Enamelled pt. Canns wrote Liberty and no Excise @ 4d., 2s. 0d.
	Sept. 30.	To 18 Enamell Basons, 1s. 6d.
1764	Oct. 1.	To 4 Enamell Cannisters, 1s. 0d.
1769	—	To 3 pr. blue Cornicopios ornamented with gold, 3s. 0d.
1770	Nov. 6.	To 12 Hyacinth glasses, blue gilded, 2s. 0d.

A further ledger entry relates to a quantity of goods assembled by Edkins for sale abroad, but it is unknown whether they went to the Continent or farther afield. They included:

2 large Setts Enamell Jars and Beak[er]s, 11s. 0d.
3 Blue Quart Cans, 9s. 0d.
12 Enamell halfpint Cans, 5s. 0d.
12 blue basins, 8s. 0d.

There is also an entry for "12 Blue halfpint Cans at 8s. 0d.", which shows that the latter glass was more costly at the time than the opaque-white.

In spite of the fact that both his son and his grandson gave currency to it, the long-standing Edkins story has been doubted as regards detail in recent years. For one thing, the prices for which he executed his work (for example, "4 Enamell Cannisters 1s.") casts doubt on the medium in which he worked. It was once widely assumed that he fired his painting in a kiln to "fix" it, but it has been suggested as more probable that he used ordinary oil colours, or gold applied on varnish: termed "cold" decoration.

The cream jug illustrated in Fig. 7 is an example of "cold" painting, and shows how the brushwork chips away with age and use. In many instances such work has vanished without leaving a trace, and all that remains is a plain article that apparently never bore decoration at all. Probably the majority of Edkins's painting has disappeared in the same manner.

The blue colour in glass is obtained by the addition to the primary mixture of zaffre, which is defined as "an impure oxide of cobalt". It was ready for use after having been made into a glassy mass and pulverised, and the resulting powder was known as smalt. The latter was produced in

Fig. 8: Blue finger bowl with Greek Key decoration in gold; inscribed I. Jacobs, Bristol. Circa *1810.* (*Delomosne & Son, Ltd.*)

Fig. 9: Bill-head of Isaac Jacobs, Bristol. Circa 1810. (City Museum, Bristol.)

Saxony, Germany, and imported into England through Bristol whence, no doubt, much of it was distributed to glass-houses throughout the country. For this reason it is perhaps the colour itself that gained the name "Bristol Blue", which in time has been transferred to the product displaying it.

Of the many firms in Bristol that made glass, one in particular is known to have made the blue variety: Lazarus and Isaac Jacobs. Lazarus Jacobs apparently started in business as a glass dealer, and in 1805 Isaac, presumably his son, established a glass-house which he called "The Non-Such Flint Glass Manufactory". In the following year he advertised himself as "Glass Manufacturer to His Majesty" (George III), and stated that he had ..

> opened a New Set of Rooms on purpose for the Retail Trade with a Large and Elegant assortment of Cut and Engraved Glass, both useful and ornamental, at the wholesale Prices, Specimens of the Dessert set. which I Jacobs had the honour of sending to her Majesty in burnished Gold upon Royal purple colored Glass to be seen at his Manufactory, where several Dessert sets of the same kind are now completed from Fifteen Guineas per set to any amount. Coats of Arms, Crests, and Cyphers done upon the same in the greatest style, by some of the First Artists in the Kingdom ...

No pieces of the purple glass have been recorded, but from his habit of putting his name on his products some of the blue has been identified. Finger bowls and stands, wine-glass coolers, and decanters are numbered among the dozen or so

Variations in the style of signature marked by Isaac Jacobs on some of his pieces.

surviving pieces bearing the name of Isaac Jacobs written in gold under their bases (Figs. 8, 10 and 12).

A mention of the use of blue glass finger bowls was made in 1786 by the German visitor to England, Sophie von la Roche. After lunching at Richmond with the Countess von Reventlow, wife of the Danish ambassador, she noted in her diary: "The blue glass bowls used for rinsing hands and mouth are quite delightful". Doubtless she was too polite in such company to examine the underneath in search of a mark or, being a meticulous reporter, she would have said so.

OPAQUE-WHITE, or enamel, glass originated in Venice in the sixteenth century. Thence, in 1741, Horace Walpole returned home with two dozen newly-made dessert plates made from it. Each was carefully painted in reddish-brown with a different view in the city, and they must have been a pleasing souvenir of his visit. At his house, Strawberry Hill, just outside London, they were displayed in the China Room, and this resemblance of opaque-white glass to porcelain led to its later popularity in England and elsewhere.

In this country the glass was aided in its competition with chinaware because it was not referred to in the Excise Act of 1745, and only in the Act of 1777 did it receive a mention. Then, a tax of 18s. 8d. was imposed on each hundredweight (112 lbs.), and this lead to the virtual termination of manufacture of wine-glasses with opaque-white stems and of articles made wholly of enamel glass.

Activity in England appears to have begun in

Fig. 10: Wine-glass cooler, in blue with Greek Key decoration in gold, signed by Isaac Jacobs. Circa 1810. Height $3\frac{7}{8}$ inches. (Sotheby's.)

the early 1760's, but there is no information at present as to what may have inspired it. An advertisement in *The General Evening Post* of 14th March 1761 invited offers of capital in order to extend a glass works at Glasborough, near Bilston, Staffordshire. The owners, who did not reveal their names added as a postscript:

> The present Proprietors will satisfy any Purchaser, from an Experiment lately made, that other particular Sorts of Glass (for which there is a great Demand) can be manufactured at the said Works to more considerable Advantage than any other in this Kingdom. All persons inclined to purchase Shares are desired to apply to Mr. Thomas Steward, in Birmingham.

It is not unreasonable to suggest that "the other particular Sorts of Glass" might have included opaque-white.

The date of the advertisement is just prior to one that appeared in 1764 specifically mentioning "Enamel". It announced the opening of a "flint and enamel glass manufactory" at Chepstow, Monmouthshire, by Williams, Dunbar & Co. In 1765 William Williams left the firm, and Dunbar acquired a man named Bradley as partner. They did not prosper, and all three of the men went individually to Ireland and were connected with glass enterprises there.

Below, *Fig. 11: Opaque-white vase painted in colours with a bird perched on a flowering branch. Circa 1760. Height 3 inches. (Cecil Davis, Ltd.)*

Like the blue-coloured glass, opaque-white has for long been attributed almost exclusively to Bristol, and as noted earlier some of it was painted by Michael Edkins. His grandson owned a few specimens, which he declared were the work of his ancestor and this convincing attribution has remained unchallenged until recent years. Then it began to be observed that there was a distinct link between the painting and colouring on the glass and on enamelled copper and saltglazed stoneware from South Staffordshire. The first two have a common factor, in that the layer of enamel on the metal is of similar composition to the glass.

Either Edkins must have painted large quantities of enamelled copper, of which no mention was made by his proud descendants, or the white glass resembling it was decorated elsewhere. Some support for this latter supposition is gained by the fact, mentioned earlier, that Edkins earned such trivial sums for his work. Even at the comparatively low rates paid for all types of workmanship at the time, his remuneration was remarkably meagre for the grade of skill demanded.

Further, the pottery dishes allegedly bearing the initials of Michael and Betty Edkins, and said to have been decorated by him, have no artistic resemblance in their painting to either glass or enamelled copper. The whole subject is still being

Below left, *Fig. 12: Stand for wine-glass cooler illustrated in Fig. 10; crested with a stag's head, and signed by Isaac Jacobs. Circa 1810. Diameter 7¾ inches. (Sotheby's.)* **Below,** *Fig. 13: Opaque-white candlestick with a spirally-ribbed stem, painted in colours with sprigs and sprays of flowers. Circa 1760. Height 9 inches. (Sotheby's.)*

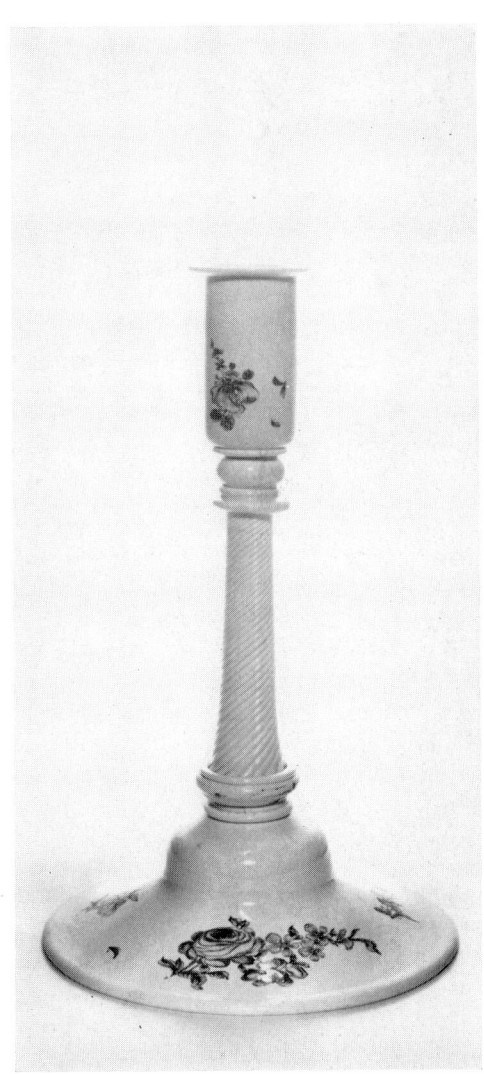

explored, and it is possible that the true rôle of the Bristol artist will eventually be determined. At the same time, the exact origin of much of the glass may also become known; for the present, it is attributed to South Staffordshire.

It is possible to make opaque-white glass by two methods: by the addition to a mixture of clear glass of either arsenic or oxide of tin. The latter was the basis of the opaque glaze on pottery made in England at Lambeth, Bristol, Liverpool and elsewhere (the so-called delftware or tin-enamelled earthenware), and it was adopted by the glass-makers for their ware made in imitation of china. Tin oxide helped to make a dense white or creamy-white glass which is quite different in appearance from contemporaneous wares made in Germany and Spain, and from Victorian English "milk glass". All of these are only semi-opaque, with traces of opalescence and occasionally a near-transparent pontil-mark.

In 1966 it was discovered that James Giles, well-known to students and collectors of English porcelain, also painted and decorated glass. Giles was one of a few men in business in eighteenth century London as decorators of chinaware, which they bought in the white from various manufactories. His advertisements in the press in the 1760's announced that he had a large stock on hand of Worcester china, both plain and decorated, at his first-floor showroom in Cockspur Street, adding:

> Ladies and Gentlemen may depend upon having their Commands executed immediately, and painted to any Pattern they shall chuse.

Giles had a kiln at Kentish Town for firing the painting, and had premises in Berwick Street which he occupied from at least 1749. He died in 1780, but had retired from business six years earlier, when he gave up the Cockspur Street showroom and sent some of the contents to be sold by auction.

The sale was held by James Christie, occupied five days from 21st March 1774, and was catalogued as:

> Part of the Stock in Trade of Mr. James Giles Chinaman and Enameller, Quitting that Business... together with an Assortment of cut and gilt Glass.

Opposite, *South Staffordshire opaque-white glass vase painted in colours with Chinese figures dancing round a standard. Circa 1760. Height 7 inches. (Christie's.)*

Fig. 14: Opaque-white tea caddy painted in colours, the cover mounted in gilt metal. Circa 1760. Height 5 inches. (Victoria and Albert Museum.)

Auction-catalogues of two centuries ago seldom wasted many words in describing the lots on offer, but the anonymous compiler has provided a few clues for posterity. It has proved possible to identify an opaque-white glass beaker in the Corning Museum of Glass, Corning, N.Y., as tallying with one in the sale. In addition, a number of other varieties of decoration can now be attributed with confidence to Giles and his employees (*frontispiece*).

It is not known where James Giles obtained his supplies of glass, but as the china he handled came from Worcester and elsewhere it is not unlikely that the glass also came from a distance. Equally, of course, it might have been manufactured in London. None of it bears distinguishing marks, and none has yet been found to exhibit special characteristics. For the time being, therefore, the source must remain unknown.

Opaque-white glass is a fragile material, and the majority of examples made in the eighteenth century have probably been smashed long ago. Surviving pieces cover a fairly wide range, and include candlesticks (Fig. 13), finger bowls, scent bottles, tea caddies (Fig. 14), vases of Oriental shape and often with painting or gilding of Chinese inspiration (page 15), and condiment bottles.

Some of the caddies and bottles are inscribed with the names of their contents, and in the case of the latter the wording is occasionally in Dutch. As Newcastle upon Tyne had a thriving export trade with Holland, it is likely that they were made at one of the many glass-houses in the city. Also perhaps of North country origin are rare examples decorated with printed patterns.

Printing of this kind was an art practised successfully in Liverpool. There, John Sadler and Guy Green were partners in a Printed Ware Manufactory between about 1757 and 1780, to which pottery and porcelain makers sent their products for decoration (see examples in *Signature* 2, Fig. 16, and *Signature* 3, Fig. 14). Such work may also have been executed in the Birmingham area, where enamelled copper articles were decorated by the same process from 1751, or near London, at Battersea, between 1753 and 1756.

The recent discoveries about Michael Edkins and James Giles, mentioned above, are due to the researches of Mr. R. J. Charleston, Keeper of the Department of Ceramics, Victoria and Albert Museum, London.

© *Geoffrey Wills, 1968.*

13

Left, walking-stic[ks] of coloured and cle[ar] glass, fourth fro[m] right filled with co[n]fectionery. Avera[ge] length 39 inches. (R[t.] Hon. The Viscou[nt] Boyd of Merto[n,] C.H.) **Below,** gro[up] of hand bells. Heigh[t] 9¾ to 14½ inches. (The Viscounte[ss] Boyd of Merton.)

Novelties and 'Friggers'

STRICTLY speaking, "Friggers" is the glass-makers' word for pieces made in their spare time: trifling objects to take home to family and friends and to keep on the mantelshelf. In the course of time, the list has been extended considerably, and the word is often used nowadays to embrace a whole range of wares produced in quantity for sale to the public in the ordinary way of business. They include such diverse things as rolling-pins, hand-bells, models of birds on "fountains", sailing ships, and many others. All are made of glass, clear or coloured or mixed, and some show skilful craftsmanship in their execution. Most, or all, of them are known also by the name of the place where they are supposed to have been made: Nailsea.

Nailsea is situated a few miles to the west of Bristol, and an early mention of it in connection with glass-making appeared in the *Bristol Gazette* on 6th May 1790. A brief paragraph read:

> On Thursday last a fire broke out in the new glass-house at Nailsea belonging to Mr. J. R. Lucas, which burnt part of the roof, but by timely assistance, the other parts of the buildings belonging to both crown glass-houses were preserved.

Two years earlier, on 2nd August 1788, another local newspaper, *Felix Farley's Bristol Journal*, had printed an advertisement which ran:

> John Robert Lucas, intending to confine himself solely to the Crown Glass and Bottle Glass Manufactures wishes to dispose of the

Above left, *Fig. 1: Cup of bottle glass splashed with white, the rim with opaque-white stringing. Circa 1800. Height 3¼ inches.* **Left,** *Fig. 2: Jug similar to the cup in Fig. 1 and of about the same date. Height 6 inches. (Both pieces, County Museum, Truro.)*

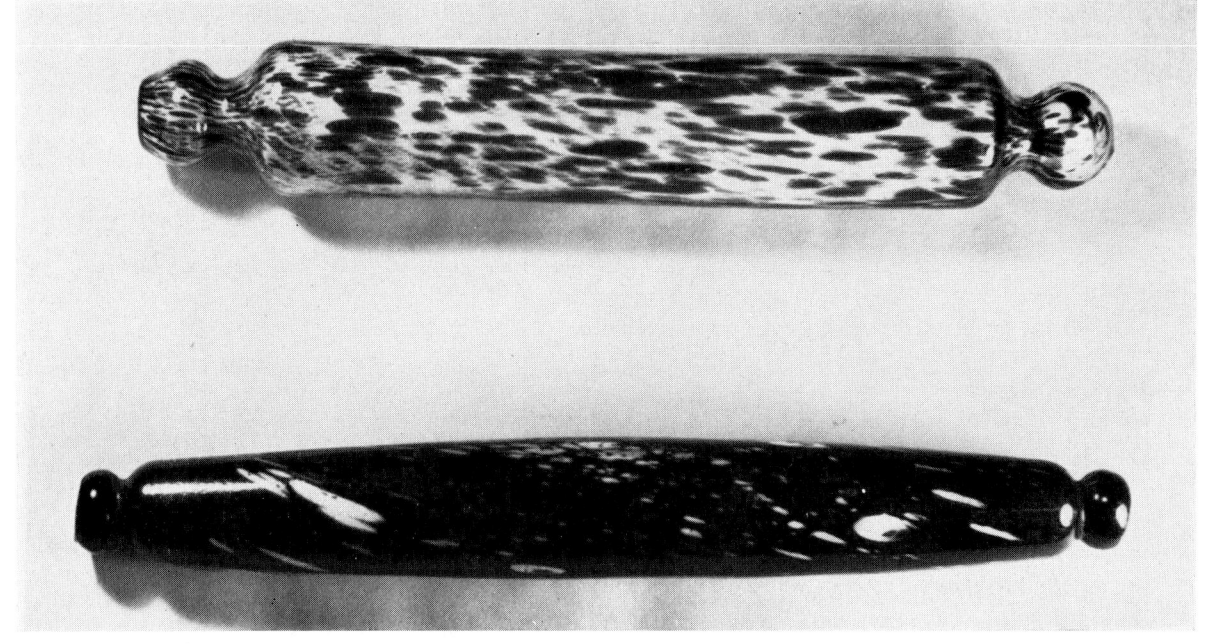

Fig. 3: Rolling-pins; (top) white glass splashed with red and blue; (bottom) bottle glass with white streaks and splashes. Early 19th century. Length 15½ inches. (County Museum, Truro.)

Beer and Cyder business which he has many years carried on in Nicholas Street.

Thus it is plain that Lucas established himself in the glass trade in order to make bottles and window glass; the latter by the "Crown" process which was originally introduced from Normandy.

In 1793 a change of partners in the firm took place, and the name of William Chance appeared. His son, Robert Lucas Chance, managed the concern between 1810 and 1815, and a few years later purchased The British Crown Glass Company, of Spon Lane, Birmingham. There, Chance and his descendants introduced many improvements in sheet glass manufacture and in the making of lenses for lighthouses.

The fact that bottle glass was taxed at a lower rate than flint very probably led to the idea of making simple domestic wares from it. The innovation is invariably said to have been due to J. R. Lucas, but his company made their bottles at Bristol and, as noted in the first-quoted newspaper paragraph, reserved their Nailsea premises for crown glass. It is possible that the domestic wares were a sideline unpublicised at the time, or that their making did not commence until some years after the factory first opened.

The so-called Nailsea pieces often took the form

of jugs made from a green-brown metal, and decorated with random white splashes of "enamel". Alternatively, or in addition, the white ornament was coiled in stringing round rims (Figs. 1 and 2). Such pieces were undoubtedly made at several factories, although at present there is little or no information about their source.

A jug in the Victoria and Albert Museum is attributed by tradition to Wrockwardine, Shropshire, and as it has flecks of yellow for ornament in place of the more usual white it is supposed that the colour can signify the origin of similar examples. In the same county, Hopton Wafers, near Cleobury Mortimer, was a further known source of this rustic ware. It is said also that it was made in Sunderland, and in Warrington, Lancashire.

A white-splashed green bottle, also in the Victoria and Albert Museum, bears a seal with the initials *J.S. J.M.*, the date 1827 and the town-name *Stirling*. It has been assumed it was made at Alloa, Clackmannanshire, which is only a short distance from Stirling and where a glass-house is known to have existed. Thus, it would appear without doubt that these pieces were made up and down the country during the first quarter of the nineteenth century, and for lack of definite characteristics are attributed to Nailsea. Rightly or wrongly, it is not unreasonable under the circumstances.

In addition to the articles of ornamented bottle glass, others of a more sophisticated type were perhaps made at Nailsea. They follow a style first introduced into Europe from Venice some centuries earlier, and incorporate coloured festoons, stripes and splashes within clear or coloured glass (see page 15). Their manufacture is said to have been due to the initiative of R. L. Chance, who took a keen interest in his craft and its development. He is supposed to have brought workers to Nailsea from France, and they lived there in a row of cottages named "French Rank". Again, similar wares were made at numerous other centres and it is rarely possible to name the source with any certainty.

The pocket-flasks attributed to Nailsea are among the most pleasing of this type of glassware. They were made either in a straightforward single form, or as twin bottles with the openings slightly

Fig. 4: Silvered witch ball with metal suspension plate. Nineteenth century. Diameter 15 inches.

twisted (see page 15). The latter are known as "gimmel" flasks, and are stated to have been bought by young lovers who plighted their troth by drinking simultaneously from the mouths of the article. Some of the flasks were provided with corks, and others were given neck-mounts and screwed caps of Britannia metal.

A type of opaque-white glass, but completely lacking the density of the eighteenth century variety (see *Signature* 12), is sometimes accredited to Nailsea. It has a milk-and-water appearance with an opalescent sheen, and is usually quite roughly made. Some examples of small jugs are inscribed in unfired colours with homely warnings like "Be canny with the Cream", or "Think on me". Similar inscriptions are to be found on objects in coloured glass, all of which were made to be sold cheaply in quantity.

Among the most frequently found articles made in both bottle glass and coloured clear glass are rolling-pins. Many and various are the theories that have been advanced to account for their popularity, and to give these prosaic objects a romantic and saleable background. It has been suggested that they were used for storing salt, for smuggling rum, for filling with tea or confectionery and, in fact, they might seem to have existed for every purpose except the obvious and mundane one of rolling pastry (Fig. 3).

Some examples of rolling-pins are engraved with devices and legends, which suggest they were given as love tokens. A few depict sailing-ships, and this may have given rise to the suggestion that they were used for smuggling rum. Others are "cold" painted (in unfired oil-colours) with similar pictures and wording to the engraved ones.

Rivalling rolling-pins as repositories of improbable legend are witch-balls: glass globes that were made in various sizes and colours. They can be found vari-coloured or single-colour, or with the interior mirrored. Some have a hole in which a metal fitting is fixed, so that the ball can be suspended, others are completely globular like large cricket-balls. This last type are said to have been made to rest on the tops of jugs, so protecting their contents from dust and flies.

The hanging type of ball is, we are told, a later version of a flask of holy water which was placed

Above, *Fig. 5: Saltcellar silvered within the double walls. Nineteenth century. Diameter 3¾ inches. (County Museum, Truro.)* **Right,** *Fig. 6: "Buy my fine singing Glasses", engraving by Pierce Tempest after Marcel Laroon, published in 1711.*

Buy my fine singing Glasses
Achetez des Trompettes de verre

Above, *Fig. 8: Linen smoother. Circa 1800. Diameter 4¾ inches. (County Museum, Truro.)*

Left, *Fig. 7: Birds at a fountain, in clear and coloured glass. Nineteenth century. Height 19¼ inches. (Howard Phillips.)*

in a room to keep evil spirits at bay. Equally, the same authority asserts, they were given as presents "with a wish for prosperity and long life", and were then called "Wish Balls".

Perhaps they had no particular significance in the realms of mumbo-jumbo, and were just decorative curiosities. Certainly the silvered variety fulfills the latter requirement, and hanging in a room they are equivalent to a convex mirror. Of these last Thomas Sheraton wrote in 1803 that "the perspective of the rooms in which they are suspended presents itself on the surface and produces an agreeable effect" (Fig. 4).

Silvering was used also on items of tableware, such as sugar bowls and salt-cellars (Fig. 5). They were made with a double wall, silvered inside and then sealed so that the ultra-thin coating of metal did not deteriorate or get worn. There was a fashion in the nineteenth century (and later) for china coated to produce the same effect, but the thin layer of silvering was prone to show signs of wear. Once it was scratched and worn away the effect was lost, and the true nature of the article revealed; alas, the silvery-looking teapot was not made from the precious metal and was only a poor man's version.

ATTRIBUTED generously to Nailsea are walking-sticks and shepherd's crooks made of glass (*frontispiece*), which are to be numbered among the more impractical uses of the material. Here, again, legend steps in, and according to an author writing in 1847:

> The most curious of their [the Devonians'] general superstitions is that of the glass rod, which they set up clean in their houses, and wipe clean every morning, under the idea that all diseases from malaria will gather about the rod innoxiously. It is twisted in the form of a walking stick, and is from 4 to 8 feet long.

A more understandable use of such objects was as walking-sticks, and that they were employed in this way is made clear from early nineteenth century reports in the press. Mention is made at the same time of other aberrations in glass, of which surviving specimens are usually claimed, willy-nilly, for Nailsea. Typical of numerous printed references is one less often quoted than many others:

> On the 12th of September 1823 the inhabitants of Newcastle and Gateshead were gratified with a . . . procession through the streets of the principal workmen employed in several of the glass-houses. It was composed of the workmen of the Northumberland, the South Shields, the Wear (Sunderland), the Durham and British (Gateshead), the Stourbridge (Gateshead), and the North Shields glass companies, each distinguished by appropriate flags. The hat of almost every person in it was decorated with a glass feather, whilst a glass star sparkled on the breast, and a chain or collar of variegated glass hung round the neck; some wore sashes round the waist. Each man carried in his hand a staff, with a cross piece on the top, displaying one or more curious or beautiful specimens of art. These elevations afforded a sight of the different vessels, con-

Below, *Fig. 9: Sugar stirrers or crushers. Nineteenth century. Length $4\frac{1}{4}$-$5\frac{1}{2}$ inches.*

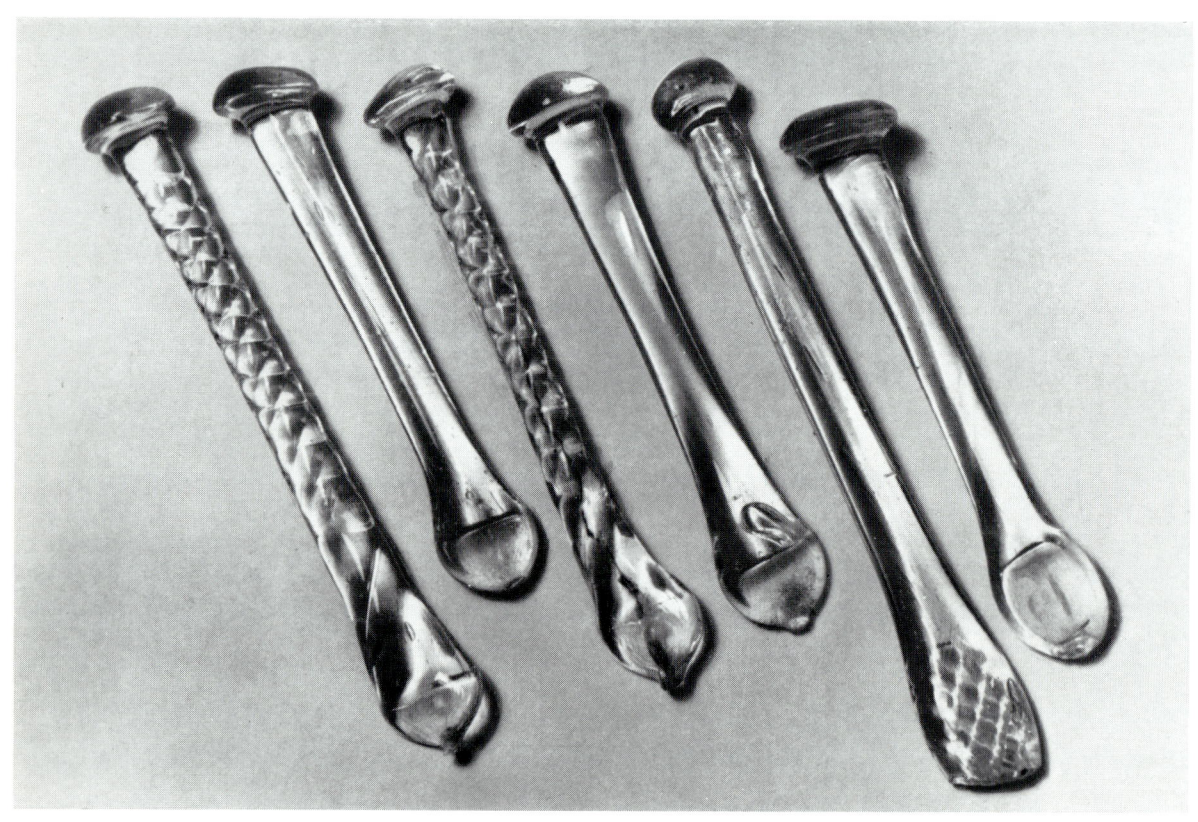

sisting of a profusion of decanters, glasses, goblets, jugs, bowls, dishes, etc. A salute was fired several times from a fort mounted with glass cannon, to the astonishment of the spectators; a glass bugle which sounded the halts, and played several marches, was much admired for its sweetness and correctness of tone. Many of the men wore glass hats and carried glass swords.

Similar processions were reported in the eighteenth century press as taking place at Bristol.

The mention of bugles in the above notice serves as a reminder of a connection between glass and music that has often been commented upon. The breaking of wine-glasses by robust singing was a popular feat at one time, and numerous theories were debated to account for its success. In the early eighteenth century there were competing claims for the excellence at the sport of a Dane named Drayer, a Dutchman who "could only shout in pieces thin medicine rummers", and a Scot named Sherbourne who spoke several languages and "is a prodigious rake and heavily in debt". Whether these last qualities assisted him or not is unknown, but he amazed his friends by his performances at vocal glass-shattering.

The knowledge that a glass bowl could be tuned by putting water into it was made use of in the 1740's. The composer Gluck claimed he had invented an instrument embodying 26 such glasses, and then in 1757 Benjamin Franklin mechanised it. The notes were obtained by rubbing a finger along the wetted rims of the bowls, and Franklin made them revolve in a shallow trough so that they were continually wet to the touch of the operator. Another type of glass-based instrument employed bars or rods of different lengths, and these were struck with small hammers.

Simple trumpets of glass were made at one time, although it is uncertain whether they were intended for serious use. A street-seller demonstrating one, and holding others, is depicted in an engraving illustrated in Fig. 6. Equally impractical are hand-bells of glass, which were made in many colours and shapes during the nineteenth century (*frontispiece*).

While most glass wares were made in specially-built establishments with large furnaces, it was

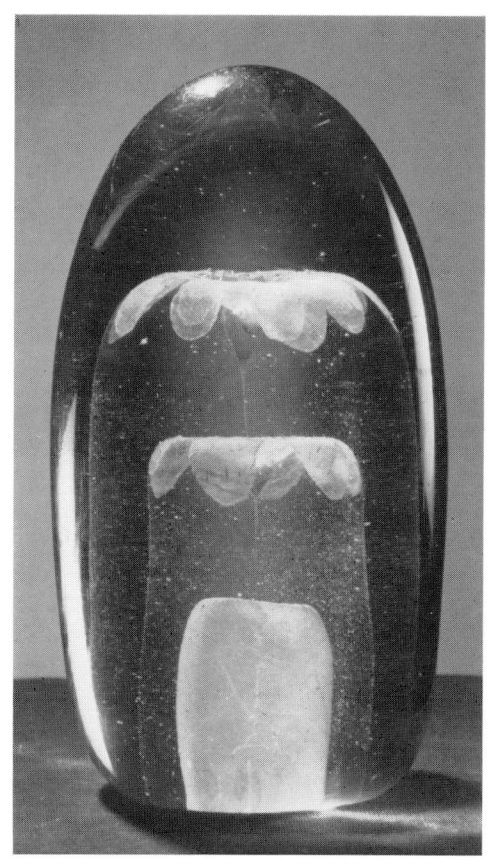

Above, *Fig. 10: Doorstop or paperweight of green glass containing a "floral" pattern. Late nineteenth century. Height 5 inches. (Victoria and Albert Museum.)*

Fig. 11: Scent bottle with a "sulphide" of King George IV, probably made by Apsley Pellatt at the Falcon Glassworks, Blackfriars, London. Circa 1820. Height about 6 inches. (Delomosne & Son, Ltd.)

also possible to do some types of work with very simple apparatus. Heat was supplied by a lamp fed with oil, and the glass was in the form of clear or coloured rods and tubes which melted easily. In 1696 a man named Grillet, probably a Frenchman, advertised that he made all kinds of objects "enamelled and of glass, different postures of all kinds, Animals, Plants, Trees, Flowers and Fruit, together with all manner of representations to the life". In 1710, a Dutchman, Nicolaus de Geus, was making similar trifles at a house opposite Somerset House, in the Strand.

The making of such objects calls for skill, but the finished work was generally more "amusing" or "curious" than artistically important. Miniature representations of fox-hunts at the gallop, sailing-ships in full rig, and groups of peacocks perched on trees or in the midst of fountains are among the relics that survive. Much of it is difficult to date with any accuracy, and some of it, perhaps the peacocks, may have been true "friggers", made after working time at the furnace.

The example of birds at a fountain illustrated in Fig. 7 is a good one of its kind. The fountain is made of a criss-crossing network of glass rod, the birds are of enamel (white) glass with coloured details, and their tails are of glass spun or drawn into very fine threads. It owes its good condition to having been kept under a blown glass dome.

CERTAIN rarities in glass do not fit easily into the normal categories into which the subject is divided, and it is convenient to discuss them here. The unusual-looking object illustrated in Fig. 8, looking like an inverted mushroom, is a linen-smoother. The bobbin-pattern stem assures a good grip, and at the same time gives it a misleading appearance of age. Similar examples are sometimes dated to the early eighteenth century, but they are perhaps no older than about 1800.

Also with a rather more antiquated look than is justified by their age, are sugar crushers or stirrers (Fig. 9). They were probably made in quantity throughout the nineteenth century, and can still be found without too much difficulty. As can be seen, they vary in pattern, but all have a domed top and a spade-like end. The diamond design on them would have been impressed with pincers while they were still in a molten state.

Similarly of unsophisticated appearance are green bottle-glass doorstops or paperweights, which date from the second half of the nineteenth century and later. They enclose patterns of bubbles or vaguely floral forms that are difficult to describe adequately (Fig. 10). They were made in the North of England, and some have been recorded bearing a mark used by a factory in Wakefield.

Other surviving novelties indicate by their careful finish that they were made for limited sale to the wealthier members of the public. Several makers produced articles of this kind, but the best known was Apsley Pellatt, owner of a glass-house in Southwark, South London.

Pellatt patented in 1819 his method of making what are variously described as "cameo incrustations", "sulphides" and "crystallo-ceramies". They comprised a silvery-looking object embedded within clear glass, but it was admitted by the English patentee that he had acquired the idea from the French. The enclosed decorations took the form of profile reliefs of prominent persons, crests and so forth, and were made of a type of porcelain that would not melt or distort when the molten glass was placed round it. It was also necessary that it should expand and contract at the same rate as glass, or fracture would result, and that it should not emit gas-bubbles when heated. Altogether these were formidable requirements to meet, but Pellatt managed to overcome the difficulties and produced attractive results.

The "sulphides" were used to decorate a range of articles which included scent-bottles (Fig. 11), jugs, candlesticks, and knife-rests. Cameo portraits include those of George III and his sons, and small-sized figures of classical goddesses and cupids. The articles they ornament are heavily cut in the fashionable manner of the 1820's.

"Crystallo-ceramies" continued to be produced by Pellatt's firm until the middle years of the nineteenth century, but they were expensive to make and never reached the stage of mass production. Later, the same process was used by John Ford of the Holyrood glassworks, Edinburgh. As very similar work was done on the Continent and in the United States of America, it is some-

Fig. 12: Scent bottle inset with a plaque of Wedgwood jasperware. Late 18th century. Height 2¾ inches. (Josiah Wedgwood & Sons, Ltd.)

times no easy matter to determine the date and country of origin of examples.

Pellatt's occasional use of classical subjects for his cameos reflects the long-lasting public taste for the style largely introduced in the 1760's by Robert Adam. In pottery it was propagated energetically by Josiah Wedgwood, who commissioned many of the prominent artists of his time to design suitable subjects for his jasperware. Among the professionals he employed was John Flaxman, the sculptor, but he also used work by amateurs. Two of them were Lady Diana Beauclerk and Lady Templetown, and a plaque designed by the latter is mounted on the front of a glass scent-bottle, illustrated in Fig. 12.

Fig. 13: Portrait plaque of John Adam, brother and partner of the architect Robert Adam; by James Tassie, 1791. (Sotheby's.)

Right, *a variety of "Friggers"; bugles, 10 and 5½ inches; "Jacob's Ladder", 12 inches; pig flask, 9 inches; bellows bottle, 12½ inches; two hats, 3 and 2 inches; pipe, 16 inches; sock darner, 7 inches. (Ian Weston, Esq.)*

Right, *single and gemmel flasks with looped decoration, and a splashed bottle. Height (flasks) 6½ to 10 inches; (bottle) 5 inches. (Ian Weston, Esq.)*

Page 15

Fig. 14: Goblet decorated by John Davenport's patented process of 1806; the small label bearing the word "Patent" is seen on the left of the base by the stem. Height 5¼ inches. (H. L. Douch, Esq.)

Many of Wedgwood's plaques were portraits of his contemporaries, from King George III downwards. Some were modelled especially for the purpose of reproducing their features in jasperware, and others Josiah purchased from sculptors and artists who had already taken likenesses. One of the suppliers was a Scot named James Tassie, who devised a special glass composition in which he made many of his cameos. He made several thousand different items, including copies of antique engraved gems which were much sought after by collectors of the time.

Some of the Tassie portraits were modelled in one with the plain background, but many were just a head and shoulders of the subject. This latter was sold mounted on a coloured opaque glass background and framed neatly in a blackened pearwood oval. Usually the name of the sitter and date are found on the truncation, with the signature of James Tassie, or his nephew William, who succeeded to his business (Fig. 13).

Finally, illustrated in Fig. 14 is a goblet dating from *circa* 1810, showing a gentleman loading his gun with powder while his hound lies curled at his feet. The method of decoration is an unusual one, and is the result of a process patented in 1806 by John Davenport, the Staffordshire potter. The surface was coated with a thin layer of powdered glass in the form of a paste, and then the design was scratched in it. The remaining powder was carefully heated until it fused to the surface, and the finished effect is not unlike engraving executed with acid. It is often confused with the latter, but Davenport added under the base of his glasses a small oblong label with the word "Patent" written on it.

© *Geoffrey Wills, 1968.*

14

Victorian Glass: Part 1

Coloured glass made in 1850-1855: (left to right) red cased in white with cut, painted, and gilt decoration, height 10¼ inches; apple green opaline with gilding, height 7 inches; white opaline, painted and gilt, height 9¾ inches. (R. & M. Andrade, Ltd.)

Cut ornament, such a characteristic feature of late Georgian glassware, continued to be fashionable into the reign of Queen Victoria. It altered in style during the 1830's, and the complicated diamond patterns were superseded by the use of plain slices running the length of an article and giving it a series of flat or concave surfaces. To achieve the best effect from these, the piece was made longer or taller in relation to its width or diameter, and at the same time the overall shape was simplified.

The new silhouette is to be seen in the decanter, which changed from being a dumpy object bristling with sharp points, and became a slimmer one with flat sides (Fig. 1, and *Signature* 4, Fig. 13). For those who preferred a different shape, there was a revival of the late seventeenth century "shaft and globe" pattern: a globular body with a tall and slender neck (Fig. 7).

There were, in fact, alternatives available for the buyer of most glass articles. He could choose between slight or heavy cutting, numerous shapes and, later, various colours, according to his taste and pocket. The range was so wide that it is difficult to state which particular style was the most popular at any one time. Most of them were on the market, with large or small differences in detail, throughout the period.

During the early years of Victoria's reign there was a large and increasing output of articles made by mechanical means. With steam-power being employed in every possible manner, it might be expected that it would have been harnessed to the production of glassware. Although it was used to some extent for driving cutting and wheel-engraving machinery, the actual making remained largely unaltered. The time-tested methods remained in use, but were gradually adapted to producing a larger output per man in a given period of time.

The employment of moulds had for some decades been commonplace in making such things as square-based case bottles and, particularly in Ireland, decanters. In that country, the lower parts of the decanter bodies were frequently given a fluted pattern, and the bases bore the names of their makers or vendors in raised lettering. Moulding was a simple method of ensuring that articles were each of a similar size and shape, and at the same time it led to a higher rate of production by eliminating some of the work of hand and eye.

While many pieces in the first half of the nineteenth century were made by blowing into moulds, they were frequently finished in the traditional manner by cutting on the wheel. This removes any external sign of moulding, as it takes away the tell-tale thin raised line left where the halves of the mould met. The other sign of the process is less obvious as it occurs on the inside of a vessel, which will be found to follow exactly the shaping of the outer surface but in reverse. That is to say, the raised parts of the exterior become concavities within. Both of these indications are readily understandable, because the process of blowing forces the molten metal into every nook and cranny of the mould, and does this from the *inside* outwards.

A different process, but likewise aimed at making glass more cheaply and in large quantities, was press-moulding. It was introduced in the late 1820's, but although originating in England in the first instance it was developed in the United States. Its use here was principally in the later years of the nineteenth century, and it is more apposite to deal with it in *Signature* 15, which is devoted to later Victorian glass.

In 1845 the Excise duty was at last abolished, and the trade freed from restraint and taxation that had shackled it for a hundred years. Some twelve years earlier there had been an inquiry by the Commissioners of Excise into the state of the industry, and numerous makers gave evidence. One of them made clear the disabilities suffered under the law as it then stood:

> Our business and our premises are placed under the arbitrary control of a class of men to

Fig. 1: Decanter of clear glass stained red and cut. Circa 1840. Height 13¼ inches.

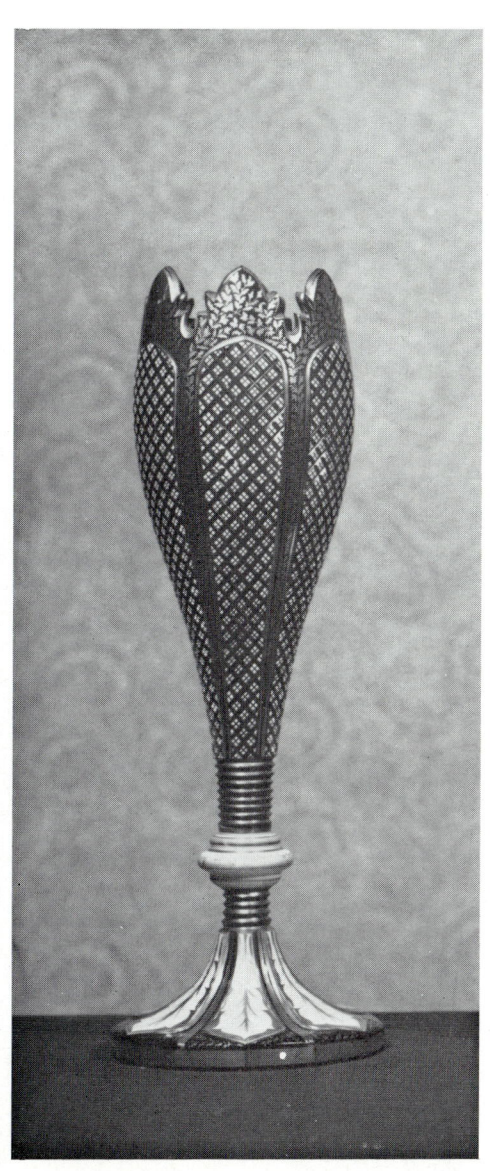

Fig. 2: One of a pair of vases of ruby glass cased in white and decorated with cutting and gilding. Circa 1850. Height about 12 inches. The pair are illustrated on the front cover of this Signature. *(Delomosne & Son, Ltd.)*

whose will and caprice it is most irksome to have to submit and this under a system of regulations most ungraciously inquisitorial. We cannot enter into parts of our own premises without their permission; we can do no one single act in the conduct of our own business without having previously notified our intention to the officers placed over us. We have in the course of the week's operations to serve some sixty or seventy notices on these, our masters, and this under heavy penalties of from £200 to £500 for every separate neglect.

The result of the inquiry was summarised by the Commissioners as follows:

(1) that in their opinion evasion of the duty could not be prevented by any addition to the laws or regulations; (2) that the regulations presented a great impediment and in many cases a complete bar in the way of those experimental researches which are necessary for the adequate pursuit of objects connected with some of the important branches of Science; and (3) that they also operate as a direct hindrance to our successful competition in the glass trade with foreign countries.

The mention in section 1 above of evasion of duty was a reference to the numerous small concerns, operated by one or more men, who ran tiny "backroom" glass-houses. They supplied their little furnaces mainly with broken glass, and were able to make a profit through evading payment of duty. It was estimated that £65,000-worth of these illicit articles were sold in London in the course of a year, but there is, of course, no means of knowing whether this was an exaggeration or not. Also, the types of such wares and their appearance are equally unascertainable, as none have been identified.

THE result of repealing the duty is not easy to assess at this date. Some writers have assumed that it led to a sudden surge of activity on the part of the glass-makers, and that they one and all took to producing new types of ware which the rigours of the past had prevented being made. No doubt the ending of taxation inspired new designs and new varieties of material, but an undoubted stimulus must have been a series of highly successful public displays. They culminated in the enormously popular Great Exhibition held quite soon after 1845; six years later in 1851.

At various dates from 1798 onwards the French had held national exhibitions, and various local ones were held in this country during the early nineteenth century. A more ambitious display was attempted by the newly-chartered Royal Society of Arts in 1847, who made it their endeavour to improve the design of all kinds of manufactured goods. The manufacturers themselves showed little interest in the project, and the scheme would have lapsed had not three of the Society's officials "spent three whole days travelling about London in four-wheel cabs calling on manufacturers and shopkeepers, till they had at last succeeded by personal entreaty in persuading some of them to send sufficient goods to fill the exhibition room".

The 1847 exhibition was attended by 20,000 visitors, a similar display in 1848 was seen by 73,000, and in the following year the crowd numbered over

Fig. 3: Glass in the Bohemian style, made by Rice Harris & Son, Islington Glass Works, Birmingham, 1851.

100,000. With this series of successes in mind the Society proposed a more ambitious exhibition for 1851, and their President, the Prince Consort, was consulted. It was he who decided that its scope should be international, and he to whom must be given considerable credit for its eventual success. It was first suggested that it be held in Leicester Square; but when Henry Cole, a dynamic member of the Society's Council, put forward his opinion that the Square might not be large enough for the purpose, the Prince requested an alternative. Cole named Hyde Park, and on the President's instruction he went there to locate a suitable spot. As is well known, he found one, and before long the enormous iron and glass building, known later as the Crystal Palace, was erected.

One of the important remaining features of the so-named *Great Exhibition of the Works of Industry of all Nations* 1851 is a meticulously-prepared catalogue. It was issued in three fat volumes with a fourth supplementary volume to complete it, and

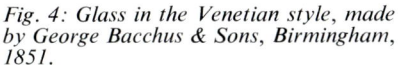

Fig. 4: Glass in the Venetian style, made by George Bacchus & Sons, Birmingham, 1851.

Page 7

Fig. 5: Jug and goblets of cut, engraved, gilt and enamelled blue glass, made by George Bacchus & Sons, Birmingham, 1851.

the set contains a total of more than 1,500 pages. All of the exhibits were described, even if only briefly, and many were illustrated. The available reproduction processes relied largely on the human element, and the principal one in use, the woodcut, is not entirely satisfactory for all objects. However, in spite of shortcomings, the woodcuts do convey some impression of the glass displayed in Hyde Park by British makers (Figs. 3 to 6).

Glass was catalogued in Volume II, and comprised Class 24 of section III of the exhibition. No fewer than one hundred firms displayed their goods, although a proportion of them showed stained glass, sheet glass of various kinds, and such things as glass curtain poles, water-pipes, picture frames and domes for preserving ornaments from dust which are outside the scope of this review.

For sheer size and glitter the exhibit of Messrs. F. & C. Osler, of Birmingham, dwarfed all else. In the very centre of the long building, where two short transepts joined the main avenue, was a fountain standing 27 feet in height and containing more than 4 tons of glass in its construction. It was arranged in three tiers and stood in a marble basin, into which fell streams of water from jets arranged at various levels. All critics at the time reported that it was a most striking spectacle, rivalled perhaps by a much smaller fountain pungently and effectively advertising the merits of a brand of eau-de-Cologne.

The size, also, of a chandelier shown by the long-established firm of Perry (formerly Parker) of Fleet Street, London, evoked considerable comment. It held 144 candles, but one writer admired it less than an example with 80 candles displayed by another British firm.

The foregoing articles were of clear glass and made the utmost of its properties, but the feature of the exhibition was the quantity and variety of coloured pieces to be seen there. Such wares had been coming into the country for some years, but until after 1845 it had been almost impossible to do anything here to compete with the imports. By 1851, the foreign article was being equalled or excelled in appearance, although probably not in most instances in price.

The makers centred on Birmingham and Stourbridge concentrated on coloured and clear glass of several types. The colour was sometimes "solid" with the article made throughout from glass of the chosen colour, or it was "cased". In the latter instance a blob of clear glass was covered with a coating of coloured, and the whole was then blown to the required shape. Often more than one different colour was applied over another, and cutting revealed the successive layers. A cheap substitute took the form of a stain giving a very thin surface cover, and which could be cut through to show the clear underlayer in contrast (Fig. 1).

The most popular colour was certainly red, and articles such as vases and dishes were made from clear glass coated with opaque-white and then with red. Shaped "windows" were cut through both layers, and given oblique edges to show the inner layer as a frame. Alternatively, red glass articles were coated with opaque-white which was cut to leave panels. The latter were often given gilded edges and carefully painted in colours with

Fig. 6: Candelabra and candlesticks, the large candelabrum in the foreground standing 8 ft. 6 inches high and the property of Queen Victoria; made by F. & C. Osler, Broad Street, Birmingham, and Oxford Street, London, 1851.

Fig. 7: Decanter of ruby glass cased in white and cut, made by George Bacchus & Sons, Birmingham. Circa 1850. Height 12¼ inches. (Victoria and Albert Museum.)

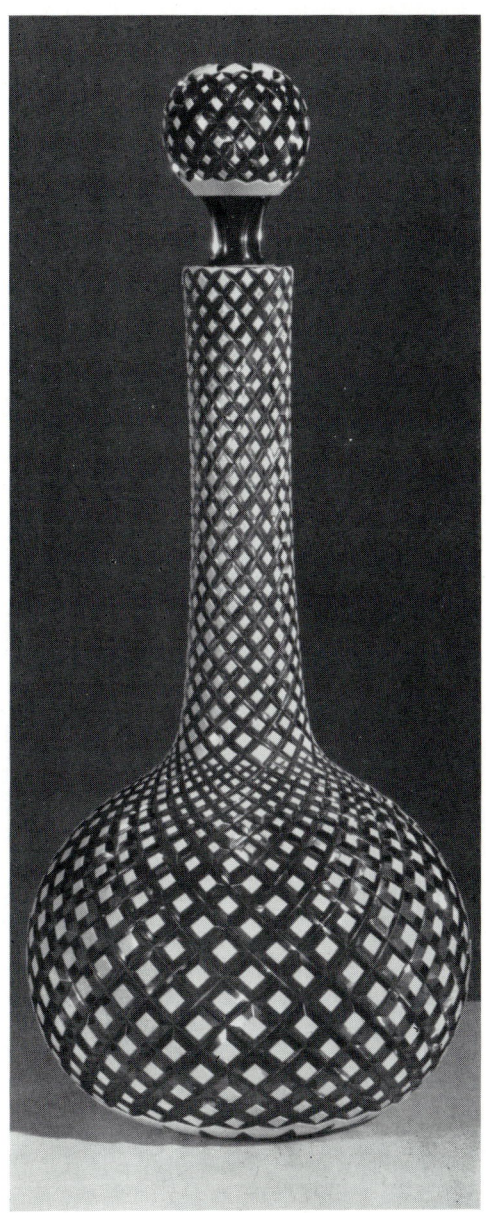

sprays of flowers while a contrasting effect was gained by diamond-cutting (Fig. 6, and see *Signature* 6, Fig. 16).

While most exhibitors in Hyde Park showed one or more examples of coloured glass, principally in ruby or blue, others displayed a variety that rivalled the rainbow. Davis, Greathead & Green, of Stourbridge, came into the latter category, and had the following, amongst other items:

> Lustres, in ruby and chrysoprase, with flint drops, cut and enamelled and frosted.
> Liqueur bottles, ruby, blue and green, coated on flint. A great variety of vases, jars and scent-jars for holding flowers, &c., in the Egyptian, Etruscan, and Grecian styles; many of them cut, coated, gilt, painted in enamel colours, after the antique, with figures, ornaments, flowers, landscapes, and marine views, of the following colours, viz., ruby, oriental blue, chrysoprase, turquoise, black, rose colour, opal-coated blue, cornelian, opal frosted, pearl opal, mazareen blue, &c. The black slabs upon which the vases stand are cut flint glass.

The names of some of the colours are open to query, but it is probable that "Oriental blue" was a bright cobalt like that on Nankin blue-and-white porcelain, "mazareen blue" was a dark shade of the same colour, and chrysoprase a bright apple-green. In contrast to this wide choice, staining was only available in two colours: red and yellow, based on the use of gold and silver, respectively. The use of staining can be recognised quite easily, for the colour is no more than a thin wash on the surface. Although it is almost as vivid in appearance as either solid-coloured or flashed glass, once it has been detected it is not difficult to distinguish from the others.

In addition to a range of transparent colours, there were as many that were semi-transparent: opal, or opaline. The true *verre Opaline* was made in several French manufactories and was reported during 1824-30 to have become the height of Paris fashion. A quantity of translucent white glass (known sometimes as "milk" glass in England and America, and as *milchglas* in Germany) had been made in several countries from the eighteenth century, but opaline differs from this kind.

Opaline glass, like others, varies greatly in its composition and appearance. The white variety, for instance, has been divided into three types: that with a slight orange opalescence; that which is a translucent white without any colour; and the third resembling alabaster with a greyish-white tint in it. All of them, whether white or coloured, were sometimes given a matt surface, and when two or more were used in the same article one might be roughened and the others left with a shiny surface. The effect was achieved by dipping the ware in hydrofluoric acid, or by grinding it on the wheel.

English opal glass was in full production by the time of the 1851 Exhibition. Whereas for many decades it had been the French ambition to excel English glass-of-lead, the tables were now turned and we set out to compete with *verre Opaline*. The firm of W. H. B. & J. Richardson had a large display of such goods in various styles. Much of it was described as painted with subjects ranging from mythological scenes to Aesop's fables (Fig. 8), and the less costly ware was ornamented with printed patterns touched-in with colour by hand.

Much opaline ware was left plain except for gilding, and relied on colour for its appeal. A frequently-found combination is white with apple-green, the rim gilded and often the body of the article encircled by a snake. This reptile appears to have enjoyed considerable popularity as an ornament on glassware in the mid-century, perhaps because it was easy to model or possibly for some deeper psychological reason. Occasionally the glass was finished by mounting it in gilded metal; a style long familiar in France, particularly for porcelain. It was not confined to table ornaments, but metal and opaline were allied in chandeliers and for wall-lights. The Birmingham firm of R. W. Winfield was prominent in manufacturing the metalwork for some of the latter, and examples are recorded shaped as flowers with gilt brass stems and stamens and green opaline blossoms.

The great quantity of coloured glass of all types that was produced in almost every country in the second quarter of the nineteenth century owed its inspiration largely to the manufactories in Bohemia, later Czecho-Slovakia. Ample local supplies of sand, lime and potash had for long enabled the landowners to establish glass-houses, which ob-

Figs. 8a and 8b: Pair of white opaline vases hand-painted with floral bouquets and gilded.

These pieces may have been made by W. H. B. & J. Richardson, Stourbridge. Circa 1850. Height about 24 inches. (Delomosne & Son, Ltd.)

tained supplies of fuel from the surrounding dense forests. Following the end of the Napoleonic wars there came a change of fashion from clear glass to coloured, and considerable research was directed towards extending the range. Between 1820 and 1830 a variety of different colours was put on the market, some of them closely imitating natural stones; a revival of a quest that had originated centuries earlier in ancient Egypt. At the same time, some of the new colours were used as "casings" and cut by craftsmen, following a tradition of lapidary skill indigenous to the region.

In addition to *verre Opaline*, the French were responsible for introducing into England the coloured glass paperweight; an object that has achieved headline importance in recent years. The technique of making the coloured glass "flowers" or "canes" was known to the Romans, but was revived in the early 1840's by a Venetian, Pietro Bigaglia. By 1846 they were being made at three famous French factories (Baccarat, St. Louis and Clichy), and two years later the Birmingham glassmakers, Bacchus, were making them. In the following year another firm in the same city, Rice Harris & Co., is known to have been manufacturing them. An example containing a cane lettered IGW, presumably the initials of their address, the Islington Glass Works, is in a United States collection.

Identified English versions of the paperweights are of the simpler floral or "*millefiore*" (literally thousand flowers) type. They lack the ingenious variety of design achieved by the French, and are less brilliant in colour (Fig. 10). Bacchus exhibited their paperweights at at least one provincial exhibition, but there is no record of their having shown them in 1851. Possibly by that date they had ceased making them and had left the field clear to the French.

Although coloured pieces were dominant in the early 1850's, there was no lack of cut clear glass. In addition to the large fountain and chandeliers mentioned above, many of the 1851 exhibitors showed wares of the type in which English metal and workmanship were unequalled. W. H. B. & J. Richardson of Stourbridge displayed a variety of pieces for the dining-table, and similar articles were shown by Davis, Greathead and Green of the same town. In London, Powell's, of the Whitefriars glass works, and Apsley Pellatt of Blackfriars were well represented (Fig. 12), and each was awarded a Prize Medal; the former for their glass pipes, and the latter for their cut crystal.

In spite of its great popularity here and on the Continent, as well as in the United States, the English cut glass was not without its critics. No less an authority than the great John Ruskin pronounced judgement on it in his *Stones of Venice*, published in 1853. He wrote words with which many nowadays agree wholeheartedly, but which at the time must have seemed outrageous to the multitude who unthinkingly admired what they had so recently seen in profusion in the Crystal Palace.

His words are worth reprinting:

> . . . *all cut glass* is barbarous: for the cutting conceals its ductility, and confuses it with

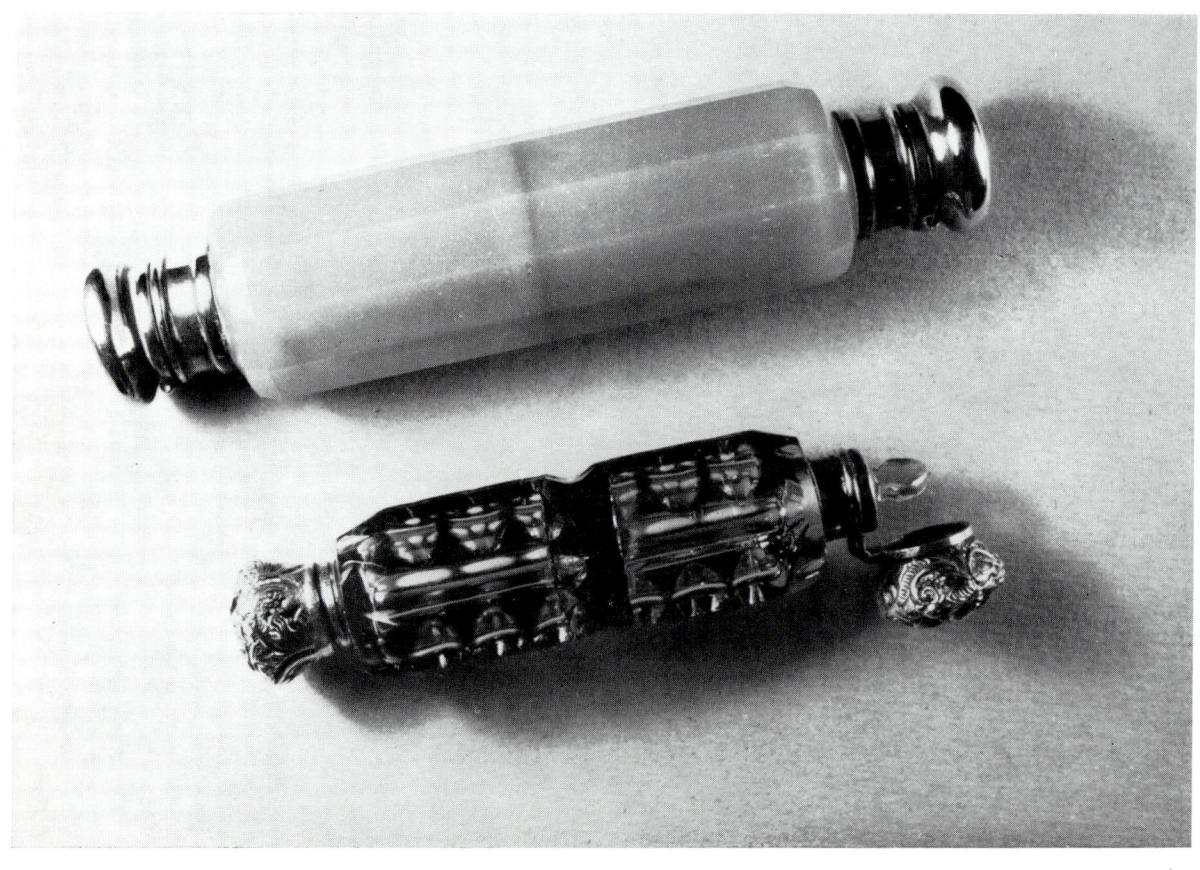

Below, *Fig. 9: Scent bottles: (top) apple green opaline, length 5 inches; (bottom) clear glass cased in dark green cut with "windows", length 4 inches. Circa 1850-60. (Mrs. P. Sedgwick.)*

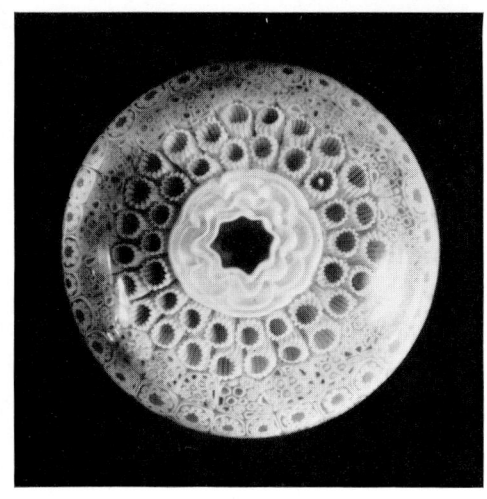

crystal [natural rock crystal]. Also, all very neat, finished, and perfect form in glass is barbarous: for this fails in proclaiming another of its great virtues; namely, the ease with which its light substance can be moulded or blown into any form, so long as perfect accuracy be not required. . . . no delicate outlines are to be attempted, but only such fantastic and fickle grace as the mind of the workman can conceive and execute on the instant. The more wild, extravagant, and grotesque in their gracefulness the forms are, the better. . . while we triumphantly set forth its transparency, we are also frankly to admit its fragility, and therefore not to waste much time upon it, nor put any real art into it when intended for daily use. No workman ought ever to spend more than an hour in the making of any glass vessel.

Ruskin was far from being completely alone in his outlook, and a small quantity of glass had been

Above, *Fig. 10: Paperweight of clear glass inset with shaped and coloured "canes", probably made by George Bacchus & Sons, Birmingham.* Circa 1850. *Diameter* 3½ *inches.* **Below,** *Fig. 11: Elaborately cut table wares shown at the Great Exhibition by W. H. B. & J. Richardson, Stourbridge.* (*From the* Art Journal Illustrated Catalogue.)

Fig. 12: Apsley Pellatt's Falcon Glasshouse, Blackfriars, London. Steel-engraving by M. J. Starling after Thomas Allom. Circa 1830. (Mansell Collection.)

designed and made a few years before he made public his views. Foremost amongst the few who were then attempting to improve taste, was Henry Cole. In 1847, when he was in the employ of the Civil Service at the Public Record Office in London, he launched a firm which he named "Summerly's Art Manufactures". Although Cole himself designed some chinaware and exhibited it successfully under his pseudonym of Felix Summerly, his firm was formed to commission designs from others. These were then sold to manufacturers of silver, china and so forth who paid a royalty on sales, while, in return, Cole attended to publicity.

One of the Summerly artists was Richard Redgrave, R.A., who designed for them an attractive and simple series of carafes and glasses decorated with painted tall leaves and with a gilt rim. They were put on the market in 1847, and a few examples have been preserved. The simplicity of the design of these glass articles, and of some of his other promotions, was in complete contrast to most of what was then popular. Even with the aid of Cole's energetic salesmanship it is doubtful if commercial success, if any, was other than very small. Like other pioneer ventures, it probably receives more attention today from art-historians than it did from the entire British public when its productions were on sale.

© *Geoffrey Wills, 1968.*

15

Victorian Glass: Part 2

Opposite, *a group of late Victorian coloured glass:* (back to front) Purple "slag" tumbler with Davidson's mark, height 4½ inches; red and clear bowl, diameter 5¼ inches; pink satin pot, diameter 3¼ inches; blue slag bowl with Sowerby's mark, width 3½ inches, painted white press-moulded bowl with Sowerby's mark, diameter 3½ inches; red and clear small vase, height 3½ inches; press-moulded yellow hand-candlestick, width 4½ inches, mould-blown green and white scent bottle, length 3 inches.

Below left, *Fig. 1: Drinking glass from a set by Philip Webb and made by James Powell & Sons, Whitefriars, London. Circa 1860. Height 5 inches. (Victoria and Albert Museum.)* **Below right,** *Fig. 2: Pink glass plaque overlaid with white and carved with a scene depicting Venus and Cupid in a landscape, signed by George Woodall. Circa 1890. Diameter 16 inches. (Sotheby's, now in the Corning Museum of Glass, Corning, N.Y.)*

THE glass made during the later part of Queen Victoria's reign has received consideration from a rapidly increasing number of collectors during the past decade or two. The enormous quantity of ware that was made has meant that much of it is still fairly plentiful, but it is collected so keenly that it does not remain on the market for long. Some varieties are rarer than others, and many have been given a status and monetary value far beyond their merit.

A large proportion of the ware made between about 1860 and 1900 was made for a quick sale at a low price, and it usually proclaims this by its appearance. While the majority of glass surviving from those years is of the commonplace variety, it must not be thought that it was the only output of late Victorian glass-houses. Some of them gave considerable attention to making goods of high

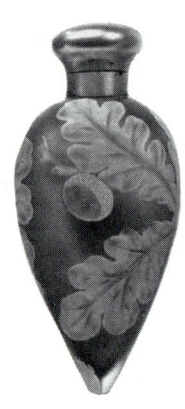

Fig. 3: Three scent bottles made by Thomas Webb & Sons of Stourbridge: (top to bottom), green with white oak leaves and acorns, length 4 inches; pink with white shells and seaweed, height 2¼ inches; turquoise-blue with white honeysuckle sprays, length 5½ inches. Circa 1885. (Christie's)

quality in both design and material. Because these better articles were made in comparatively small numbers and are now scarce, they seldom receive the attention they deserve.

The attempt by Henry Cole to produce more tasteful articles in glass, china and silver was a premature one (see *Signature* 14), and when his "Felix Summerly's Manufactures" ceased business in 1849 its short life was doubtless quickly forgotten. Cole, however, was closely connected with the organisation of the 1851 Exhibition, and one of the results of its success was the eventual establishment of schools of design in various parts of the country. In addition, the Treasury authorized the Board of Trade in 1851 to spend £5,000 on "such articles of manufacture, shown in the Exhibition, as it might seem desirable to acquire for purposes of study".

The committee appointed to deal with the matter duly spent a total of £4,470 16s. 5d., and trusted that what they had acquired would form the nucleus of "a Museum of Manufactures". In due course, some of the profits from the Exhibition were used to buy a large area of land in South Kensington, and on a portion of it was built a museum, later named the Victoria and Albert museum. It was under the superintendence of Henry Cole for its first twenty years, and to the purchases of 1851 were continually added a variety of articles of all countries and periods.

The influence of the new museum, the man in charge of it, and the Schools of Art that began to flourish, slowly had an effect on all industries. Not least in the manufacture of glass, where there was a movement towards reviving old patterns and a cross-current of new ideas attempting to improve upon them. The leader in this revolt against stale industrial design was William Morris, who did not confine his attention to any one form of the applied arts but endeavoured to enhance them all. Furniture, tapestry, stained-glass, wallpaper and fabrics were among the goods and chattels that received attention from Morris and his followers: a body of workers who were duly dubbed collectively "The Arts and Crafts" movement.

In 1859 Morris commissioned an architect, Philip Webb, to design for him, amongst much else, a set of table glasses. They were manufactured by James Powell & Sons, of Whitefriars, London, and it is thought that the glass illustrated in Fig. 1 is one of them. They were made for the personal use of Morris in a house he had had designed and built, but before long he turned from amateur interior decorator to professional.

As a retail outlet he established the firm of Morris, Marshall, Faulkner & Co., in Red Lion Square, London, and issued a prospectus announcing a willingness to undertake "church decoration, carving, stained glass, metal-work, paper-hangings, chintzes and carpets". It has been stated that the first things they sold were some of the Webb-designed glasses. The effect of the "Arts and Crafts" activity was not great as regards mass-produced glass or other items during the period, but eventually it gathered strength, and became the foundation of much twentieth-century work.

Powell's of Whitefriars, who removed in the 1920's from the City of London to Wealdstone, Middlesex, was managed by Harry J. Powell between 1875 and 1915. He was a keen experimenter and designer, and in his book, *Glass-making in England*, noted some of the events that impressed him during his term at the works. Among them he noted that blue and straw-coloured "opal" glass was being made and exported to the United States in 1877-9, and at about the same time experiments were being made to produce irridescent surfaces using acids and by other methods. A decade later he recorded the making of soda-lime glass (instead of the English flint, or glass-of-lead) for producing copies of Venetian wares and in imitation of ancient Roman glass. One entry is especially evocative: "1885. Bulbs for incandescent electric light made by hand in considerable quantities".

Venetian achievements had never been completely forgotten, and there was plenty of English glass "in the Venetian style" in the 1851 Exhibition. There was, however, a more general revival of interest in the ware during the last quarter of the nineteenth century. The glass-houses in Murano had slowly been re-vitalised and reached fresh heights under Antonio Salviati, who once again established a world-wide demand for the products of the long-dormant industry. He reproduced and

Fig. 4: Tumbler etched with a pattern of plants and butterflies. Late nineteenth century. Height 4¼ inches.

Fig. 5: The "Elgin Jug", engraved by F. E. Kny, a Bohemian craftsman working with Thomas Webb & Sons, Stourbridge. Exhibited at Paris in 1878. Height, 14¼ inches. (Victoria and Albert Museum.)

modified the old designs, and brought back into use most of the traditional processes. With the keen encouragement of A. H. Layard, the excavator of the ruins of Nineveh and subsequently a politician, Salviati opened a retail shop in St. James's Street, London. The hand-blown articles on sale were welcomed by many as a refreshing antidote to the English wares available in the 1870's. Comparing them with the Venetian, one critic described ours as displaying "angularity of form, lumpy ornament, deep incisions, and solidity of material".

Powell was not the only manufacturer to turn back the clock two centuries and compete with the Venetians by imitating their work. The pale tints, thinly-blown metal and Muranese shapes were aped in many objects, and the influence of the imported ware can be discerned in cheap as well as in expensive glass of the time.

The creation of artificial irridescence, referred to by Powell, was also due to foreign inspiration. This time it was Bohemia, where the brilliantly-coloured surface acquired by ancient glass during lengthy burial in the earth was formed instantaneously by chemical means. Great secrecy prevailed as to details of the process, and there were whispered references to something named "pink salts". Several makers in England conducted experiments to produce the desired effect and a certain amount of such glass was made, but it cannot be said to have become widely popular in this country.

A revival comparable to that of early Roman glass took place also with regard to the later and more sophisticated productions of the Empire. The focal point of this was the Portland Vase, which had been exhibited since 1810 in the British Museum. There had been an interval of seven months from 7th February 1845, when the vase had had to be withdrawn from public view after it had been wantonly smashed by a visitor, and earlier it had had almost as much publicity when it had been borrowed by Josiah Wedgwood so that he could make copies of it in his celebrated jasperware.

Although there was doubt for fully a century afterwards, Wedgwood published the fact that the vase was not carved, as some thought, from natural stone, but was made of glass. The object had been blown in dark blue glass and then coated with opaque-white, the latter being cut through with immense skill to form the decorative frieze on it.

A clever Stourbridge craftsman, John Northwood, took up a challenge from a local glass-maker and, in the intervals of running his business as a glass decorator, copied the original vase. Unfortunately, when it was almost finished and was being touched with warm hands on a frosty morning, it cracked and, later, broke in two: a catastrophe due to unequal expansion of the two kinds of glass that formed it. This was a sad occurrence, as a considerable amount of time had been spent on it, but it certainly underlined the superior knowledge of glass-making possessed by an anonymous Roman of some 1,800 years prior. Nothing daunted, Northwood decided to finish his task after gluing the parts together, and the vase, after occupying him the three years 1873-76 in making, eventually joined the original in the British Museum.

The comparative success of the copy, and the publicity attending it, led some of the Stourbridge makers to market pieces decorated in a similar manner. Webb's and Richardson's were the firms concerned, and the principal artists employed in the work were Northwood and the brothers George and Thomas Woodall.

Whereas the original Portland Vase had been painstakingly engraved and carved by its maker, Northwood accelerated his task. He first used a bath of acid to remove quickly and easily all the unwanted portions of the white layer, and then he ground on the wheel as much as he could of the remaining pattern. He was left with a white glass layer outlined in the shape of the pattern, and with the general hollows roughly indicated. The final detailed work was carved laboriously by hand, using sharp steel tools with paraffin to give them a "bite".

The same methods were used for the manufacture of cameo-decorated pieces on a commercial scale. Plaques depicting mythological figures, dancing maidens and similar subjects each took several years to make from start to finish, and could cost

Fig. 6: Cream jug, cut and polished in the so-called "rock crystal" style, the silver mount hall-marked 1881. Height $3\frac{1}{4}$ inches.

Fig. 7: Night-light holders and shades. Circa 1890. (Geoffrey A. Godden, Esq., F.R.S.A.)

at the time as much as £1,000 apiece (Fig. 2). Less ambitious examples of the work, such as scent-bottles and small decorative vases, carved with floral patterns, were made in larger quantities and sold for much smaller sums (Fig. 3).

The carved work was usually in opaque-white, but the background colour varied. Many shades of all colours were produced, and they were polished, made matt or given a rough "chipped" surface. Many of the important pieces were signed by their carvers, and occasionally the date when the work was finished was added.

John Northwood was connected with a number of improvements and devices affecting glass decorating during the period. He experimented with the use of acid to etch designs on glass in place of the costly hand process of engraving it. The piece to be ornamented was, in much the same manner as the Portland Vase copy described above, protected with a coating of paint or wax, then scratched with the design and immersed in acid. Later, a process employing transfers printed with a special ink was used. Metal templates assisted accuracy and speed for hand-etching, and by 1865 a type of lathe had been devised for scratching on the waxed article such repetitive patterns as interlinked circles and the familiar Greek Key (Fig. 4).

A result of the intensive study of old glass that took place was an advance in technical skill, which is apparent in many small and unpretentious articles. The earlier use of trapped air bubbles, which led from a simple tear to a complicated air-twist, was carried a stage farther forward. A group of bubbles was manipulated between two layers of contrasting-coloured glass so as to form a regular pattern. Use was made also of lumps of clear and coloured glass tooled into floral shapes, and applied to the sides of vases and bowls.

The clever craftsmanship of most of these pieces is often overlooked, because their shapes and colours do not conform to modern taste. Further, surfaces were frequently treated with acid to give a matt or "satin" finish that is equally unappealing to many at the present day. As the clarity and reflective quality of glass are its principal virtues, it is argued, with considerable justice, that to obscure them both is to change the appearance of the material for the worse.

There was a large output of blown ruby-coloured glass, often decorated with contrasting additions of clear glass (*frontispiece*). Covered sugar bowls, vases and saltcellars are among the many articles made in this style. The colour varies in tone from deep to pale, and it has had a large band of devoted collectors for many years. It is admired particularly across the Atlantic, where it is known as "Cranberry" glass.

The use of paraffin for domestic lighting, which began to increase rapidly in the 1860's, called for large numbers of suitable lamps. Those for standing on a table were given a tall stem of glass or metal supporting a glass reservoir for the oil, and surmounted by more glass in the form of a shade. All these parts were clear or coloured, and decorated to suit the taste of the time and the purse of each category of buyer. Hand lamps of similar pattern lacked a stem, but were equally varied in design.

Some of the unusual tints and types of glass were utilised in the making of night-light shades, which were enormously popular in the 1880's. They owed their widespread use to the plentiful publicity gained for them by Samuel Clarke, a maker of candles. His night-lights had a double wick

Fig. 8: Gilt metal stand fitted with holders for Clarke's "Fairy" night-lights and flowers, made of Webb's "Queen's Burmese Ware" painted with floral sprays. Height 8 inches.
(*Sotheby's.*)

Above, *Fig. 9: Press-moulding; the molten glass is dropped into the closed mould. (Glass Manufacturers' Federation.)*

of rush that burned with a good oval flame for anything between four and eleven hours. By enclosing them within glass domes, which had a hole in the top for ventilation, the lights were protected from draughts and gave a steady glow.

They were introduced shortly before 1886 under the name of "Fairy" lights, and followed by modified versions called "Fairy-Pyramid" and "Wee Fairy". Clarke also patented the trade names "Burglar's Horror" and "Cricklite", the latter a simplified version with a clear glass cover. Competitors were not lacking, and produced similar articles with comparable names like "Glow-worm" and "Bijou".

Public interest in these trifles was stimulated not only by extensive advertising, but also by a rapid succession of styles (Fig. 7). These culminated in the making of shades from "Queen's Burmese Ware": a matt-surfaced material shading gradually from yellow to deep pink, which may be thought to bear a closer resemblance to confectionery than to glass. It was invented and patented in 1885 by the Mount Washington Glass Company, of New Bedford, Massachusetts, and some samples were submitted for the approval of Queen Victoria. The English rights were purchased by Thomas Webb & Sons of Stourbridge, who began to manu-

Above, *Fig. 10: The mould opened and the article revealed after pressing. (Glass Manufacturers' Federation.)*

facture it in the following year and put it on sale with the royal prefix to its name.

Webb's did not limit their use of the "Ware" to night-lights, but made small vases and other objects from it. Many of them bear the name of the firm beneath the base, where it was acid-etched together with "Queen's Burmese Ware" and one or more patent numbers (Fig. 8).

ONE of the biggest advances in glass-making during the nineteenth century was the adoption of the technique of press-moulding, which brought attractive-looking articles within the reach of millions who could not afford the hand-made product. The process was a simple one, although it still placed considerable reliance on human judgement and could not be described as being mechanised. The worker placed a pre-determined quantity of molten glass into a mould, and brought down a plunger that squeezed the material into every crevice. The plunger was then raised, the mould opened (unless for a flat object, when hinging was unnecessary) and the glass article removed (Figs. 9 and 10).

The ware could be given any chosen pattern on its exterior, and the plunger could be smooth or bear a suitable design. The biggest difficulty encountered was due to the rapid cooling that occurred when the glass was used in small quantities, and this sometimes led to flawed work. The molten mass began to harden before the plunger could press it evenly right up to the top of the mould, and imperfections are to be found sometimes below the rims of tumblers and similar tall pieces. At first, the article to be re-heated was held on a pontil in the normal manner, and where it was removed the tell-tale mark remains. Later pieces do not show this, because they were gripped in spring-loaded claws at the end of a rod, which left no signs of its use.

The article emerged with a ruffled surface from contact with the mould, and to cure this it was held for a short while in an oil-flame; the latter usually under steam or air pressure. The outside surface began to melt, and in so doing smoothed out most of the inequalities and gave it a gloss. The piece was then ready to join the hundreds or thousands of others slowly cooling, or annealling, prior to being despatched from the factory.

Three big firms were the principal ones in the industry, and all were in the north-east of England. They were Sowerby's and George Davidson & Co., of Gateshead, and Greener & Co., of Sunderland. Each used a mark on much of its output: (see right)

Although these appear often beneath a base, there is no invariable rule, and when they are on the inside of an article they can easily be overlooked. All three marks are raised from the surface, and are not always very distinct.

A proportion of the glassware made by these firms, and by others, is to be found bearing a small raised diamond-shaped mark. Sometimes it is on its own, and sometimes in addition to the makers' mark. In the centre of it appears *Rd*, an abbreviation of the word *registered*, meaning that the design of the article was registered at the Patent Office in London. Numerals and letters in the corners of the diamond indicate the year, month and day of the month, as well as other details, and can be de-coded from lists published in books on chinamarks. After 1884 a series of numerals, without any diamond, was used, and are prefixed by *Rd. No.* The date, when found, will reveal the year in which the pattern was registered, and does not imply that the object itself was necessarily made then (Fig. 12).

Both clear and tinted varieties of glass were press-moulded, and their composition was similar to that used by the Bohemian makers. The flint type of metal was not only expensive, but it was found that results almost as good could be obtained by using a formula with lime as one of the ingredients. This gave a bright-looking article, was sufficiently durable for most uses, and could be turned out cheaply. An opaque-white type gave a close approximation to china, and tinted in any of a half-dozen or so colours it was made into ornaments (see page 15).

THE much-admired "Slag" glass is undoubtedly the most avidly collected of pressed wares at the present day. Its name is due to the fact that one of its constituents is waste slag from blast-furnaces. This was readily obtained in the north-east from any of the numerous iron works, and as it

Left, *marks found on press-moulded wares; (top to bottom) Sowerby's Ellison Glass Works, Gateshead; Henry Greener, Sunderland; George Davidson, Gateshead. (Enlarged: the actual marks each measure about ½″ in height.)*

Right, *Fig. 11: An advertisement published in 1887 for Sowerby's Ellison Glass Works. (Geoffrey A. Godden, Esq., F.R.S.A.)*

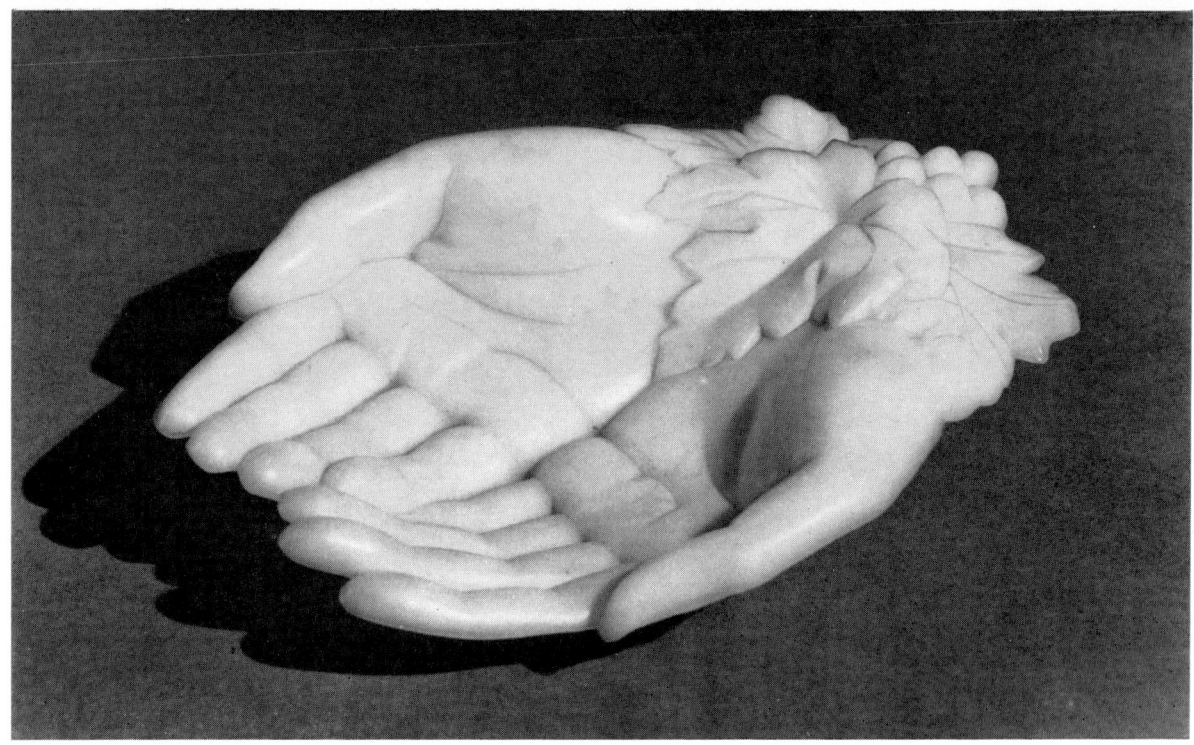

seems to have been collected during the evening it was also known as "End of Day" glass. In time, this has been misconstrued as implying that the mixture was compounded in the glass-house at the end of the day, and that it was the result of mixing all the cullet and waste in the nearly-empty pots.

In fact, it has been pointed out, this is completely wrong. The slag was weighed up and added in just as scientific a manner as the other ingredients and the operation was performed at any hour of the day or night between a Monday morning and a Saturday night. The resulting material was an opaque glass, veined and streaked like marble, which was made in a dark purple and other colours (*frontispiece*). Sowerby's advertised in 1880 that

> They have a wide reputation for Vitro-Porcelain Dessert ware, Vases, &c., in turquoise and opal colours, Malachite, Agate and Sorpini in fancy vases, flower pots, &c.

The term "Vitro-Porcelain" underlines the fact that the glass was something of a cross-breed, and the makers did their best to sell to both markets: the glass and the chinaware. Greener's advertised similarly that they made "Opal, Malachite and

Above, *Fig. 12: Grape dish of white glass with a matt or satin finish, marked beneath the base* PATENTED AUG 31 1875. *Probably made by John Ford of Edinburgh. Length 7¾ inches.*

Opposite, *a group of press-moulded wares, mostly made by Sowerby's of Gateshead. Circa 1880. (Mrs. G. C. S. Coode.)*

Fig. 13: *White vase in the form of a hand holding a cornucopia. Circa 1880. Height about 7 inches.*

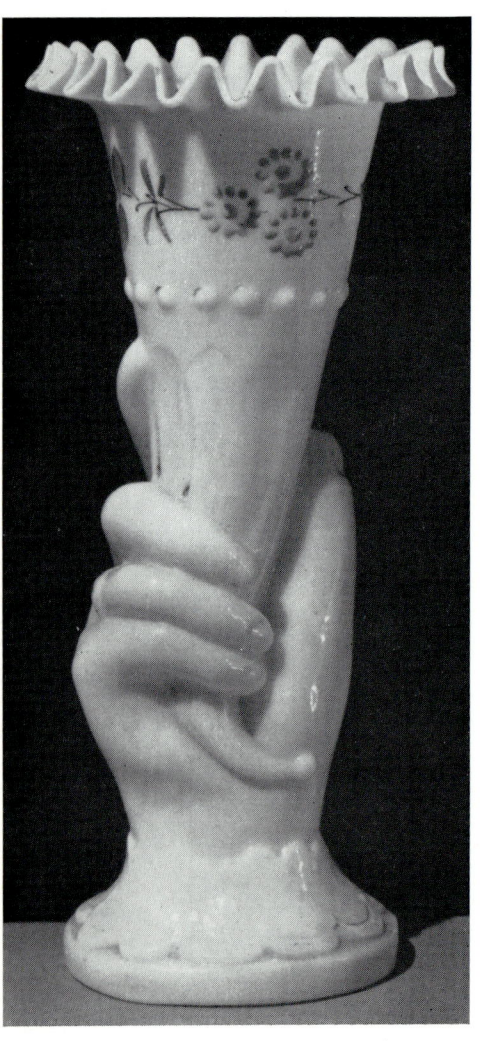

Blue or Black Majolica", but as pottery-makers of the time also mis-used the term "majolica" it was probably inevitable that the glass-makers should do the same.

The various firms manufactured a wide range of goods in the different kinds of pressed glass. Many of them were of small size, and in the form of "fancy" pots for one purpose and another. They were limited at first as regards height because of the process, but the difficulty was later overcome. Plates and other flat pieces were never a trouble, and opaque-white and tinted ones were made in sets for dessert. The earlier pressed glass was made in close imitation of hand cut examples, but later specific designs were executed for pressed work. These made use of small dots or lace-like patterns, that were beyond the scope of the wheel and were very effective when moulded.

Favourite Victorian models of boots and shoes were made, and the equally well-loved vase in the form of a human hand (Fig. 13) was turned out by the hundred. The Gladstone bag appeared in the shape of a small vase, and salt-cellars masqueraded occasionally as railway engines. The celebrations in 1887 and 1897 of Queen Victoria's 50 and 60 years' reign, respectively, brought forth an avalanche of commemorative pieces of many kinds, all of which were appropriately inscribed.

During the whole of the second half of the Victorian period, from about 1860 to 1900, the English glass industry, while free of taxation at home, was plagued by competition from abroad. This was a bane at all levels: the higher-priced articles could hold their own on the quality of their metal and their workmanship, but there was a continual influx of novelties to captivate the public and divert money to foreign makers. In the cheap grades, the competition was no less intense, but in spite of bearing heavier manufacturing costs the English manufacturers managed to keep their heads above water.

Imports rose very rapidly, and figures tell the story. In 1861 glass goods to the value of £354,024 came into the country, while by 1880 the figure had rocketed to £1,776,472. If nothing else, it proves that an abundance of glassware was made, and much remains for the pleasure of collectors.

© *Geoffrey Wills, 1968.*

16

Modern Glass

Left, *Westminster Abbey, London, showing six of the sixteen chandeliers presented by members of the Guinness family in 1965 to celebrate the 900th anniversary of the founding of the Abbey. The chandeliers were made by Waterford Glass Ltd., of Waterford, Ireland; each is 9 ft 6 ins. in height and weighs 2½ cwt. (280 lbs.) (By courtesy British Travel Assoc.)*

Below, *Fig. 1: Iridescent green vase with English silver mount hallmarked 1903. Height 5 inches.*

ENGLISH glassmakers have been for long almost exclusively occupied in filling a world-wide demand for high quality cut crystal of conventional type. Deep cutting in heavy metal has retained its popularity with scarcely any intermission since it was introduced in the eighteenth century, and it remains recognised in this country, and many others, as true "English glass". Ever since John Ruskin boldly spoke against its barbarism it has had its detractors, but their protests have been largely ineffectual in influencing the taste of the public.

Wedding and other commemorative gifts still take the form of glittering pieces of cut glass, the largest the donor can afford to buy, which are destined to become treasured possessions. With craftsmen trained in its making and decoration, and furnaces and workshops equipped to the same end, it is only to be expected that the makers have continued on their profitable path.

At the beginning of the century the discriminating were buying Tiffany's Art Nouveau fantasies in glass, notably his iridescent "Favrile". The mass market, in England and in much of the remainder of the world, was supplied as it had been for several decades from the many glassworks in central Europe: Bohemia, later Czecho-Slovakia. There, cheap raw materials and ceaseless introductions of new shapes and styles, together with plentiful labour resulted in an enormous output at highly competitive prices. True, the wares did not match up to the quality made in England and other countries, but cheapness and novelty compensated for this.

In France at about the same time there was activity among the experimental or "studio" glassmakers who followed in the footsteps of Emile Gallé. His work was very different in appearance from that of Tiffany, although both of them owed

Fig. 2: Claret decanter and stopper, 1913, height 13 inches; goblet, 1920, height 9 inches. Both made by James Powell & Sons (Whitefriars) Ltd. (Victoria and Albert Museum.)

a lot to the current interest in Japanese art. Both, too, were attracted by floral and other natural forms.

Gallé is remembered for a particular type of ware in which he employed one or more casings in different colours on an opaque or semi-opaque base. The casings were rarely of a single pure colour, but were usually streaked or blotched and then cut in the manner of cameos. As with English cameo glass both acid and wheel-engraving were used, but the Frenchman's results were more free than ours. His had a distinctive ruggedness, far removed from the rigid classicism of the Portland Vase which inspired John Northwood and his fellow craftsmen.

Tiffany's iridescent glass had plenty of copyists in his own country, the United States, and in Europe the Bohemians were hard at work making imitations by 1900. The work of Gallé, however, seems either to have met with a smaller demand, or to have proved beyond the resources of the large-scale manufacturers. Certainly, in England neither of the men can be said to have caused a revolution in glass design: Webb's exhibited their "Bronze" iridescent ware in Paris in 1878, but nothing like Emile Gallé's work would seem to have been attempted.

The free-blown forms used by Tiffany were well within the scope of any competent glass-blower and the surface colourings could have been attained after experiment, but Gallé's vases and other articles were in many instances individually-created works in a technique that would not have come easily to rigidly-disciplined operatives. It is no exaggeration to say that in the first quarter of the twentieth century little artistically important glass was produced in England, but the demands of war and the cessation of foreign supplies drove the industry to devising and improving many new types of glass for military purposes.

With the ending of the war there came a general re-appraisal of design in many countries, and domestic glassware came under scrutiny with everything else. A large and important exhibition of decorative art held in Paris in 1925 focused attention on the subject, and smaller displays held in other capitals had the same effect. A Swedish exhibition in London in 1932 brought glassware from that country before an audience to most of whom it was completely new.

As a result of this world-wide activity some of the English firms set about recruiting artists to design in the newer idiom. Reliance continued to be placed on clear metal, as opposed to coloured, and on cutting to emphasise its qualities. The outcome was a partial switch from the old-style complicated criss-cross cutting to a more subtle use of facets and straight lines. Much depended on the skill of the designer, who was in many instances working in a medium which he grew to understand as he proceeded, but the man at the wheel remained no less important than in the past.

It cannot be said that the new style made much headway with the general public, who were content to continue buying that with which they had long been familiar. The war which began in 1939 once again forced the industry to devote its energies to the vital task of providing military supplies, and the making of salad bowls and wine-glasses became of minor importance.

Even before hostilities terminated, the Board of Trade set up the Council of Industrial Design, of which the purpose was to encourage "the improvement of design in the products of British Industry". It has display centres in London and Glasgow, which can be visited by the public and where selected articles are on show. Of equal importance, it provides an advisory service to manufacturers, and gives instruction on design appreciation to those who can do so much to influence taste: salesmen and trade-buyers.

Public appreciation has been advanced by the spread of television, a medium ideally suited to the purpose: one object displayed on a screen in the home has a far greater impact than twenty described in words only. Again, the popularity of foreign travel has widened mental horizons, and slightly lessened innate conservatism of taste.

Both Gallé and Tiffany have formed part of the 1960's renaissance of Art Nouveau, and original works by them have risen steeply in price on the market. There has been a noticeable spread in the use of free-blown forms relying on tinting for much of their effect. The pioneering work of Alfred Powell, once of Whitefriars but whose firm moved outside the city to Wealdstone, Middlesex, in 1922,

Fig. 3: Engraved green glass decanter with silver stopper, made by James Powell & Sons (Whitefriars) Ltd., 1920. Height 11 inches. (Victoria and Albert Museum.)

has been generally recognised, and his successors uphold his reputation.

Purchasers are offered a wide choice of articles, mostly in simple shapes and often with thin walls contrasted against a heavy and glittering base. Colours embrace the spectrum, with smoky greys and greens harking back to the old *Waldglas* and *verre de fougère*, but normally without the bubbles and impurities that are present in the old material. This is not, however, invariably the case, as Powell's have made pieces with deliberate "faults" of those kinds in order to give them an "antique" appearance.

Shapes vary from the tall and thin to the squat, with something for every taste. Such a galaxy may make it difficult for future art-historians to decide exactly what was most sought after.

At the same time, the shops display plenty of traditional cut crystal in near-eighteenth century shapes, and there is little sign of interest in it waning now or in the foreseeable future. The high reputation for cutting established by the Irish manufactories in the late eighteenth/early nineteenth centuries is being kept alive by establishments in Waterford (frontispiece and Fig. 14) and, farther to the north of the country, Galway.

A development of recent years has been the

Fig. 4: Water jug and tumbler, from a suite of tableware presented to H.R.H. Princess Elizabeth on the occasion of her marriage, November 20th, 1947, by the British Glass Industry. (Photograph: Glass Manufacturers' Federation.)

starting of a factory in Devonshire under the auspices of Dartington Hall, which brought craftsmen from abroad to inaugurate the venture. The wheel turns full circle, and this event can be seen as a recurrence of what took place 400 years earlier when a party of Venetians came to London (Fig. 15).

That we do not rely entirely on workers from other countries is proved by the existence of the flourishing Royal College of Art, London, which includes a Department of Industrial Glass to teach design and industrial processes. At Stourbridge there is a School with its own furnaces, where design and its practical application are taught, and the same is carried out at Edinburgh College of Art and elsewhere. Much of the work produced by the students is interesting and promising, but Mrs. Ada Polak remarks that "It seems difficult, however, to exploit in the industry the young talent from the schools".

Many other critics make similar complaints, and suggest that our glassmakers lack a spirit of adventure in marketing new shapes or in revitalising old ones, and in devising fresh techniques to enlarge the scope of the material. In their

Fig. 5: Vase made to commemorate the Coronation of Queen Elizabeth II, 1953; made by Stuart & Sons, Stourbridge, Worcestershire. (Photograph: Glass Manufacturers' Federation.)

Below, *Figs. 6 and 7: Vases designed by John Luxton, A.R.C.A., 1967, and made by Stuart & Sons, Stourbridge. Heights 8½ inches (top) and 9 inches. (Photographs: Council of Industrial Design.)*
Right, *Fig. 8: Wineglass designed by F. G. Stuart, 1964, and made by Stuart & Sons, Stourbridge. Height 7½ inches. (Photograph: Council of Industrial Design.)*

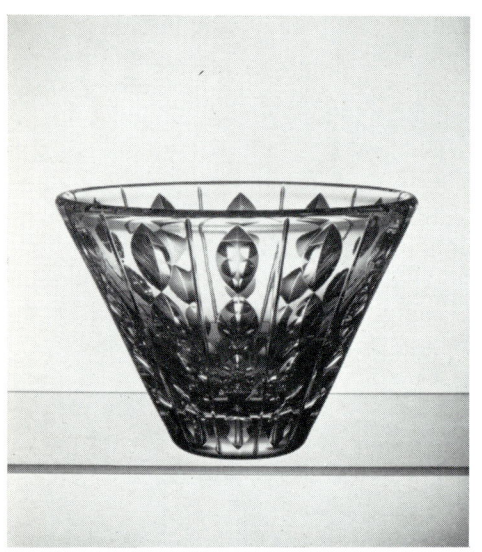

defence it must be pointed out that there remains a persistent demand for the traditional wares, and that the craftsmen of any nation can only work within their own capabilities both of taste and techniques. Although attempts are made from time to time to escape from these restrictions, it would seem that, up to the present at any rate, our talents are expressed at their best in "cut crystal". Its "barbarism" is a matter of opinion, and the public taste and purse are the arbiters.

* * * * *

Fig. 9: Ship's decanter designed by T. Jones, 1963, and made by Stevens & Williams Ltd., Brierley Hill, Staffordshire. (Photograph: Council of Industrial Design.)

Gas and oil light had called for large numbers of simple globular shades, more to assist the buring process than for decoration. Most of them were plain, but some were decorated with etching and the more expensive ones boasted cutting. Perhaps the most decorative were the large red glass examples made for portable oil heaters in the late nineteenth century, where the psychological effect of a ruby-coloured glow was possibly more warming than the heat from the flame within.

The ubiquitous Tiffany was early in the field, and with the advent of electricity he collaborated with Thomas Alva Edison in producing shades to disguise the stark bulb. He used his glass in various shapes, and in the true spirit of Art Nouveau produced in 1902 his "Lily Cluster": bronze-stalked electrically-lighted lilies with shaped gold iridescent shades. His most popular introduction was made from pieces of coloured glass held together with lead strips in the manner of a stained-glass window.

As was the case with his other wares, Tiffany's lampshades were for the few rather than for the multitude. The latter had, for several decades, a choice of shades of opal glass, with or without a trifle of painted ornament on it. Alternatively, there was a type with a frilled edge ranging from semi-opaque to clear in pink or green. Then, in the thirties it began to be realised that there were enormous potentialities for making this neglected object more attractive in appearance and more practical in effect. It should not only look well, but perform this part of its job without obscuring too much of the light.

Innumerable patterns are now available, many of them taking advantage of skilful cutting for their effect and others relying more on shape and surface texture. The competition of transparent plastics, in this field and others, has undoubtedly stimulated the glass industry to meet a very real threat to its prosperity.

* * * * *

JUST as the eighteenth century makers tried for some years to vie with the china trade by producing an opaque-white material, so in recent years a further onslaught on the potters has been made. Heat-resisting glass, for many years sold in the shape of casseroles, dishes and bowls for use in cooking and serving hot foods, has had its range extended. Now, cups, saucers and plates are made from it, and a proportion is sold decorated with coloured patterns.

* * * * *

MENTION must be made of one type of glass decorating that has achieved prominence in recent years in England and which, like cutting, emphasises the beauty of glass-of-lead while benefiting from its qualities. In the eighteenth century there was a considerable export trade from the Newcastle glass-houses to Holland, and many of the distinctive drinking-glasses from the area (see *Signature* 2) have been found there. While some were decorated before being sent abroad, many were embellished with engraving after arrival and such wheel-engraved glasses often bear inscriptions in the Dutch language.

A different and distinctive type of ornament was practised by a small number of Dutchmen, probably all amateurs, but who preferred to use for it the brilliant English type of glass rather than their own duller variety. The work was done with the aid of a splinter of diamond set in a handle, which was tapped lightly with a hammer to produce a tiny dot or a short line on the surface of the piece. The best-known exponent of the art was a man named Frans Greenwood, of Rotterdam, who

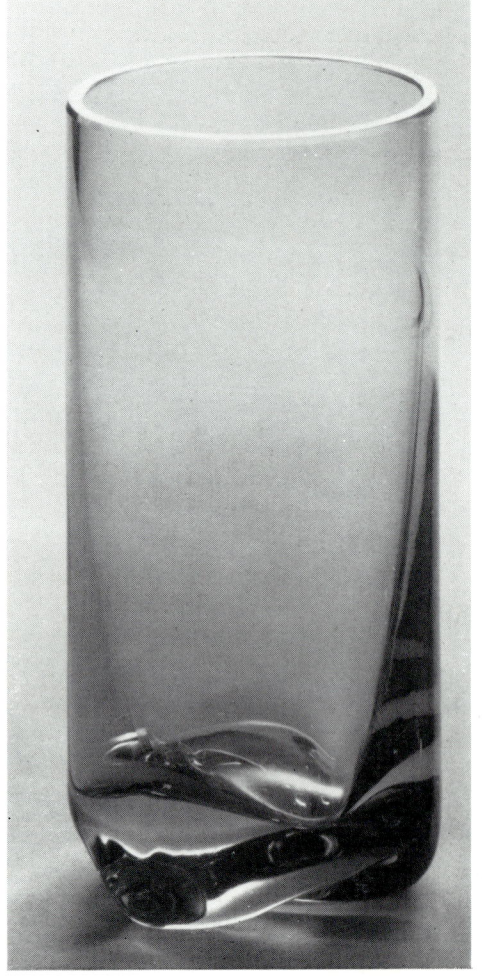

Fig. 10: *Vase designed by Angus Sillars, 1966, and made by Strathearn Glass, Ltd., Crieff, Perthshire. Height 9¼ inches. (Photograph: Council of Industrial Design.)*

Fig. 11: Ice jug made in clear, "soot", "peat" and "twilight" glass by Caithness Glass, Ltd., Wick, Caithness, from 1962. Capacity 2½ pints. (Photograph: Council of Industrial Design.)

lived between 1680 and 1761 and, judged by his surname, was probably of English origin. Work of the same type was done by David Wolff and Aert Schouman, and all three men, as well as some others, occasionally signed their work.

The effect of stipple-engraving is that of a shadowy picture, in which the high-lights are made with the diamond and polished untouched portions form contrasting shadows. At its best, the delicate work is so slight as to be almost unnoticeable, and this semi-invisibility is one of its charms. The most noteworthy present-day practitioner of stippling is Laurence Whistler, who began by using old glasses for his work but now has them made to his own design at the Whitefriars glassworks (Fig. 12).

* * * * *

To conclude this series of *Signatures* it is appropriate to give the collector, or potential collector, some advice as to what to look for in old English and Irish glass. To the uninitiated all look alike, old and new, British and foreign, but it should not take a keen student long to master the elementary differences. Once a start has been made, it will be found an absorbing subject in a fascinating and rewarding field.

A necessity in collecting, and this applies to any branch of it, is to possess an understanding of the manufacturing processes involved at various dates. Thus, while it is remembered that the pontil mark was usually ground away from glasses, decanters and other articles after about 1800, there is no certainty that a piece bearing one is of earlier date. Any forger making "old" glass will have no difficulty at all in providing a convincing-looking scar. Conversely, the absence of a pontil mark on an apparently mid-eighteenth century article should arouse instant suspicions.

In judging the age of glass, shape is of paramount importance, and the more the eye is trained by looking at first-rate authentic examples the easier it becomes to sort wheat from chaff. A man reproducing something at a later date cannot help including in it a look of his own times. The example of painting will clarify the point: the Victorian

Fig. 12: Goblet, the bowl stipple-engraved by Laurence Whistler with a view of Ince Castle, Cornwall. Height 10¼ inches. (Hon. Simon Lennox-Boyd.)

artist "creating" or copying a Rubens will unconsciously give the human face the traits of his period. Because of this, the almond-shaped nineteenth century female visage peers forth from innumerable pseudo-Flemish masterpieces alleged to be of early seventeenth century date. From comparable indications, a modern copy of an old glass is recognised by the expert for what it really is.

Prior to the invention of Ravenscroft's glass-of-lead, which did not come into use until about 1675 English and foreign pieces are difficult or impossible to differentiate. After that date, following the widespread use of lead oxide in English glass-houses, the resemblance largely ended. However it must be pointed out that the manufacture of soda glass did not cease completely, and in the nineteenth century, especially in the Newcastle area, large quantities were made.

The dissimilar appearances of lead and soda glass are not always obvious, but there are two straightforward tests which can be applied and should settle any doubts. While they will only be required on rare occasions, it may be useful to note them here so that they are readily available.

A small drop of hydrofluoric acid together with a small drop of ammonium sulphide is applied carefully to the glass in question. If any lead is present it turns black, and if there is none it does not. A precaution to be taken is to test in an inconspicuous place, because the acid eats into the surface and leaves it dull. So if the test has to be employed, it should be used beneath the foot perhaps near the pontil mark. It is important to wash away afterwards all traces of the acid, as it is a dangerous liquid.

Alternatively, testing by means of an ultra-violet lamp is completely harmless to the article and does not involve the use of any chemicals. It will be found that lead glass fluoresces only slightly in a violet-blue colour, but soda glass gives a strong and instantly recognisable reaction in a brilliant greenish-yellow.

A useful visual test for genuineness is to check whether there are normal signs of wear on a piece. Beneath the foot of a wine glass, for instance, where it would have had years of contact with table tops, it should be correspondingly scored at

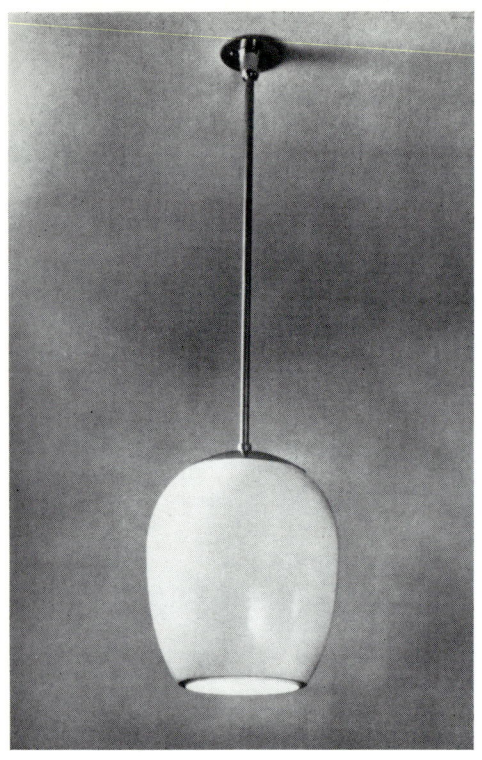

Left, *Fig. 13: Opal glass and metal pendant electric-light fitting, designed and made by Troughton & Young (Lighting) Ltd., London, from 1951. Overall length, 31 inches. (Photograph: Council of Industrial Design.)*

Right, *Three vases from a series designed by G. P. Baxter for Whitefriars Glass, Ltd., in 1966. (Left) the texture derived from burnt wood and nail heads, height $8\frac{1}{4}$ inches; (centre and right) the texture derived from wood bark, heights 2 and 6 inches. (Glass Manufacturers' Federation.)*

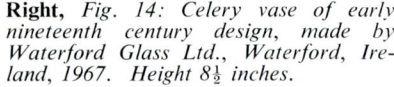

Right, *Fig. 14: Celery vase of early nineteenth century design, made by Waterford Glass Ltd., Waterford, Ireland, 1967. Height $8\frac{1}{2}$ inches.*

Fig. 15: Square vase made in clear, "midnight" and "kingfisher" glass, by Dartington Glass, Ltd., Great Torrington, Devon. Designed by F. J. Thrower, 1967. Height 3¼ inches. (Photograph: Council of Industrial Design.)

the edge. Less obvious, and revealed usually only when the piece is angled to the light, are the myriad tiny scratches on the surface. They will have been caused by day-to-day handling during use, and by washing and dusting. It is remarkable how rough an apparently polished old surface appears when it is inspected closely.

The fashion for collecting inscribed glasses, especially those with Jacobite or Williamite sentiments, has lasted for at least eighty years, during which their value has risen considerably. They have naturally proved a target for forgers, and this was especially the case when suitable antique glasses of the correct type could be bought quite cheaply. When compared with an undoubted eighteenth century example, the re-decorated one is seen to have been executed in a clumsy manner, but it is seldom possible to place old and new side by side when a decision has to be made.

Finally, consideration must be given to the possibility of some types of ware being revived by their makers after an interval. This is occurring at the present time in the case of some of the later Victorian press-moulded wares, for which there is a big demand. Slag, for instance, is currently being made again by Davidson's of Gateshead, and the new productions are in the same shapes and bear the same mark as the old (*Signature* 15, page 12). An unworn shiny surface, newly-ground rim beneath the base, and a blurred mark are indications of the modern article.

The aspiring expert should not only handle and examine all the genuine glass possible, but visits to museums, even where only a distant viewing is feasible, are of great value in training the eye. To augment experience in handling the real thing, books and magazine articles will inform the reader of discoveries and opinions, and keep his knowledge of the subject up to date.

*　　*　　*　　*　　*

The author takes this opportunity of thanking those who so kindly loaned prints or allowed photographs to be taken, and whose names are acknowledged against the illustrations.

© *Geoffrey Wills, 1968.*

INDEX

Numerals in bold type (thus, **1**) refer to individual *Signatures*, while those in ordinary type (thus, 1) are page numbers. Italics (thus, *1*) refer to figure numbers in each *Signature*, except where they are definitely stated to be page references (thus, *p. 15*).

Adam, John	**13**, *13*.
Robert	**7**, 9, *frontispiece, 5*; **13**, 14.
"Air-twist"	**2**, 11, *7*; **3**, *3, 7, 8, 9, 11, 12*; **5**, 14, *12, 2.*
Akerman, John & Isaac	**11**, 13.
Ale glasses	**3**, *5, 7, 8.*
"Amen" glasses	**11**, *6, 2.*
Annealing	**9**, *9.*
Argand lamp	**6**, 8; **7**, 12.
Aventurine glass	**12**, *3.*
Bacchus & Sons, Birmingham	**14**, *4, 5, 10.*
Baillie, Lady Grizell	**5**, 10, 16.
Baluster stems	**2**, 8.
Barilla	**1**, 9, 10.
Bedford: Cecil Higgins Art Gallery	**4**, *2, 2*; **5**, *2.*
Beilby, William & Mary	**11**, 14, *frontispiece, 14.*
Belfast: Ulster Museum	**11**, *7.*
Bells (hand-bells)	**13**, *3, 11, frontispiece.*
Betts, Thomas	**11**, 13.
Bishop (Bischoppe), Hawley	**4**, *4.*
Blades, John	**7**, 15.
"Boot" glasses	**3**, *3, 5.*
Bottle-making	**9**, *9*; **10**, 6, 13.
Bowes, Sir Jerome	**1**, 8.
Bowles, John, & Wm. Lillington	**4**, *6.*
Bowls (see also Punch bowls)	**5**, 3, *frontispiece, 1, 2, 3, 13*; **8**, *1, 2, 3*; **11**, 5, *1.*
Brighton: Royal Pavilion	**7**, 12, *9.*
Bristol	**10**, 7, 13, *10, 11*; **12**, 7, *4, 5, 6, 8, 9, 10, 12.*
Bristol: City Museum	**12**, 8, *9.*
Britannic Society	**1**, *9.*
Bunyan, John	**3**, 15.
Bute, John, Earl of	**3**, *3, 5.*
"Butler Buggin Bowls"	**11**, 5, *1.*
Caithness Glass Ltd., Wick	**16**, *11.*
Cameo-glass	**15**, 7, *2, 3.*
"Cameo incrustations"	**13**, 13, *11.*
Candelabra	**6**, 13, *10, 11, 12, 13, 14, 15*; **14**, *6.*

(i)

Candlesticks	**6**, 4, *frontispiece, 1, 2, 3, 4, 5, 6, 7, 12, 13*; **14**, *6.*
"Captain" glasses	**5**, 11, *9.*
Case bottles	**10**, 5, *p. 15.*
Cassilari, Josepo	**1**, *2.*
Caudle	**4**, *8.*
Champagne	**3**, 6, *9.*
Chance, William & R. L.	**13**, *4.*
Chandeliers	**7**, 3, *frontispiece, 1, 2, 3, 4, 5, 6, 7, 8, 9, 10*; **16**, *frontispiece.*
Cider	**3**, *8.*
Claret	**3**, *9*; **4**, 14, *3.*
Clarke, Samuel	**15**, 9, 7, *8.*
Coins in glasses	**1**, 14, 5, 6, *7.*
Cold painting	**12**, 9, *7.*
Cole, Sir Henry	**14**, 7, 16; **15**, *4.*
"Colour-twist" stems	**2**, 12, *8*; **3**, *2.*
Cordial glasses	**2**, *13*; **3**, 9, *3, 10, 11.*
Cork Glass Co.	**8**, 13, 8, *12.*
Cork glass cutters	**8**, 14, *11.*
Council of Industrial Design	**16**, 5, 6, 7, 8, 9, 10, 11, 13, *15.*
Creamware pottery	**2**, *16*; **3**, *14.*
Crisselling	**1**, *12*; **4**, 2, *2*; **5**, 3, *3.*
Cruets	**5**, 11; **12**, *4.*
"Crystallo-ceramies"	**13**, 13, *11.*
Cullet	**5**, *4.*
Custard glasses	**3**, 4, *4.*
Cutting	**6**, 6, *14*; **11**, 11; **14**, 3, *14*; **16**, 3, *9.*
Daffy's Elixir	**10**, *10.*
Dagnia family	**2**, *14.*
Dartington Glass Ltd., Torrington	**16**, 7, *15.*
Davenport, John	**13**, 16, *14.*
Davidson, George & Co., Gateshead	**15**, 12, *frontispiece*; **16**, *16.*
Davis, Greathead & Green, Stourbridge	**14**, 11, *14.*
Decanters	**4**, 10, *3, 7, 8, 9, 10, 11, 12, 13, 14, 15*; **8**, 12, *7, 10, 12*; **11**, *9*; **12**, *frontispiece, 4, 5*; **14**, *1, 7*; **16**, 2, *3.*
Decanters, Ship's	**4**, 14, *14*; **16**, *9.*
"Deceptive" glasses	**3**, 2, *3.*
Delany, Mrs. (Mary Granville)	**7**, *5.*
Delftware (pottery)	**9**, 6, *1*; **12**, *8.*
Dickens, Charles	**10**, *10.*
Dier, John and Jone	**1**, 7, *1.*
Digby, Sir Kenelm	**9**, *5.*
Doorstops	**13**, *10.*
Drams	**3**, 2, *1.*
Duncan, Admiral Viscount	**1**, 13, *14.*
Edkins, Michael & William	**12**, *7.*

Enamelling	**11**, 14, *frontispiece, 11, 12, 13, 14*; **12**, 7, *6, 11, 13, p. 15, 14*.
"End of Day" glass	**15**, 14, *frontispiece*.
Engraved wineglasses	**3**, 5, *6, 7, 12, 16*; **11**, 8, *3, 4, 5, 6, 7, 8, 9*; **12**, *2*; **16**, *12*.
Epergnes..	**5**, 11, *10*.
Etching	**13**, 16; **15**, 8, *4*.
Evelyn, John	**1**, 12; **3**, 6.
Ewers (see Jugs)	
Excise Duties	**2**, 10; **8**, 7; **10**, 11; **12**, 11; **13**, 4; **14**, 4.
Facet-cut stems..	**1**, *11*; **2**, *9*; **3**, 7.
"Fairy" night-lights	**15**, 9, *7, 8*.
Falkland, Lucius Henry Cary, Viscount ..	**9**, 13, *8*.
Farquhar, George	**3**, 7.
"Favrile" glass..	**16**, 3.
Finger bowls	**4**, *3*; **5**, 13, *15*; **12**, 4, *8*.
Firing glasses	**3**, 2, *3*.
Flasks	**13**, 5, *p. 15*.
Flip glasses	**2**, 16.
Folded foot	**2**, 9.
Franklin, Benjamin	**13**, 11.
"Friggers"	**13**, 3, *7, p. 15*.
Gallé, Emile	**16**, 4.
Gas lighting	**6**, 9; **7**, 12.
Gatchell, Jonathan & George	**8**, 12, 13.
Geare, Wenyfrid	**1**, 8, *3*.
Gilding	**11**, 16, *15*; **12**, *frontispiece, 4, 5, 8, 10, 12*.
Giles, James	**12**, 14, *frontispiece*.
Gin	**2**, 15.
Glasse, Mrs. Hannah	**5**, 11.
Glass-houses in 1696	**9**, 10.
Glass Manufacturers' Federation ..	**9**, 9; **15**, *9, 10*; **16**, *4, 5, p. 15*.
Glass Sellers' Company	**2**, 7; **5**, 3; **9**, 7.
Goblets	**1**, 2, *1—14*; **14**, 5; **16**, *12*.
Greene, John, & Michael Measey ..	**2**, 4; **4**, 4; **12**, 4.
Greener & Co., Sunderland	**15**, 12, *frontispiece*.
Greenwood, Frans	**16**, 11.
Gumley, John	**7**, 6.
Haedy, Christopher	**11**, 13.
Harris, Rice & Co., Birmingham ..	**14**, 13, *3*.
Harrison, William	**1**, 5.
Heidegger, John James	**7**, 5.
Hill, John	**8**, 12.
Hogarth, William	**2**, 15, *12*; **7**, 5.
Holden, Henry	**4**, 5; **9**, 5.
Holinshed, Raphael	**1**, 4.
Houghton, John	**9**, 9.

Howell, James	1, 9; 3, 9, 11.
Irish glass	8, 3, *frontispiece*, *1—12;* **16**, 6, *frontispiece*, *14*.
Jackson, Francis, & John Straw	2, 14.
Jacobite glass	11, 6, *2, 3, 4, 5, 6, 13*.
Jacobs, Lazarus & Isaac	12, 10, *4, 8, 10, 12*.
Jamestown, Virginia	9, 13, 16, *11, 12*.
Johnson, Jerom	6, 13; **13**, 13.
Johnson, Dr. Samuel	2, 8; **3**, 12, 13.
Jugs, Claret	4, 14, *3*.
cream and milk..	4, 7, *4*; **15**, 6.
water	4, 2, *1, 2, 3, 4*; 8, 12, *8, 9*; **14**, *5*; **15**, *5*; **16**, *4, 11*.
King's Lynn	2, 14, *11*.
Knollys, Sir Francis	1, *10*.
Kny, Frederick E.	15, *5*.
Lacemaker's lamp	6, 8, *8*.
"Lazy Susan"	5, 11.
Lead oxide	1, 13; **5**, 4; **16**, 13.
Linen smoothers	13, 12, *8*.
London: London Museum	1, *5, 7, 9, 12*; **5**, *3, 4*; **9**, 8.
Royal College of Art	16, 7.
Sir John Soane's Museum ..	7, 11, *5*.
Victoria & Albert Museum ..	1, 7, *1, 3, 4*; **2**, *2*; **6**, *10*; **9**, *2*; **11**, 6, *frontispiece*, *1*; **12**, 12, *1, 6, 14*; **13**, 5, *10*; **14**, 7; **15**, 4, *1*; **16**, 2, *3*.
Westminster Abbey	16, *frontispiece*.
Lorraine glassworkers	6, 4; **9**, 3; **16**, 7.
Lucas, John Robert	13, 3.
Lustres	6, 16, *16*.
Mansell, Sir Robert	9, 5; **12**, 4.
Marvering	9, *9*.
Masonic glasses	1, *12*.
"Master" glasses	5, 11, *9*.
Mead	3, 11, *13*.
Merchants' marks	1, 7, *2*; **9**, 16, *frontispiece*, *15*.
Merese	5, 7.
Methuen Treaty	3, 9; **10**, 3.
Misson, François-Maximilien	1, 12.
Monteith..	5, 13.
Morelli, Alessio	2, 4.
Morris, William	15, 5, *1*.
Mumm	3, 12.
Musical glasses..	13, 11, *6*.
Nailsea	13, 3, *frontispiece*, *1, 2*.
Neri, Antonio	1, 11.
Neve, Richard	2, 12.

Newcastle glass	**2**, 12, *10*; **4**, 16, *15*; **12**, 16; **13**, 10; **16**, 10.
New York: Corning Museum of Glass	**1**, 7, *2*; **11**, 6, *1*; **12**, 16; **15**, 2.
"Nipt diamond waies" (NDW)	**2**, 7; **4**, 10, *7*; **5**, 7, 16, *4*, *12*; **12**, 5.
Non-Such Glass Manufactory	**12**, 10, *4*, *8*, *9*, *10*, *12*.
Northampton: Central Museum	**9**, 8, *4*, *6*.
Northwood, John	**15**, 7.
"Opaque-twist" glasses	**2**, *11*; **3**, 7, *11*, *13*, *16*; **5**, 9, *14*; **12**, 3.
Opaque-white	**12**, 11, *7*, *11*, *13*, p *15*, *14*; **13**, 6; **15**, 13.
Opaline glass	**14**, 11, *frontispiece*.
"Orange" glasses	**5**, 11, *9*.
Osler, F. & C., Birmingham	**14**, 9, *7*.
Oxford: Ashmolean Museum	**4**, 7; **11**, *13*; **12**, 5.
Paperweights	**13**, 13, *10*; **14**, 13, *10*.
Papworth, John Buonarotti	**7**, 15.
Paris: Musée de Cluny	**1**, 6.
Parker, William	**7**, 12, *9*; **14**, 9.
Pellatt, Apsley	**13**, 13, *11*; **14**, 14, *12*.
Pepys, Samuel	**3**, 12.
Pewterers' Company	**1**, 6, *2*.
Pincering (see "Nipt diamond waies")	**5**, 7.
Plot, Dr. Robert	**5**, 3.
Plymouth: City Museum & Art Gallery	**3**, *4*; **4**, 10, *13*; **5**, *11*.
Pontil mark	**2**, 9; **9**, 8; **10**, 7, *14*; **16**, 11.
Port	**3**, 9; **10**, 3.
Portland Vase	**15**, 7; **16**, 4.
Posset pots	**4**, 8, *5*, *6*.
Potter, Barbara	**1**, 11, *4*.
Poulett, John, Earl	**10**, 9, *8*.
Powell & Sons, James (see also Whitefriars Glass Ltd.)	**15**, 5, *1*; **16**, 6.
Powell, Ricketts, & Filer	**10**, 14, *11*.
Press-moulding	**15**, 11, *frontispiece*, 9, *10*, *11*, p. *15*.
Pretender, Young (and Old)	**11**, 6, *2*, *3*, *4*, *5*, *6*, *13*.
Printed decoration	**12**, 6.
Prunts	**1**, 5, *6*; **2**, 7, *2*; **4**, 9; **5**, 12.
Punch	**2**, *16*; **3**, 13, *14*.
Punch bowls	**5**, 7, *4*, *5*, *6*.
Punch (and toddy) lifters	**3**, 14, *15*.
Purl	**2**, 8.
"Queen's Burmese Ware"	**15**, 10, *8*.
Ratafia	**3**, 10, 15, *16*.
Ravenscroft, George	**1**, 12; **2**, 6, *2*; **4**, 2, *2*, *5*; **5**, 3, *1*, *2*; **11**, 5, *1*; **16**, 13.
Richardson, W. H. B. & J., Stourbridge	**14**, 12, 13, *8a*, *8b*, *11*.
Ricketts, Henry & Co.	**10**, 14, *1*, *2*, *10*.
Rochefoucauld, F. de la	**5**, 13.

Roche, Sophie von La..	6, 9; **12**, 11.
Rococo	**2**, 11.
Rolling pins	**13**, 3, 6, *3*.
Römers	**2**, 6, 16, *2*.
Rummers	**2**, 15, *14*, *15*; **3**, 6.
Ruskin, John	**11**, 11; **14**, 14; **16**, 3.
Salt cellars	**5**, 12, *11*; **8**, *frontispiece*, *6*; **13**, 5.
Saltram, Devon..	**7**, 11, *frontispiece*.
Salvers	**5**, 8, *7*.
Scent bottles	**12**, 6; **13**, 13, 16, *11*, *12*; **14**, 9; **15**, 3.
Schmelzglas	**12**, 3.
Schouman, Aert	**16**, 11.
Sealed glass (see also Wine bottles)	**1**, 13; **2**, 2; **4**, 2, 2, 5; **5**, 4, *1*, 2.
Shrub	**3**, 15.
"Silesian" stem	**2**, 9, *5*, *7*; **6**, 5, *3*; **12**, 5.
Silvering..	**13**, 9, *4*, *5*.
Silver hall-marks	**5**, 11.
"Slag" glass	**15**, 13, *frontispiece*.
Sowerby's Ellison Glass Works	**15**, 12, *frontispiece*, *11*, *p. 15*.
Stevens & Williams Ltd., Stourbridge	**16**, 9.
Stirrup-cups	**3**, 3, *5*.
Stoppers, decanter	**4**, 10, 15; **5**, 11.
Strathearn Glass Ltd., Crieff	**16**, 10.
String rim	**9**, 8; **10**, 3.
Stuart & Sons, Stourbridge..	**16**, 5, 6, 7, 8.
Sugar crushers or stirrers	**13**, 12, *9*.
"Sulphides"	**13**, 13, *11*.
"Summerly, Felix"	**14**, 16; **15**, 4.
Sweetmeat glasses	**5**, 16, *9*, *12*, *14*.
Syllabub	**3**, 16.
Tantalus	**4**, 13.
Tapersticks	**6**, 7, *9*.
Tassie, James & William	**13**, 16, *13*.
Tea caddies	**8**, *frontispiece*; **12**, *14*.
Tiffany, Louis Comfort	**16**, 3.
Toddy	**3**, 16.
Toledo, Ohio: Museum of Art	**11**, *14*.
Troughton & Young (Lighting), Ltd.	**16**, *13*.
Trumpets..	**13**, 11, *6*.
Truro, Cornwall: County Museum..	**3**, *15*; **6**, 8, *9*; **9**, *7*; **10**, *frontispiece*, *p. 15*; **12**, *7*.
Tumblers..	**2**, 16; **15**, *frontispiece*, *4*; **16**, 4.
Twiss, William..	**5**, 13.
Vases	**8**, *3*, *4*, *5*; **12**, *4*, *11*, *p. 15*; **14**, *frontispiece*, *2*, *8a*, *8b*; **15**, *13*; **16**, *1*, *5*, *6*, *7*, *10*, *p. 15*, *14*, *15*.
Venetian (and Venetian style) glass	**1**, 12; **2**, 3; **4**, 4; **11**, 3; **12**, 3; **13**, 5; **14**, 4; **15**, 5.

Verre de fougère	**9**, 4; **16**, 6.
Verzelini, Giacomo	**1**, 4, 6, 7, 8, *1, 2, 3*; **2**, 1.
"Vitro-Porcelain"	**15**, 14, *frontispiece, p. 15*.
Waldglas	**9**, 4; **16**, 4.
Walking sticks	**13**, 9, *frontispiece*.
Wall lights	**7**, 15, *11, 12, 13*.
Walpole, Hon. Horace	**1**, 7; **12**, 11.
Washington, D.C.: Smithsonian Institution	**9**, 15, *14*.
Waterford	**8**, 11; **16**, 7, *frontispiece, 14*.
Water glasses	**5**, 13.
Waterloo Glass Co., Cork	**8**, 14, *9, 10*.
Webb, Philip	**15**, 4, *1*.
Webb, Thomas & Sons, Stourbridge	**15**, 10, *3, 5*; **16**, 4.
Wedgwood, Josiah	**3**, *14*; **6**, 7, 15, *frontispiece, 7, 14*; **13**, 14, *12*; **15**, 6.
Whistler, Laurence	**16**, 11, *12*.
Whitefriars Glass Ltd. (see also Powell, James & Son)	**16**, 6, 11, *p. 15*.
Wilkes, John	**3**, 8.
Williamite glasses	**11**, 11, *7*.
Williamsburg, Virginia	**9**, 14.
Wine bottles	**9**, 10.
Wineglass coolers	**4**, *3*; **5**, 13, 15; **12**, *10, 12*.
Witch balls	**13**, 6, *4*.
Wolff, David	**16**, 11.
Woodall, George	**15**, *2*.
Wormeley, Ralph	**7**, *3*.
Yard-of-ale	**3**, 6.
Zaffre	**12**, 9.